Five Studies in Japanese Politics

Edited by

ROBERT E. WARD

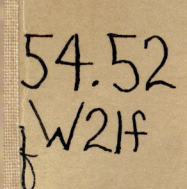

Ann Arbor: The University of Michigan Press
Center for Japanese Studies · Occasional Papers No. 7

Five Studies in Japanese Politics

Edited by

ROBERT E. WARD

Ann Arbor: The University of Michigan Press
Center for Japanese Studies · Occasional Papers No. 7
1957

Copyright © 1957
by the
University of Michigan

University of Michigan Center for Japanese Studies
Director: John W. Hall
Associate Editor: Rosannah C. Steinhoff

The Occasional Papers of the Center for Japanese Studies are published by the University of Michigan Press.

Sales correspondence should be directed to the University of Michigan Press, 412 Maynard St., Ann Arbor, Michigan.

Editorial correspondence should be directed to the Center for Japanese Studies, 622 Haven Hall, the University of Michigan, Ann Arbor, Michigan.

LITHOPRINTED IN THE UNITED STATES OF AMERICA BY
BRAUN-BRUMFIELD, INC., ANN ARBOR, MICHIGAN, 1957

PREFACE

The Center for Japanese Studies at the University of Michigan is primarily concerned with the graduate and post-doctoral training of area specialists in the Japanese field. A major portion of the program is focused upon research training and the provision of facilities for the conduct of advanced research both in the United States and Japan. At Ann Arbor these activities are centered in the Center's interdisciplinary research seminar, which it has been my privilege to direct for the past five years. In Japan they have normally been associated with the Center's Field Station at Okayama City in southwestern Honshu. Over the years a notable series of publications has emerged from both sources. Many of these, such as the Center's well-known bibliographical series or Dr. Edward Norbeck's study of Takashima, a Japanese fishing community, have been separately published in book form. Numerous other briefer contributions have appeared in a variety of professional journals or in the first four numbers of the Center's publication, Occasional Papers. In 1956, however, a policy was inaugurated of devoting each issue of the Occasional Papers to a particular aspect of Japanese culture. Thus No. 5 presented two parallel anthropological studies of Japanese agricultural villages done at the Field Station by Doctors John B. Cornell and Robert J. Smith. The present issue continues this policy with the publication of five studies in the general field of Japanese law and politics.

Three of the five papers fall in the category of politics. Dr. Paul S. Dull, Professor of Political Science at the University of Oregon, has contributed a study of a neglected but most important figure in Japanese politics, the local "boss." The work is based upon Professor Dull's experiences as a research associate at the Center's Okayama Field Station. Mr. Alfred B. Clubok's paper represents work done for the master's degree at Ann Arbor. It derives from library rather than field research, but provides some very useful insights into the geographical and demographic patterning of "conservative" political strength in Japan as manifested in the five most recent general elections of members of the House of Representatives. Mr. William Amidon's study of the political history and contemporary economic and political significance of the island of Sakhalin also represents a student contribution. It was done in the Center's interdisciplinary seminar in partial fulfillment of the requirements for the master's degree.

The remaining two articles are oriented toward legal problems. Professor Shuichi Sugai of Kyoto University's Law School wrote his paper while serving as an Exchange Fellow of the Kyoto American Studies Program at the Center in Ann Arbor. His study provides a most informative analysis of recent developments in the Japanese police system and well exemplifies the extent to which the so-called "reverse course" movement has affected the reforms initiated by the Allied Occupation. Dr. Dan F. Henderson's bibliographical essay on sources for the study of Tokugawa law and legal institutions differs from the preceding articles in the sense that its author has had no official connection with the Center for Japanese Studies. The work was done at the University of California at Berkeley, and in Japan. In our opinion, however, Dr. Henderson's material is so useful, and this sort of informed and authoritative guidance normally is so difficult to acquire, that we felt it must be made publicly available.

It is our hope that scholars and students in the Asian field generally will find these contributions to the study of Japanese law and politics suggestive and useful. We look forward to the publication of further issues of the Occasional Papers similarly focused upon other major aspects of Japanese culture.

Robert E. Ward

CONTENTS

	Page
The Japanese Police System .... Shuichi Sugai	1
Maeda Shoichi: A Case Study of a Japanese Political Boss .... Paul S. Dull	15
Japanese Conservative Politics 1947-1955 .... Alfred B. Clubok	21
The Issue of Sakhalin in Russo-Japanese Relations .... William C. Amidon	60
Japanese Legal History of the Tokugawa Period: Scholars and Sources .... Dan F. Henderson	100

THE JAPANESE POLICE SYSTEM

Shuichi Sugai

One of the objects of the most drastic reforms made by the Allied Occupation Forces in accordance with their policies to democratize Japan was the Japanese police system. The so-called "Police Law" was one of the enactments directed toward democratization and was in effect seven years—from December, 1947 through June, 1954. Two years after the end of the Occupation, however, and over the vehement opposition of the Socialists, a new legislation was rammed through the National Diet by the conservative parties, completely revising this Police Law. At the present time the Japanese police system is said to have nearly reverted to the pre-war system of some seventy years' prior standing.

Now that the confusion attending the bitter struggle over the police situation has abated and the perspective is somewhat cleared, it seems time to assess the innovations introduced by the Occupation into the Japanese police system and to examine their effect. This paper is an attempt to evaluate in relation to this field some of the major influences of the Occupation's introduction of American democratic institutions diametrically opposed to those of the traditionally authoritarian governmental pattern of Japan.

The revision of the Police Law is one of the most significant indices of the backswing of the pendulum in Japanese governmental policies and legislation. It is also symptomatic of the problems posed by the possible amendment of the Japanese Constitution itself, which has represented an even more important Occupation achievement; for the fate of the Police Law may be said to foreshadow that of basic law. The Japanese police system was chosen for this study because of its significance in estimating the present Japanese revisionist movement in respect to Occupation policies in the governmental field. This study of the Police Law is therefore presented as an indication of the fate of the whole Occupation system.

Pre-war Japanese Police System[1]

The emergence of Japan's police system dates from 1874 (the seventh year of Meiji). In that year, a reform was made in the police functions, which were removed from the jurisdiction of the Ministry of Justice to that of the Ministry of Home Affairs. In addition, the Metropolitan Police Board was newly established in the Tokyo Prefecture. Elsewhere prefectural governors were to have police jurisdiction. General jurisdiction over police affairs in the whole country was in the hands of the Ministry of Home Affairs which appointed the prefectural governors and the Chief of the Metropolitan Police Board. These, in turn, handled local police affairs, operating under the control and supervision of the Home Ministry. There were police-station chiefs under the chief of the Metropolitan Police Board and prefectural governors.

Salaries, travel allowances, etc., of police officers above inspector's rank were paid from the national treasury; other expenses, such as maintaining policemen in lower ranks, and providing and keeping up office buildings, were mainly met by local taxes but partially subsidized by the national government—the ratio of subsidies being four-tenths of all expenses for the Metropolitan Police Board and one-sixth for other prefectures. (Office building, repair and other office expenses of the Metropolitan Police Board were, however, entirely paid by the national treasury.)

This was, on the whole, a unified, close-knit national police system which followed a very simple pattern of complete control and supervision exercised from the top of the police pyramid downwards. Although there were later changes and improvements, the foundations of the Japanese police system were laid down at this time.

The prime mover behind the scenes of the 1874 reform was none other than Daikeishi (The Great Superintendent), Kawaji Toshiyoshi, who traveled abroad in 1872 and 1873 to make a survey of western police systems and was later appointed the first Chief of the Metropolitan Police Board. After his return home, Kawaji tendered recommendations to the government on police reorganization, nearly all of which were adopted and incorporated in the subsequent reform. His recommendations included differentiation of the organizations for judicial and police functions; assumption of local police functions by prefectural governors; establishment of a separate office for the metropolitan police affairs of the national capital; decreasing the number of local watchmen or substituting governmental policemen for them; and recruiting policemen from the ranks of unemployed samurai. These recommendations were keynoted in the preface to his report, which is translated as follows:

> The police are a daily cure and remedy to a state, as everyday hygiene is to an individual. The police are able to protect good citizens and nurture the active force of a country. For this reason, those who desired to make their imperial powers glorious and extend their territories paid attention to these facts. Napoleon I was one of them. To cite a more recent example, Prussia has been able to annex surrounding countries and display her glory over the world, because her police are capable of preserving peace within and around the country and exploring the internal condition and circumstances of foreign countries. Even the great power of France has not been her match because of this aptitude. Therefore, the establishment of the police is an absolute necessity in strengthening the state and setting up relations with foreign nations.

To emphasize, Superintendent Kawaji drew a comparison (not wholly accurate) between continental and British police systems:

> Autocratic monarchies have to make their monarchical powers glorious. For this reason, all three countries, Russia, Prussia and France maintain their police at governmental expense. In St. Petersburg, Russia, they are under the jurisdiction of the Prefect of Police. In Paris, France, they are called "royal police" and their Chief of Police consults every morning with the Sovereign. Prussia has taken its model from the Napoleonic system and maintains most splendid police.... Three other countries, England, Holland and Belgium rely on police systems financed at local expense. But London is a prosperous metropolis with wealthy citizens and lively commerce, and the people contribute with pleasure to the support of their police. The present conditions of our country do not bear comparison with this.

This passage reveals his leaning towards the continental rather than the British system. The British Metropolitan Police Board (Scotland Yard) was already at that time a nationalized police unit, and is an exception to the ordinary British police forces which were organized on the basis of local autonomy. In referring to the "London" police, Kawaji may have been thinking of the City of London Police, which was, as it is now, supported at the local expense.

Kawaji was considering police organization along lines of monarchical principles, and it was not by accident that the Japanese police system followed the Continental pattern of a centralized national police system. This characteristic is also evidenced by the powers given to police agencies, which combined legislative, judicial and administrative powers after the Continental pattern.

The powers of police agencies came to be defined by the Meiji Constitution of 1889 and other subsequent legislation. Article IX of the said Constitution stipulated:

> The Emperor issues, or causes to be issued, the Ordinances necessary for the carrying out of the laws, for the maintenance of the public peace and order, and for the promotion of the welfare of the subjects. But no Ordinance shall in any way alter any of the existing laws.

The Emperor was thus able to issue or let other governmental agencies issue ordinances necessary for the maintenance of public peace and order, provided those ordinances did not conflict with the statutes passed by the Diet. On the basis of this constitutional provision, the Emperor, the Home Ministry, the Metropolitan Police Board and prefectural governors were enabled to, and did in fact, issue numerous ordinances for police purposes, which were accompanied by the necessary penalty provision against their violation, and which had the force of law. These so-called "police ordinances" were issued in those fields that were not already covered by statutes, as, for instance, public health and trade licensing, and they became quite important. Thus the police agencies had and were exercising a sub-legislative power.

The Ikeizaisokketsurei (Law of the Summary Procedure for Police Offenses) of 1885 provided that the chiefs of the police stations could prosecute and adjudicate summarily the so-called Ikeizai, i.e., "police offenses." These were later enumerated in Keisatsuhansho-batsurei (Ordinance on the Penalties of Police Offenses. This ordinance changed the name of police offenses from Ikeizai to Keisatsuhan) of 1908, and comprised offenses punishable with detention less than thirty days and with fines of less than twenty yen. The chiefs of police stations were enabled to exercise a prevotal power, playing a double role of prosecutor and judge in cases of minor offenses.

The Gyoseishikkoho (Law of Administrative Execution) of 1900 gave police officials these powers: to detain until sunset of the next day persons who needed protection or who were suspected of endangering the public safety (the so-called "protective and preventive custodies"); to take weapons and other pernicious objects into custody for a limited period; to enter premises under specified circumstances; to subject certain persons to medical examination and hospitalization; to use or dispose of real or personal properties under certain circumstances; and to enforce laws by specified measures of compulsory execution, ranging from performance by proxy and fines, to the use of physical force. All of these powers were to be exercised without recourse to permissions and warrants issued by judicial authorities.

The Japanese police agencies thus possessed legislative, judicial and quasi-judicial powers as well as administrative authority.

Raymond B. Fosdick who made a careful comparative study of Anglo-American and European police systems in European Police Systems (1915) said (p. 15, et seqq.):

> In Great Britain the police are the servants of the community.... They are civil employees, whose primary duty is the preservation of public security. In the execution of this duty they have no powers not possessed by any other citizen.... In sharp contrast the Continental theory, which evolved from the necessities of autocratic government, makes of the police force the strong arm of the ruling classes. The Continental policeman is the servant of the Crown or the higher authorities; the people have no share in his duties, nor, indeed, any connection with them. He possesses powers greatly exceeding those of the citizen.

This characterization of the Continental police applied very aptly to the old Japanese police system--as may be shown by a few salient instances of the actual use of such police force in Japan.

In 1877, three years after the initiation of the Metropolitan Police Board, a brigade of its forces contributed greatly in quelling the Saigo Rebellion in Kyushu. In 1887, ten years later, the police were used effectively to expel in less than three days 570 anti-government politicians from within a seven-mile radius of Tokyo City. In 1897, the then Minister and Vice-Minister of Home Affairs interfered extensively with the general election for the Diet, utilizing prefectural governors and their police forces to obstruct the election of opposition candidates. From Taisho (1912-1925) to the beginning of the Showa period (1926-   ), in the era of the parliamentary cabinet system, the police were invariably used to some extent for similar purposes by the ruling party. After 1925, the police were very efficient in enforcing the Peace Preservation Law and in ferreting out and suppressing any subversive movements. After 1928, the police officials in charge of enforcing this law formed a special unit called the "Special High Police," control of which by-passed prefectural governors and was directly in the hands of the Home Ministry.

From the inception of the modern system, Japanese police were recruited from among the unemployed ex-samurai. This method of choosing men was singularly effective in guaranteeing their staunchness and relative immunity from corruption because of a system of morality peculiar to the former warrior class. On the other hand, this practice had certain drawbacks, in that it tended to develop in the police an attitude of disrespect and superciliousness toward the people.

That the Japanese police were a very convenient tool of the government is further shown by the multifarious functions performed by the police agencies. For instance, Keishichokansei (Ordinance on the Organization of the Metropolitan Police Board) of 1913 listed as the responsibilities of the Metropolitan Police Board: police and fire protection, public health administration, and mediation of labor disputes, as well as administration of the Factory Law, Minimum Age Law for Industrial Laborers, Labor Accidents Compensation Law, Labor Accidents Compensation Insurance Law, and Health Insurance Law.

For anyone seeking a judicial remedy against illegal police measures, the recourse of appeal to an independent judicial tribunal was hardly to be found. Under the pre-war judicial system, the ordinary courts had no jurisdiction in administrative law cases, which were rather under the jurisdiction of Gyoseisaibansho (Tribunal of Administrative Litigation) within the executive branch of government. The jurisdiction of Gyoseisaibansho was limited to specific matters enumerated in the statutes and among police measures only trade licensing cases were reviewable. Therefore, those who suffered damages from illegal police actions were able only to sue individual policemen who committed flagrantly illegal acts. There was no state liability in such police cases.

Reform by the Occupation[2]

From September, 1945, the beginning of the Occupation, to December, 1947, the pre-war Japanese police system preserved its precarious life with minor internal changes. In the meantime, police reorganization plans were in progress both within the Japanese government and the Occupation Forces. The Japanese government, i.e., the Ministry of Home Affairs, was considering a limited decentralization of the police in accordance with the "fundamental human rights" and "local autonomy" ideas which were to be embodied in the new Constitution and the Local Autonomy Law. By the time these came into force, however, in May, 1947, the Ministry of Home Affairs itself was near its end. It was dissolved on December 31, 1947 by order of the Occupation.

In the Occupation Forces, there were two sections involved in the reorganization of the Japanese police system. One was the Public Safety Division of the Civil Intelligence Section and the other was the Government Section of General Headquarters, Supreme Commander for the Allied Powers. Under the direction of the Chief of the Public Safety

Division, studies of the Japanese police were made by Mr. Lewis J. Valentine of the New York City Police Department, and Mr. Oscar G. Olander, Commissioner of the Michigan State Police Force. They tendered reports on reorganization of the system, the former covering the municipal police and the latter covering the rural police. In February, 1947, the Japanese Cabinet presented the draft of a plan based on the Valentine and Olander reports. These had recommended that in all municipalities of over fifty thousand population autonomous police forces be established, patterned after the New York City Police, and that a national rural police system be set up to serve rural areas and cities of less than fifty thousand. The Government Section of General Headquarters objected to this plan on the grounds that it did not provide sufficient decentralization of authority and would have delayed decentralization until the new local autonomous bodies had demonstrated proficiency in self-government.

The Katayama government of the Socialist Party was formed in June, 1947, and at the request of the Government Section of General Headquarters a Cabinet Committee on Judicial and Police System was appointed to make studies on the police reorganization. The result of this study was a revised police reorganization plan, which Prime Minister Katayama submitted to General MacArthur on September 3. The General replied to this with a letter of September 16, 1947, which was to the effect that the plan proposed by the Japanese government provided only for a limited and gradual decentralization and retained many of the principles of the old centralized structure, and suggested in detail an immediate and nearly complete decentralization. With the cooperation of General Headquarters, the Japanese Government drafted and submitted a bill, based upon the principles laid down in General MacArthur's letter, which was enacted into law by the National Diet on December 7, 1947.

The reforms of 1947 came under four headings: deconcentrating the powers of police agencies, decentralizing such agencies, putting them under popular control, and neutralizing them politically.

In the effort toward deconcentration of power, fire protection, public health and other such administrative functions extraneous to police functions proper were removed from police agencies and transferred to appropriate agencies. The responsibilities of police agencies were thus limited to protection of life, person and property, detection of crimes, apprehension of criminals and preservation of public order. The police agencies were shorn of their former sub-legislative and judicial functions and became simple administrative agencies. They could no longer issue ordinances, nor adjudicate minor offenses.

To bring about decentralization, autonomous police units were established in all the cities, towns, or villages of five thousand population or more. Thus, Japan came to have more than sixteen hundred independent municipal police forces with a total strength of ninety-five thousand men. On the other hand, the towns and villages of less than five thousand population were policed by the National Rural Police, which consisted of only thirty thousand men. Centralization was limited to certain matters to be handled at the national level (i.e., standards, identification, communications, training, scientific crime detection and statistics) and to grave emergency cases, in the event of which the Prime Minister should possess certain exceptional police powers.

In the matter of increasing popular control the Public Safety Commissions were to be made up of citizens who were not tainted by any bureaucratic experience. These were to be appointed by the Prime Minister, the prefectural governors and the local mayors subject to the consent of the Diet and local assemblies, respectively, and were to have control and supervision of the police forces. The idea was to put decentralized police forces under popular control by means of Public Safety Commissions made up of laymen. The Municipal Public Safety Commissions had complete legal control over the chiefs of the Municipal Police. Control of the National Rural Police was divided: the Prefectural Public Safety

Commissions had only "operational control" over the prefectural units, while the National Public Safety Commission had "administrative" control over the chief of the National Rural Police. (It later became evident that the Prefectural Public Safety Commissions' control over the superintendents of prefectural units of the rural police was rather inadequate, for those commissions had not the power to hire and fire such officers.) Although not popularly elected, the members of municipal and prefectural Public Safety Commissions were subject to recall by the local citizens.

To prevent the use of police agencies for political schemes, the Public Safety Commissions were to be non-partisan and politically neutral bodies, quite separate from the heads of the executive branch of the central and local governments. The Prime Minister, the prefectural governors, and mayors had no legal means of influencing Public Safety Commissions in their exercise of official functions. For instance, Prime Minister Yoshida could not have the National Public Safety Commission discharge his Chief of the National Rural Police from office. Although the move to make the police organization independent of politics was designed as a safeguard, it also had the undesirable result of keeping the central government from receiving much of the vital information collected by the various police agencies.

The Japanese government's police reorganization planners and Prime Minister Katayama himself, as mentioned above, firmly opposed the drastic decentralization, arguing that it would disrupt the efficiency and power of the Japanese police. On the same grounds, they requested an increase in the authorized number of men from 93,935 to 125,000, in view of the fact that the Japanese Army had been abolished.

While approving the request for the increase in the number of men, the Occupation authorities countered the plea for a better integrated police by stressing the urgent need for "democratization" and the consequent inadvisability of retaining a centralized national police. The Japanese government still seemed to retain, however, the belief that decentralization meant a weakening of over-all police strength. The two views remained opposed, but a number of significant later events seemed to prove the Japanese government's point.

The new municipal police forces were established in March, 1948. A month later, the separate schools for Korean residents had to be closed down in accordance with a new educational system, and Korean children were inducted into Japanese schools. In Kobe City more than one thousand Koreans held demonstrations protesting the closing of the schools; they formed mobs, cut telephone wires and broke into the Hyogo prefectural office building. The governor of Hyogo Prefecture, the Mayor of Kobe and the City Police Chief—who were in conference at the time—were coerced into signing a document acceding to demands made by the mob. The riot was instigated by Communists, and was only an example of similar events occurring at the same time all over the country. A few days later, Prime Minister Yoshida, answering questions in the National Diet, said that before the enactment of the new Police Law, he had had a premonition that such things would happen as a consequence of separating the municipal and national rural police. These events illustrated, he said, the law's defects in terms of public safety, and such defects must be eliminated at the earliest opportunity.

In April, 1948, in the town of Honjo in Saitama Prefecture, a newspaper reporter wrote an exposé of the corruption among the town assemblymen and police who were in collusion with gangsters. He was threatened and assaulted. The case was interpreted by the National Rural Police headquarters as a symptom of the way in which municipal police had come to be controlled by local assemblymen tied up with blackmarketeers and gangsters.

In June, 1949, operations of the government-owned suburban railroad lines in the Tokyo-Yokohama area were stopped because of a large-scale strike of the railroad workers. Many cases of violence and other offenses accompanied the strike. These also were cited by the government to strengthen their argument for a thoroughgoing reexamination of the police system. The government declared that such disturbances were mainly caused by the weakness of the police system, especially of the municipal police. It was said that the government was unable to obtain necessary information from the police units owing to the separation and lack of close cooperation between the government and the police. The government, therefore, claimed that the police system itself had to be revised to provide permanently for coordinated counter measures against such disorders.

Out of these events a minor issue arose in July, 1949, concerning the government-police relationship. Prime Minister Yoshida requested the National Public Safety Commission to consider the removal of National Rural Police Chief Saito, who allegedly had been uncooperative with the government in settling the June incident. The Commission refused to comply with the government's request and retained Saito in office.

Then on June 30, 1949, the Taira City Police headquarters in Fukushima Prefecture were occupied for eight hours by a Communist-inspired mob of about seven hundred. This demonstration was in protest against a police order to remove billboards posted in front of the railroad station by a Communist district committee. In the course of the uprising, two policemen were put in the detention cell, five others were assaulted and injured, the police office building was temporarily taken possession of by the crowd and two red banners were hung in front of the building. Simultaneous riots in other cities within this prefecture were staged with the design of preventing the cooperation of the different police units. Following these events, the citizens in the Taira area organized a body of thirteen hundred vigilantes, alleging the police forces to be inadequate to cope with the situation.

Decentralization of the reorganized police system, it was claimed, had resulted in inefficiency, or weakening, of the over-all police strength, alienating government and police, impeding coordination and cooperation, and fostering mutual distrust and jealousy among the different units. In addition there had developed increased expenses, corruption of municipal police units, obstacles to the exchange of personnel among different units, and so forth. These defects were not beyond amelioration by a voluntary cooperation of the different police units. But there was a suspicion that the necessary remedial measures along this line would be half-hearted at best—if they were not deliberately sabotaged--to create an excuse for reorganizing, recentralizing, and by some means restoring the old police system.

In the meantime, the international situation changed rapidly for the worse. Already in 1949 a bolstering of the Japanese police by an armed police force was reported to be under consideration in Washington, D.C. Then in June, 1950, fighting broke out in Korea, and a month later, the National Police Reserve of seventy-five thousand men was hurriedly established to fill the gap left by the Occupation forces being mobilized for the Korean front. This new force was to be under the Prime Minister's personal control, entirely separate from the ordinary police and free from interference by any public safety commission. It was to be equipped with American weapons, including mortars and machine guns, clothed in American-type uniforms, and drilled in army fashion. This seemed at first glance to solve the problem of strengthening the present Japanese police system, but later developments made it clear that further changes were desired.

In April, 1951, General MacArthur was relieved of the office of Supreme Commander for the Allied Powers. On May 2, 1951, his successor, General Matthew B. Ridgeway, announced the policy of relaxing Occupation control. For the Japanese Government, this was a signal for revising the Police Law. In June of that year an amendment of the Police Law was submitted and passed through the Diet, authorizing smaller communities having their own municipal police units to decide by referendum whether they wished a merger with the National Rural Police. The first wave of referenda held between June and September of 1951 showed that nearly eighty per cent of the total number of communities concerned, or 1028 towns and villages, favored the abolition of their own police forces and the surrender of their jurisdiction to the National Rural Police. The National Rural Police, by absorbing such municipal police forces, which totaled more than thirteen thousand men, considerably increased both its jurisdictional area and its numerical strength. Such referenda were repeated every year thereafter.

The next steps toward a return to the pre-war police system were to abolish the remaining municipal forces, then bring about their absorption into National Rural Police, thus finally accomplishing a recentralization. The government and the National Rural Police were waiting only for an opportunity to take such steps.

The 1954 Reform and Centralization of the Japanese Police System[3]

In line with the new policies adopted by General Ridgeway, the Japanese government set up the Ordinance Review Advisory Committee which was to reexamine the ordinances and laws introduced at the behest of the Occupation Forces and report on the desirability of continuing their existence. In July, 1951, this committee expressed its views in respect to the abolition of municipal police forces and their absorption into the National Rural Police and suggested that all agencies with police functions be unified under a Ministry of Public Safety.

Political circumstances seemed to demand that every possible action be taken to bring the police system to its maximum effectiveness. In February, 1952, the Chief of the Special Investigation Bureau under the Attorney General's Office declared the Communist Party membership in Japan to be from 300,000 to 350,000 of which 80,000 to 100,000 were regular party members. Seventy per cent of the party organization had gone underground, on the alert for armed rebellion. At the same time, the Chief of the National Rural Police stated to a Diet committee that the Communist activities were being directed toward policemen. As indications he cited the following: an illegal Communist publication, "How to Raise Flower Bulbs," No. 32 (November, 1951), which had the subtitle "In order to overcome the delay of operations against the police"; incidents of violence, such as the murder of the Chief of the Public Safety Division of the Sapporo City Police in Hokkaido, and the riot against policemen in a town in the prefecture of Nagano; the distribution of postcards and handbills threatening policemen; attacks with stones, etc. There were, he claimed, more than six hundred such cases in 1951. Anti-American and "anti-colonialism" demonstrations were raging in all of the key cities of the country. The purpose of these outbreaks was to obstruct the conclusion of the administrative agreements between the United States and Japan in accordance with the Peace Treaty, and, later, to prevent the enactment of the Anti-Subversive Act (Hakaikatsudoboshiho). Unrest over such issues continued in 1952. In this year the Communists were using crude home-made bombs and bottled inflammable chemicals in their terrorist activities against the police, tax officials and public prosecutors.

In February, 1953, the National Diet received a bill to revise the Police Law and to establish under a Minister of State a national police board within the central government, which would relegate the National Public Safety Commission to the status of an advisory agency. In addition it was proposed to establish prefectural police forces, the chiefs of which were to be appointed by the Chief of the National Police Board, which would supersede the National Rural Police and Municipal Police forces. Cities of more than 500,000 population, however, were to be allowed to retain their own police units. This bill was not passed by the Diet, because the National Rural Police and prefectures would not agree to the continuance of autonomous police units in these major cities, and because the weight of the Progressive Party and the Socialists was opposed to the government at that time on a budgetary issue.

In January, 1954, a new and more successful bill to revise the Police Law was submitted to the Lower House of the National Diet. This time the Progressives were more cooperative with the government; the National Rural Police and prefectures also approved this bill, because the Municipal Police forces were to be abolished altogether. The new bill provided that the National Public Safety Commission, headed by a Minister of State, was to be the superior organ instead of the National Police Board as in the 1953 bill. The police board itself came under the said commission. The Prime Minister was to appoint the Chief of the National Police Board with the advice (and not necessarily the consent) of the commission. Among other functions the National Police Board was to handle nationally important matters, such as major disasters and riots.

Further provisions of the bill called for the National Rural Police and Municipal Police forces to be abolished and replaced by Prefectural Police forces. The Chief of the Tokyo-To Police was to be appointed by the Prime Minister with the advice of the National Public Safety Commission. The Chiefs of other Prefectural Police forces were to be appointed by the Chief of the National Police Board with the advice of the National Public Safety Commission. The Chiefs of the Prefectural Police forces were to appoint the personnel of their forces with the consent of the Prefectural Public Safety Commission. With the exception of salaries to those police officers above the rank of superintendent, who were to be national rather than local officials, the expenses of the Prefectural Police were to be defrayed by prefectures, using local taxes and national subsidies. Communication, criminal identification, material equipment, and expenses for any other operations conducted on a national scale were to be financed by the national treasury.

The most controversial points in the new bill were the appointment of key officers by the Prime Minister and by the Chief of the National Police Board, and the abolition of the police forces of the five major cities. In the Lower House, the bill was amended to conciliate the Progressives and the five big cities. The Progressives consented to the amended bill under the erroneous impression that since the current session was nearly over the Upper House would take no action, and the bill would be killed.

The amendments of the bill introduced two major changes: (1) The Chief of the National Police Board should be appointed by the National Public Safety Commission with the approval of the Prime Minister. The Chief of the Tokyo-To Police should be appointed by the National Public Safety Commission with the consent of the Tokyo-To Public Safety Commission and the approval of the Prime Minister. The Chiefs of Prefectural Police should be appointed by the National Public Safety Commission with the consent of the Prefectural Public Safety Commission. This amendment meant that the National Public Safety Commission was restored to its former position instead of being demoted to an advisory agency. (2) The abolition of the police forces of major cities was so controverted between prefectures pro, and the five big cities contra, that a dilatory compromise, which was not a compromise at all, was offered, to the effect that the inactivation of the five municipal police forces should be put off for one year, or until July, 1955.

The period of session of the National Diet was to expire on May 22, although the more important bills, including the revision of the Police Law, had not yet been acted upon by the Upper House. There the Socialists were bitterly opposed to the revision of the Police Law on three counts. They foresaw that the chairmanship of a Minister of State in the National Public Safety Commission could be used as a bridgehead for a move to put the police under political influence. Further, they recognized the anti-democratic tendency of the bill, and last but not least, they resisted the intended abolition of municipal police forces. Meanwhile the period of session had necessarily been extended again and again between May 22 and June 3.

On the night of June 3-4, the Socialist Diet members, pushed to the extreme, staged a riot to prevent the chairman of the Lower House from entering the assembly. A few minutes past the midnight deadline, still outside the doors of the meeting room, the chairman had to declare the resolution to extend the period two more days, the fourth of such resolutions. Feelings were running so high by this time that two hundred policemen had to be summoned to bring belated order to the House. Subsequently, the Socialists claimed the extension to be legally null and void and absented themselves when a fifth extension of the period finally resulted in a vote. On June 8, with no Socialist members present, the revision of the Police Law was passed by the conservative members of the House of Councillors.

The Government's justification of the revision was stated in the Diet by Minister of Justice Inukai. In part, his statement reads:

The present Police Law which was enacted as one of the more important of the Occupation policies, was, no doubt, an epoch-making and important legislation, reforming from the ground up the prewar Japanese police system and putting emphasis on the ideals of democratic police. However, being enacted in a hurry, reflecting the then-prevailing "international circumstances" [This is a Japanese euphemism for the Occupation—S.S.], it had many points which were not suitable to our national circumstances and was not free from defects which in actual practice produced inefficiency and bad economy. It had been widely recognized from the beginning that sooner or later, a thorough-going revision would be necessary in order to cure and correct such errors and defects. That is to say, the present police system is dual, consisting of National Rural Police and City, Town and Village Autonomous Police units. The National Rural Police governing towns and villages has too much the character of national police without local autonomy of any kind, while the Municipal Police governing cities has, on the other hand, too great a measure of complete autonomy, lacking the character of national police. The consequence of this dualism is that there are police systems of different types in existence in cities on one hand and in towns and villages on the other, and that this dual system has some features which are not suitable to the operation of modern police functions, which should naturally combine both national and local characteristics. Furthermore, the City, Town and Village Autonomous Police, being organized and operated independently in each city, town or village—despite the fact that functional areas of public safety are rapidly becoming broader and broader—the responsibility is divided among many units under this multiple police system and their organic coordination is obstructed to a considerable extent. Of course, in the past years, efforts were made to establish friendly relationships and to smooth mutual contact and coordination among different police units by personnel exchange and agreements of cooperation; but such finesse in maneuvering had limitations in view of the defects inherent in the structure itself, and the existence of blind spots, caused by the multiple division into different police units, has been hampering an efficient operation of the police. In addition to this, the fact that such shortcomings had a pernicious influence in terms of clear-cut responsibility for national public safety is still fresh in the nation's memory from various "incidents" which have happened frequently in these years. On the other hand, from the point of view of a desirable reform in public administration and finance, the duplication of facilities and personnel of the National Rural Police and Municipal Police has unnecessarily introduced greater complexity and increased the economical burden, and consequently the necessity for fundamental reorganization is now being recognized in current public opinion....

When, and if, this revision comes into force, it is expected that by a simplification of structure, thirty thousand men in police personnel and nine billion yen in police expenses will be saved....

This explanation enumerates the alleged defects of the 1947 police system and may be considered to epitomize the criticisms from the Japanese government's side, even to constitute an official epitaph to the Occupation-sponsored policies on the police system. Actually it remains doubtful whether any sincere efforts had been made within the given framework to cure the defects which were not certainly incurable. It is also interesting to note that the official explanation implies that the 1954 system of prefectural police units constitutes a synthesis of the former two extremes of National Rural Police and Municipal Police. It was one of the issues raised when the new police bill was in debate in the National Diet— that is, whether the prefectural police units were nearer in nature to the Municipal Police or to the National Rural Police.

The National Public Safety Commission and the National Police Board are the national superstructures over the entire prefectural police forces and are purely national agencies in character. The National Public Safety Commission consists of a chairman, who is a Minister of State appointed by the Prime Minister, and five commissioners who are themselves appointed by the Prime Minister with the consent of the two Houses of the National Diet. The chairman convokes the Commission, and votes only in case of a tie among the commissioners, whose quorum is three. While the commissioners have a guarantee of tenure, the Minister of State as chairman holds the office during the Prime Minister's pleasure. The Commission appoints the Chief of the Police Board with the approval of the Prime Minister. The National Public Safety Commission in addition to national matters handles certain local affairs, such as major disasters and riots, which may be of national significance. That these agencies were regular national organs was beyond dispute, and the issue raised in the National Diet concerned for the most part the ambiguous nature of the prefectural police units.

The character of the new prefectural police forces is undoubtedly that of a nationalized police: (1) The chiefs of the prefectural police forces are, along with high police officers of those forces, national government officials, and the power of their appointment rests with the National Public Safety Commission, although the consent of the Prefectural Public Safety Commission is required. (2) Theoretically the Prefectural Public Safety Commission has the power of operational control over the Prefectural Police units, but control over the Chief of the Prefectural Police is in nature one of general supervision and is only advisory, if not illusory, in view of past experience. (3) All of the more important police functions are regulated by national statutes, and very little is left to the initiative of the Prefectural Public Safety Commissions. (4) The salaries, allowances and like expenditures of police personnel are all governed by standards established by the central authorities; the prefectural assemblies have little to say about such disbursements although these expenses are defrayed by the prefectures themselves. (5) The authorized number of police personnel, their distribution in terms of the differentiation of ranks, the organization of police headquarters, the arrangement and location of police stations, etc., are all regulated by the standards established by the central authorities; here again the prefectures make only minor decisions. (6) One motive behind the 1954 reform was the desire to eliminate the weaknesses inherent in the municipal police systems forced upon Japan by the Occupation. (7) The long-standing tradition of the national police system, which had been very effective since early Meiji, is still a very strong influence in the present approaches to the problem of police organization.

The 1954 system cannot, however, be said to be an exact duplicate of the pre-war system. In the present system, the National Public Safety Commission, although headed by a Minister of State, still maintains the appearance of an independent top-level agency. Then, too, the pre-war system presented the paradox of being in theory a centralized national system, yet actually to some extent decentralized, inasmuch as the prefectural governors had considerable latitude in the determination of policies in police affairs. But in the 1954 system the prefectural governors, as locally elected officials, do not possess any power of policy determination in this field, and their substitutes, the Prefectural Public

Safety Commissions, are limited and hamstrung in their own power of control over the police—as was shown with respect to the 1947 system—and, hence, the centralization is much more conspicuous than in the pre-war system.

Conclusion[4]

The Occupation-sponsored program of decentralizing the police system was considered to be an "unrealistic" failure. The Japanese Government, the National Rural Police, the prefectures and the high ranking police officers, who were to become national rather than local officials according to the new law, all favored the 1954 bill. Only the Socialists and the representatives of the major cities opposed it. Public opinion was divided. The intensity of opposition to the new bill in the Diet was shown by the uproar over extending the period of session so that the measure could be voted upon. But the police recentralization bill was passed by the majority of the Diet reconstituted by the conservative parties of Liberals and Progressives.

Excluding the military forces, the Japanese police have been a last rampart, or ultima ratio, of the government since early Meiji against malcontent and subversive elements. Since Japan has been, or is at least considered to have been, in a perpetual state of crisis and emergency, the authoritarian form of police has been thought a necessity. Stripped of its centralized national police by the 1947 reform, the government felt that Japan had become dangerously vulnerable, in view of her precarious position between two camps in the international struggles, and her more than ample share of domestic discontent and unrest. It was thought that she had no choice but to return to the authoritarian organizational principle of the pre-war police system.

Japan's propensity for administrative centralization has another basis, that of practical economy. In a public relations pamphlet of the Kyoto Prefectural Police, published on the occasion of the 1954 revision, a former National Rural Police official, looking back to the Occupation period, wrote:

> I should like to congratulate from my heart the present reform of the [police] system, by pointing at the problems which I have been pondering these six years.... Under the old system, valid before March, 1948, one section chief was in charge of and able to handle criminal investigation in the whole prefecture. But after the disintegration of this system, and even after the 1951 abolition of the town police, more than ten division and section chiefs cropped up in accordance with the law in several city and National Rural Police and divided the former one-man job among too many officials. These police staffs required not only personnel expenses but also motorcars, official residences, office rooms, and so forth, and were quite uneconomical. Was such a system a right one?.... The chief of police and the police station chief had jurisdiction over only one-half or one-third of the area such officials controlled under the former system. They must have a lot of leisure indeed. What a squandering of able officers!....

On the other hand, by recentralization the local bodies have lost their own agents of law enforcement. The city by-laws or regulations can no longer be enforced by the city's own police. The local bodies issue their by-laws, but must rely on the national police system for their enforcement. This means, obviously, a weakening of local autonomy. At about the time of the abolition of major city police units, i.e., July, 1955, a groundless doubt arose concerning the so-called Local Anti-Demonstration By-Laws issued by the cities during the Occupation to cope with the Communist-inspired mass demonstrations, parades and assemblies. It was questioned whether such by-laws were valid after the abolition of city police. The local bodies, having no more police units of their own, have tended to refrain from issuing local ordinances in the police field; the national government was expected to take over this field. It is strange that in the controversies around the problem of centralization of the police system no one argued that it was a violation of the Constitutional provisions stipulating the principles of local autonomy.

Another of the Occupation policies, the deconcentration of powers of the pre-war police agencies, is still valid and intact. The Ordinance Review Advisory Committee recommended in July, 1951, the merger of all public safety agencies—not only the local and national police, but also the Maritime Safety Board (coast guard) of the Ministry of Transportation, the Immigration Agency, and the Special Investigation Board (counterpart of the F.B.I.) of the Attorney General's office—into a Public Safety Ministry. The Police Law Revision Bill of February, 1953, had been planned to establish a National Police Board in the Prime Minister's office, relegating the National Public Safety Commission to an advisory status. These schemes were unsuccessful attempts to revive a central agency akin to the former Home Ministry. The 1954 bill was a retreat from these lines, leaving the chairmanship of a Minister of State as a Trojan horse in the National Public Safety Commission. The police agencies are still limited to purely administrative functions of execution of laws, and their former powers of sub-legislative and judicial functions have not been restored even by the 1954 revision.

Among the Occupation policies, the neutralization or separation of police agencies from political interference has come to be somewhat marred by the introduction of a Minister of State as chairman of the National Public Safety Commission. This invasion of neutrality had to be accepted as a part of the bargain in order to establish a closer government and police relationship. The Constitutional provision that the Prime Minister exercises control and supervision over various administrative branches was, conveniently, used as a justification for this reform.

Lastly, the popular control exercised through Public Safety Commissions over the police was, on the whole, a failure. A group of lay members meeting in a committee only a few times a month was inadequate for the purpose of exerting a strong control over the experienced police—so much so, in fact, that the government was not at all reluctant to let the Public Safety Commissions remain in the police picture. The government used these as a facade to keep up the appearance of democracy in the 1954 revision.

Despite the Occupation, the bureaucratic police mentality and its "power complex" are much the same as they were before the war. The democratization of the police has not been successful. (This fact is well evidenced by careful research made by Hironaka Toshio in Nippon-no-Keisatsu, 1955, Todai-Shinsho No. 25.) It is feared on all sides that the present police attitude will be strengthened by the 1954 reform rather than otherwise.

Almost the only remaining hope of democratization in the governmental field rests with the Japanese judiciary. The power of the court and its jurisdiction vis-à-vis the public administration has been broadened and amplified by the Occupation reforms, by the Anglo-Americanization of criminal procedure, introduction of the judicial review system of administrative actions, and by the State Liability Law. Now the citizens can and do sue the government for the annulment of administrative orders and decisions, and for damages suffered by illegal acts and practices of the law enforcement officials. The police are checked in their operations to a degree never known before. The effect of this judicial system is very salutary and will remain so. The judiciary reform, one of the less acclaimed achievements of the Occupation, has been a real boon to the Japanese people, and it is hoped that it is not going to be tampered with even by possible Constitutional amendment, for it is now a deep-seated popular possession.

A Chinese proverb says that when lips are broken, teeth feel the cold. A breach was made in the wall of the Occupation policies in the form of the 1954 police reform. In the fields of the Constitutional and statutory amendments similar onslaughts and reforms will be attempted under the pretexts of "unsuitability to the national circumstances," "efficiency" and "economy." The fate of the police reform may well foreshadow that of numerous other Occupation innovations.

NOTES

1. This first section is based on Count Okuma Shigenobu, Kaikoku-Gojunenshi (History of the Fifty Years Since the Opening Up of the Country), vol. I, and Keishicho, Keishicho-shiko (History of the Metropolitan Police Board), vol. I.

2. The second section is based on The Political Reorientation of Japan, September 1945 to September 1948, Report of Government Section, Supreme Commander for the Allied Powers, and Asàhi Shimbun Shukusatsuban (Photostat Edition Asahi Newspaper), 1947-1954.

3. The third section is based on Asahi Shimbun Shukusatsuban and on Harry Emerson Wildes, Typhoon in Tokyo, New York, 1954.

4. The final section is based on Sugai Shuichi's article "Sengo Keisatsuseido no Suii" (Vicissitudes in the Police System After the War) in Toshimondaikenkyu, Osaka, January, 1955.

MAEDA SHOICHI: A CASE STUDY OF A JAPANESE POLITICAL BOSS*

Paul S. Dull

I

The dynamics of politics tend to be universal, and it is probably true that political bosses develop in all countries in one form or another. Certainly a political boss in Japan is no new phenomenon, nor has the subject been entirely overlooked in surveys of the Japanese political scene. In the present study, however, the purpose has been to supplement more general essays on political behavior by focusing attention upon one individual boss, investigating the local sources and effects of his power, and as far as possible suggesting the motives behind his activities. Although the specific qualities in the situation described here can never be exactly duplicated, it is hoped that its details will afford some insight into techniques of control and modes of obedience which are common over a large area.

The case under study seems to present a rather extreme example of "bossism." As one informant said: "You could probably look all over Japan and never find such a boss as Maeda Shoichi of Naka-chō." The extraordinary effectiveness of Maeda's exploits, however, does not mean that they are unique, except perhaps in the degree to which they have succeeded. In fact the usefulness of this composite picture of one Japanese political boss will largely depend on how well it serves to highlight similar but more obscure activities of his kind elsewhere.

The data in this case study are derived from personal interviews with Maeda's political friends and cronies as well as his opponents. Information was gathered also from town officials, politically informed persons in nearby areas, and from farmers and townspeople of Naka-chō who, though less active in politics, were nevertheless well aware of the man's influence. An interview was obtained with the ex-Procurator who repeatedly tried to prosecute Maeda, and with Maeda himself. In addition, pertinent facts were found in official records such as the town government's census register (koseki), records of criminal convictions (kiketsu hanzainin) and official court records (keiji saiban kakutei gempon), obtained from the Procurator's Office in Kō City. Certain Kō City newspapers were also consulted.

Maeda's position in the community made it necessary to use a variety of approaches with informants and to discount some of their statements. Political opponents of Maeda were fearful that he would discover what they might say against him and insisted that the interviews be arranged in secret and pledges of anonymity given. The town mayor, though also a political opponent, was an exception. He made no such demands; in fact, he tried to use the investigation to his advantage against Maeda. In questioning the common townspeople and farmers, the purpose of the interview had to be hidden. Maeda's friends, who were interviewed first, were told that Naka-chō's Farmers' Cooperative (Nōgyō Kyōdō Kumiai) was being studied along with several other such groups in the prefecture. Compliments about Maeda and his friends helped to make these people responsive. Maeda himself avoided interviews, and although he was tricked into coming to the mayor's office by a ruse in which the mayor assisted, the meeting turned out to be the least productive of all, much to the mayor's disappointment. Throughout the study rumor and fact were hard to

---
*This study is based upon materials collected by the author as research associate for the University of Michigan Center for Japanese Studies at Okayama City, Japan. The work was supported by grants from the Social Science Research Council, the Ford Board for Overseas Training and Research, and the Graduate Council of the University of Oregon. For obvious reasons, all personal and place names in this paper are fictitious.

separate, but by checking story against story, and using records as an additional test, there emerged what was felt to be a reasonably accurate picture of the whole design, if not of each particular detail. Rumors, even when they could not be substantiated, have necessarily been included in this picture. One reason is that their influence has often been strong. Further, the very fact that the truth about Maeda's activities is so elusive does much to describe the atmosphere in which he rules.

Naka-chō, the term -chō indicating an administrative area which includes not only the town proper but a larger rural area around it, is about ten miles from Kō City. According to statistics gathered July 1, 1952, it has a population of 2,162 families, or 9,555 people. It is divided into two smaller administrative areas (ōaza): Hei, the smaller, is totally agrarian; Naka, which includes the town and the rest of the rural area, is predominantly urban and has a population about three times that of Hei-ōaza. Naka-chō is reputed to have been ruled for a long time by unscrupulous bosses and its standing as a community has suffered accordingly. In addition, its inhabitants appear to undergo some social discrimination. On several occasions informants living elsewhere referred to the people of Naka-chō as rude and commented on the fact that it was difficult for Naka-chō girls to find husbands from other communities.[1]

II

Maeda Shoichi was born February 19, 1903 in Hei-ōaza, the second child and eldest son in a family of eight. His father and mother were of common rank (heimin). In 1921 his father died and Maeda inherited his father's domicile. He was not married until 1941 and there have been no children from this marriage, although a boy was adopted in 1942. In 1947, Maeda moved to a larger house in Hei-ōaza.

Maeda's schooling was scanty because he was unruly in the classroom and was often a truant. To this day he cannot write his name or count written figures—a lack most unusual in Japan. His personal characteristics do not commend him. He is taller and heavier than the average Japanese and his features are rather coarse. For months on end he wears the same rumpled and dirty Western-style tweed suit, of a loud pattern. Many say that on hot summer days he takes off his clothes in the office and conducts his business in that state. Apparently he is a coward and a bully. He is said to be afraid of drunks and to keep a sword under the mattress (futon). Unless he has friends with him he is seldom assertive or loud, but otherwise he is both. In his office and in the town legislature (chō-gikai), he habitually beats down his opponents by shouting his arguments.

His criminal career started early. He was sentenced in 1921 by the Bo Supreme Court to one year and two months in the penitentiary for the crime of arson. In 1928, he was sentenced by the Kō District Court to seven years in the penitentiary for the crime of illegal entry and burglary. His term was shortened to five years and three months by an Imperial amnesty to criminals. In 1944, he was fined twelve hundred yen by the Kō District Court for violating the National Emergency Draft Law. In 1951, he was fined thirty thousand yen by the same court for violating the Essential Goods Regulation Law.

After his release from the penitentiary in 1943 he worked his small farm. The closing years of the war, however, brought Maeda his first opportunity to acquire wealth and use it for political ends, when the government rationing of essential commodities began to be enforced. At this time he engaged in black market operations, gaining a sizable amount of capital. Shortly thereafter he started operating with the Suzuki family: the father, Jun, and two sons, Kaneo and Shige. These men had also been farmers but had branched out into dealing in goods made from igusa, a cultivated reed used in the manufacture of the mats which all Japanese have on their floors. Soon after the end of the war, Suzuki Kaneo and Maeda formed the Aison Kōgyō Kaisha, a company ostensibly engaged in making paper yarn, but actually a front for black market activities. When the company was no longer useful for such purposes, there followed some complicated financial maneuvers, including a large loan from the Chūgoku Bank of Kō City. The firm soon declared itself bankrupt, however, and only half the loan was recovered by the bank. There is little doubt that Maeda himself came out of the transaction with more money than before.

At this time the same group gained control of the Naka-chō branch of the Kō Igusa Goods Cooperative (Kō-ken Iseihin Kōgyō Kumiai, Naka-shibu). Suzuki Shige became managing director and Maeda a director. The cooperative was effectively milked and eventually went bankrupt. Although the farmers brought in high-grade igusa, this was sold on the black market solely for the profit of the administrators, who then bought cheap igusa from which the cooperative made goods which were necessarily of the poorest quality. The farmers were credited only with the profit, if any, from the sale of the cheap goods. These manipulations, of course, contributed to the group's fortunes, but brought Maeda in danger of punishment. Indeed, the Procurator wished to bring action against him but could not obtain any complaining witness fearless enough to testify in court.

During the food shortage of the last part of the war and the first post-war years, the cultivation of igusa was strictly regulated by the Japanese government in order to prevent farmers from growing this crop on land which could be used for rice. A third scheme of Maeda's was to take over the office of Chief Inspector of the Igusa Inspection Committee (Igusa Kensain), a governmental body which regulated the sale of igusa goods to keep them off the black market. There is no evidence as to how Maeda became Chief Inspector; his growing position as a dealer in igusa goods may have been a factor. There is no doubt that he used this position to promote his own black market activities and to charge illegal fees for permitting others' igusa goods to be transported. As noted before, Maeda was eventually brought to trial for this extortion and fined a nominal sum of thirty thousand yen. According to the Court records in this case, Maeda's gang attacked and beat those whom they caught trying to transport igusa goods without his stamp, or, at the least, confiscated a good share of the goods before they would permit the rest to be moved. Inasmuch as the intercepted goods were often bound for the black market, the operation was essentially a highjacking one.

Out of these often illegal operations Maeda became relatively wealthy. He used his money next to build a political machine that would add to his power in the community. In 1946 he was a candidate for the office of director of the Nōgyō Nōchi Iinkai, a precursor of the present Nōgyō Kyōdō Kumiai (Farmers' Cooperative), but was defeated because of his personal unpopularity. Some of his henchmen, however, were more successful in gaining offices within the organization, and through them he appears to have controlled it until it too went bankrupt as a result of his use of the organization for his own ends. When its successor, the Nōgyō Kyōdō Kumiai, was organized he became a director, and later its managing director. Since that time he has used this cooperative as his primary tool for exercising political control over Naka-chō as well as for increasing his own fortune and that of his friends. Unlike most farmers' cooperatives it is not run for the benefit of farmer members.

Three features of the Naka-chō Farmers' Cooperative illustrate this point and distinguish it from the usual type. Membership is open to any man who cultivates one tan (.245 acres) of land, a ridiculously low figure which admits many whose main occupation is not farming. Second, the cooperative operates no general store. Fertilizer and oil can be obtained at the main office but at a higher rate than the commercial price. In Hin-buraku (a hamlet in Hei-ōaza) the organization does operate a store in a small building which is used also as a residence, and is completely inaccessible to motor transportation. This store handles a few foodstuffs such as mikan in season, soy sauce, cuttle-fish and sugar, and a very small selection of dry-goods, such as jikatabi, tabi and zōri. An inspection of the store showed it to be dirty and cluttered, though apparently unused to much trade. It was far inferior to most farmers' cooperative stores, such as those found in nearby machi and mura. Third, Maeda has arranged that the important Farmers' Committee (Nōgyō Iinkai) which sets rice requisitioning quotas (kyōshutsu) has its headquarters in the Farmers' Cooperative building rather than in the town government office (yakuba) where it belongs as part of the town government and where it is always found elsewhere.[2] The Farmers' Committee is composed of seventeen members. Maeda is its chairman and fifteen of the sixteen remaining members belong to his faction.

Domination of the Farmers' Cooperative and the Farmers' Committee makes possible two of Maeda's strongest techniques of control: manipulation of rice requisitioning quotas and of credit. An example of the first was witnessed in the fall of 1952 when the time came for the establishing of individual rice requisitioning quotas. In Naka-ōaza the full committee devoted a whole day to a thorough field survey before quotas were set. The next day in Hei-ōaza, the stronghold of Maeda and his faction, the quotas for the farmers were determined in two hours with only a small number of pro-Maeda committee members participating. Thus Maeda and his followers set almost arbitrary quotas for their own fields, deducting considerably for insect and disease damage. What statistics could be gathered from the Farmers' Committee through an officer in the Farmers' Cooperative showed that Naka-ōaza was carrying a disproportionate share of the governmental rice requisitioning burden. The one member of the committee who was not a Maeda man reported that Maeda's quota was always practically non-existent.

Manipulation of credit is carried out by Maeda by several methods. Most of the money available to the Farmers' Cooperative comes from Maeda, whose investment is some six million yen or eighty per cent of the Farmers' Cooperative's total resources. Control of this group's funds enables Maeda to prevent loans which a farmers' cooperative would normally make. This is a considerable weapon against a farmer whose livelihood may depend on credit and who stands little chance of securing it from a commercial bank. If the Farmers' Cooperative lends money to an applicant who cannot obtain a loan elsewhere, interest rates are higher than usual. Observation of loan operations bore out the stories that loans were on a day-to-day and individual basis.

A Farm-Forestry Central Bank (Nōrin Chūō Ginko) was established by the Japanese government to enable farmers to borrow money at 2.6 sen per day and thus buy the tools necessary to increase production. Funds from this governmental bank, however, are available only through village and town agencies. In Naka-chō, the Farmers' Cooperative withholds this money from its members. When applicants have asked for loans from this fund, Maeda has said that no funds were available, so that they would borrow money from him at a higher rate of interest. The informants did not know if Maeda had drawn Naka-chō's share of funds from the Farm-Forestry Central Bank. They suspected, however, that he had himself arranged for the use of this money at 2.6 sen per day and was then lending it out at 4 sen per day.

If Maeda exploits the Farmers' Cooperative and Farmers' Committee for his own profit and to threaten financial ruin for any who may oppose him, he also uses these groups to reward his supporters. They receive the advantage of low rice requisition figures, easy credit, and lower prices for oil and fertilizer. In addition, as chairman of the Farmers' Committee and head of the Farmers' Cooperative, Maeda controls employment within both agencies and distributes jobs to his henchmen. Many informants complained that the Farmers' Cooperative had too many employees, including some twenty clerks. A comparison based on observation of other farmers' cooperatives leads to the estimate that the number of employees of the Naka-chō Farmers' Cooperative was about four times more than normal. Although apparently well aware of practices which add to the expense of the organization and make its cooperative features less attractive, farmer members dare not complain or try to get a change of officers lest their rice requisition quotas be raised and their credit restricted.

Maeda has used the town government in his third technique of gaining profit and exercising control: manipulation of taxes. He first ran for the town legislature in 1947 and was elected. Since then he has controlled it absolutely, and at most sessions he is the only member of the legislature who speaks. In the rare instances when he is opposed, he shouts threats at the top of his voice to prevent any member from complaining of his management of the Farmers' Cooperative, his vulnerable point. The town mayor (chōchō) is powerless, under the post-war system of local government, for he cannot secure legislation over the opposition of the legislature. The only proposals before this body are Maeda's.

Until the 1952 election the office of mayor was held by a supporter of Maeda. Gathering forces of opposition finally succeeded in defeating this man. However, although the new mayor opposes Maeda, his record shows him to be more anxious to capitalize on whatever power he can capture than to spearhead any reform movement. The tradition of bosses in Naka-chō does not seem to be losing vitality.

Maeda has not been able to extend his dominance beyond Naka-chō. His one-time associate, Suzuki Kaneo has risen to a high position in the Kō prefectural government. Although his younger brother, Suzuki Shige, is still associated with Maeda's machine, the elder has distributed no political favors to Maeda despite the latter's efforts; in fact, he has tried to get his younger brother to break with Maeda. Reasons for the apparent antagonism have not been established, but unverified stories suggest that Suzuki Kaneo's dislike stems from Maeda's appropriating most of the profits when the Aison Kōgyō Kaisha went bankrupt.

Maeda's influence on national elections can not be clearly determined. Politicians seek his aid at election time, and even candidates to the national Diet visit him. However, there is no evidence that he can deliver a vote where the balloting is secret and is not concerned with Naka-chō's matters. When the Socialists were in power his home was the Socialist Party (Shakaitō) headquarters for the town. At present he is an officer of the Kō-ken Liberal Party (Jiyūtō).

Other areas and techniques of control than those already described are still harder to define. Agrarian Hei-ōaza has, for a long time, feared the domination of Naka-ōaza. The rivalry and hatred between the two has extended even to the schools where Naka and Hei factions have formed and frequently battle. No matter how much the farmers of Hei-ōaza, Maeda's stronghold, dislike him personally, they feel that his power works to their advantage. Maeda makes full use of this situation. Active opposition against him from any quarter is hard to arouse because the long history of political bosses has developed in these people a tendency toward submission, which goes even beyond the usual political docility of the average Japanese farmer. Maeda himself has not often relied upon violence. He has not had to do so. Some signs of deterioration of his machine are in evidence, but so far he continues to dominate this community, and to fill his own purse and feed his sense of power.

III

There are many men like Maeda Shoichi in both rural and urban Japan. Some have criminal records; most do not. Their techniques of control vary with particular circumstances. Some make use of the institutions of the oyabun-kobun (literally, leader-follower); others use the yakuza (bullies).[3] In some cases, their rule may result in a benevolent paternalism; in many instances, "bossism" results in a selfish accumulation of power and money at the common man's expense. If one accepts the idea that democracy would be a desirable thing for Japan, as was assumed during the Occupation years, political bosses create a disturbing obstacle to its growth.

The so-called democratizing of local government in the Local Autonomy Law lessened the power of the Home Ministry and of executives in village, town and city and increased that of local legislative bodies. Such a re-arrangement of power did not guarantee a more democratic use of authority, as the case of Maeda illustrates, although the change made it possible for new faces to appear on the political scene. Democratic machinery of government provides no safeguard against bosses if the electorate is not aware of its responsibilities, or its power, and if it even thinks it improper to oppose politicians who are already dominant in the political hierarchy of Japan.

Attempts have been made to place the blame for post-war bossism in Japan on the Liberal Party.[4] This thesis seems difficult to support. Local politics seldom reflect the rivalries of the national parties. Bosses tend to ally themselves with the party in power and the Liberal Party has been in power most of the time in post-war Japan. Maeda, it will be remembered, was a Socialist during Katayama's cabinet and easily shifted to the Liberal Party when Yoshida came to power again.

If a prognosis must be made for the course of this disease in Japanese politics, it would be that the trouble will remain chronic. It is not particularly susceptible to cure by manipulation of governmental machinery or by a change in parties. It is, in fact, too deeply imbedded in Japan's political _mores_ for much immediate change to be anticipated.

NOTES

1. This fact of a hierarchy among towns and villages and social discrimination practiced among them is noted in Edward Norbeck, <u>Takashima</u>, <u>A Japanese Fishing Community</u> (University of Utah Press, 1954) p. 113.

2. Under the kyōshutsu system, the national government has required Japanese farmers to grow specified amounts of various agricultural produce, chiefly rice. The government then buys the specified amounts at a price much lower than the farmer could obtain on the commercial market. Bonuses are given to farmers who sell more than their quota to the government. The produce that remains after the meeting of the quota can be sold on the commercial market.

3. For a description of the oyabun-kobun, see Iwao Ishino, "Oyabun-kobun: A Japanese Ritual Kinship Institution," <u>American Anthropologist</u>, 55 (Dec. 1953).

4. See, for example, the <u>Shakaitō Taimsu</u> (Socialist Times), (Tōkyō edition), April 8, 1953.

JAPANESE CONSERVATIVE POLITICS 1947-1955

Alfred B. Clubok

Introduction

Since the end of the Pacific War and the subsequent occupation of Japan by American troops, the Japanese people have had six opportunities to elect or reject political leadership by means of "free and competitive" elections. The Japanese electorate not only has had the opportunity to participate in the election process, but perhaps for the first time in the history of modern Japan, the voter has been presented with a meaningful choice between political parties of the right and the left.

That the choice presented to the Japanese people is broader than that of pre-war Japan needs no verification. However, a glance at the results of the post-war elections at once indicates that the conservative tradition of pre-war Japan has carried over into the post-war political scene. Perhaps the dominance of conservative political forces in Japan is best evidenced by the fact that since the surrender the premiership has been held continuously by conservative politicians, except for a short period from May 23, 1947 to February 10, 1948 when Katayama Tetsu, President of the Socialist Party, held office. It must be remembered, however, that the Katayama Cabinet remained in office at the sufferance of the conservative parties and that at any time during this period a coalition of the two major conservative parties, the Liberal and Democratic Parties, could have expelled the Socialist-led Cabinet.

Within the conservative political movement, the Liberal Party was the dominant political group until 1955. The fact that the Liberal Party's past president, Yoshida Shigeru, was elected five times to the premiership and that, from 1949 (neglecting the split in the Party in the 1953 election) to 1955, the Party controlled a majority of seats in the House of Representatives was ample evidence of the Liberal Party's leading position.

If, then, conservative political forces are dominant in Japan, an obvious question presents itself. What do we in the West know of the dynamics of Japanese conservative politics? The Western political scientist must answer that he knows exceedingly little about the forces affecting the Japanese political scene. Perhaps even more unfortunate is the fact that, although the Occupation offered to the Western research worker an excellent opportunity to alleviate this deficiency, a disproportionately large segment of post-war political research has been directed at one peripheral aspect of Japanese politics: the post-war Socialist and Communist movements in Japan. Although this preoccupation with left wing politics in Japan is understandable in view of the world situation, it is somewhat unrealistic since it neglects the conservative elements which have politically controlled the nation.

The present study is directed at two aspects of Japanese conservative politics:

(1) An investigation of the geographical distribution of the Liberal Party's and the Conservative Block's strength, partly in terms of the traditional regional breakdown of Japan and partly in terms of the election districts. (The Conservative Block is defined as the Liberal and Democratic Parties combined.)

(2) An investigation of the urban-rural distribution of the support of the Liberal Party and the Conservative Block.

The basic hypothesis underlying the urban-rural analysis is that the Liberal Party, as well as the conservative forces as a whole, received their greatest support in rural

Japan, and that this support would decrease as the degree of urbanization of the area in question increased. This is, of course, a theory of long standing in Japanese politics, but, to the best of the author's knowledge, its validity has never been adequately demonstrated.

For each election analyzed in the study, a general survey of the election results of the House of Representatives is presented, followed by an investigation of the urban-rural distribution of the Liberal Party's and Conservative Block's strength. Based on these analyses, the final section of the text presents an indication of the Liberal Party's and the Conservative Block's geographical strongholds, and also generalized conclusions as to Liberal Party and conservative strength, vis-à-vis the urban-rural continuum.

Urban-Rural Concept

When discussing an urban-rural pattern of voting behavior, one must recognize from the outset that there is a continuous merging of urban and rural cultural characteristics. Perhaps the most adequate term for this phenomenon is the often used "urban-rural continuum." The problem, in a study such as this, is to place real communities on this continuum. When we speak of the "degree of urbanization" we are clearly indicating that the phenomena being studied can be scaled. To measure quantitatively the degree of urbanization of a community, that is, to place the community at its appropriate position on the continuum, an index must be devised. There are any number of interrelated factors which could be utilized to form this index. Population density within a community, occupation of the inhabitants, the extent of contact between the community concerned and other communities, the degree of mobility within the community, are all factors related to the degree of urbanization.

At the time this study was conducted, the only information the author had regarding a given community was its population size. This information was obtained from the Japanese Population Census of 1950.[1] There are no unincorporated areas in Japan; since all of the population are living in one of the three political subdivisions of the prefecture (ken)— city (shi), town (machi), or village (mura)—the entire Japanese voting population can be studied by sampling these communities.

The assumption made in studying these urban-rural voting patterns is that the degree of urbanization of a community is correlated to its population size. As the population of a community increases, the degree of urbanization also increases. The author realized that communities of the same population size can have different functions and, accordingly, different degrees of urbanization. However, it was felt that the degree of urbanization could be inferred, in rather broad terms, from population statistics.

Method

The population was stratified into four groups based on the population size of the community. The four strata are as follows:

Group   I - Communities with populations up to 5,000 (rural group)
Group II - Communities with populations of 5,001-30,000 (semi-rural group)
Group III - Communities with populations of 30,001-150,000 (semi-urban group)
Group IV - Communities with populations of 150,000 and above (urban group)

The first and fourth subdivisions are of primary concern in this study.

Since occupation is another useful index of urbanization, an investigation was made of occupation statistics for seven prefectures for which such data were available. The results of this investigation indicated that communities with a population of 5,000 and below had primarily rural characteristics, while communities with a population of 150,000 and above were communities with primarily urban characteristics.[2] Groups II and III were included in the study to indicate trend and were purposely left wide, vis-à-vis population, so as not to obscure the primary urban-rural pattern. The division between these intermediate groups is based on the fact that population clusters of 30,000 or more are considered in the Japanese census to be urban areas, whereas population clusters below the 30,000 limit are considered to be rural areas.

From Groups I, II, and III a simple random sample of communities was chosen. The 1950 population census was used for this purpose. It was originally decided to select one hundred samples from each group. However, time limitations made it necessary to decrease the proposed sample size. At the time this decision was forced on the author, the greater part of the work on sample Groups II and III had been completed and, accordingly, the sample size in Group I had to be decreased. The sample size for each of the first three groups is as follows: Group I, 50 communities; Group II, 100 communities; and Group III, 100 communities. The total sample size is 250 communities. There were thirty-seven communities in Japan with a population of 150,001 or more as of 1950. Consequently, all of these communities were included in Group IV. This group, then, represents an entire population and is not treated as a statistic.

One difficulty which presented itself in the selection of the samples was the consolidation of two or more communities into one political and administrative unit. This is especially prevalent at the village level, that is, in Group I and, to a lesser extent, in Group II. When consolidation occurred before the compilation of the 1950 census, it was possible to identify the original communities which were combined, since this information was included in the census data. In such cases the combined election statistics of the component parts were included in the study. When consolidation occurred after 1950 it was impossible to identify the communities which had been combined with the original sample community. Accordingly, when such cases occurred in the 1952, 1953, and 1955 election data, a replacement was selected at random.

The source of all election data utilized in the urban-rural study is the Summary of the General Election of Members of the House of Representatives, an official publication of the House of Representatives.[3] Data were collected from this source for the 1947, 1949, 1952, 1953, and 1955 elections.

An analysis of the 1946 election was not conducted for two reasons. First, the utilization of large election districts in 1946, with a consequent large number of candidates competing for office within any one constituency, made the election returns too unwieldy to be used profitably. Second, the exceedingly large number of minor party and independent candidates running for election clouded the election returns and it was believed that a meaningful analysis could not be made.

Two statistical tests were utilized in this study: (1) the Analysis of Variance, and (2) the Student Fisher T Test. All statistically significant data will be presented at the five per cent level of significance.

Election System for the House of Representatives

Although the present study does not focus on either the legal or historical aspects of the election law, a short summary of the Japanese election system is presented as a background for the analyses of the post-war elections with which this study is chiefly concerned. The Japanese election system was substantially revised in both 1945 and 1947. However, the 1945 revision was utilized only in the House of Representatives election of April 10, 1946. The provisions of the 1947 law, with minor revisions, have been in effect since its promulgation, and five post-war elections have been held under its provisions.

1945 Election Law

The first major revision of the pre-war election system was promulgated December 18, 1945.[4] The new law, however, did not represent a complete rewriting of the pre-war election code, but rather a revision and reshaping of it to meet existing conditions.

Only five provisions of the 1945 law need concern us here: the expansion of the franchise; the adoption of a large electoral district; the use of limited plural voting; the election deposit required by law; and the requirements for election.

The election law, by reducing the voting age from twenty-five to twenty years of age and by extending the franchise to women, increased the electorate from approximately 14.5 million in 1942 to approximately thirty-six million in 1946. The right to vote, however, was denied to incompetents and quasi-incompetents, to those serving prison sentences, to those receiving public or private charity, to those with no definite domicile, and to heads of noble families.

The total number of election districts was drastically reduced, with a corresponding increase in the size of the district as compared to the pre-war medium-sized constituency. In 1941 Japan was divided into 120 election districts. The distribution of the districts within the prefectures ranged from a prefecture constituting a single election district, such as Nara, Yamanashi, and Shiga, to prefectures containing six and seven districts, Osaka and Tokyo respectively. Thirty-three prefectures out of forty-six contained either two or three election districts.[5] Under the election law as amended in 1945, Japan was divided into fifty-three election districts. Thirty-nine prefectures constituted single districts, while the remaining seven prefectures were divided into two districts each. Each district elected from four to twenty-three members, one representative for every 150,000 population.

A limited plural-entry ballot was provided for in the 1945 law. Under this system each elector voted for from one to three candidates, depending upon the number of House of Representative seats assigned to the election district. The provisions under which this system operated were as follows:

1. The elector voted for one candidate in any district in which less than three seats had been assigned. However, this provision operated only in cases of by-election.

2. The elector voted for not more than two candidates in any district in which more than four and less than eleven seats had been assigned.

3. The elector voted for not more than three candidates in any district in which eleven or more seats had been assigned.

The election law required that each candidate post two thousand yen in cash or national bonds, to be forfeited to the government if the candidate failed to poll at least one-tenth of the total number of votes cast in the district divided by the number of seats assigned to the district. Finally, the law required that a candidate obtain a minimum number of votes to be elected to the House of Representatives. The requirement was that a candidate must receive not less than one-fourth of the total number of votes obtained by the respective candidates divided by the number of seats assigned to the district. In the April 10, 1946 election two seats could not be filled because of this provision. Accordingly, two constituency by-elections were required.

1947 Election Law

The House of Representatives Election Law was again revised and reached its final form slightly more than three weeks before the 1947 House of Representatives election.

The Yoshida Cabinet submitted to the Diet on March 11, 1947 a revision bill primarily concerned with the enfranchisement of certain groups, stricter supervision of the election itself, and more rigorous restrictions on campaign practices.

Both the Liberal and the Democratic Parties desired that changes be made concerning the size of the election district and the plural-entry ballot. There were two reasons for this desire for change. First,

> the plural ballot system, coupled with large plural-member constituencies, provided the voter with at least two votes in all but fourteen electoral districts, in which he had three. <u>Designed to aid new and minority parties against established organizations on the right</u> (the Liberal and Democratic Parties) it resulted in capricious voting.... The writer's chauffeur, for instance, voted for a Liberal and a Communist; many of the thirty-nine women elected admittedly owed their election to second choice 'courtesy' ballots.[6] [Underscored words are mine.—A.B.C.]

Second, the large districts made adequate election planning extremely difficult. In an election system based on a plural-member constituency, a party must attempt to ascertain its strength accurately before the election. A party must not run too few candidates and thereby pile up dead votes which could have otherwise elected one or more of the party's candidates. On the other hand, if a party runs too many candidates, it takes the chance of spreading its vote thinly and consequently losing seats which it might otherwise have won. This guessing game presents many difficulties under ordinary circumstances. When a system of large election districts and plural voting is added, a good guess is almost impossible to make.

Based primarily on these two factors, the Liberal and Democratic Parties introduced in the Diet two amendments which provided for a medium-sized election district and a single-entry ballot. These amendments were passed by the Diet on March 31, 1947. The election law as revised in 1947 retained the 1945 provisions on age and sex, and further extended the franchise so that only those persons serving prison sentences for crimes, and those persons declared incompetent or quasi-incompetent, were barred from voting.[7] Any Japanese national, twenty-five years of age or older, is eligible to hold office, except for certain categories of public officials who are not eligible while they hold such offices, e.g., judges, public procurators, and members of the national police force.

The large election district system of the 1945 revision was replaced by a medium-sized district closely resembling the pre-war districts (1928-1942). The nation was divided into 117 districts for the House of Representatives elections. Nine prefectures constituted single districts, while the remaining thirty-seven prefectures contained from two to seven districts. Each district elects from two to five members, apportioned on a basis of one per 150,000 population. A list of the election districts, along with the number of candidates to be elected in each district and the geographical areas included within each district, is included in the appendix of the election law.

The requirement of an election deposit, in cash or national bonds, was continued under the revised election law. However, the amount of the deposit was increased from two thousand <u>yen</u> in 1946 to five thousand <u>yen</u> in 1947. This increase in the amount of the deposit was, of course, necessitated by the decline in the value of the <u>yen</u>, the sole purpose of the deposit being to discourage irresponsible candidates. The deposit would be forfeited if the total popular vote which the candidate received were less than one-fifth of the aggregate vote of all candidates divided by the number of seats assigned to the election district. This provision is more stringent than its counterpart in the 1945 law, which required only one-tenth of the total vote divided by the number of seats assigned to the district. A candidate, to be elected, must receive not less than one-fourth the total number of votes for all candidates divided by the number of members to be elected from the district.

The General Election of 1946

In the five succeeding sections an analysis of the 1947, 1949, 1952, 1953, and 1955 House of Representatives elections will be presented. The 1946 election will not be analyzed in detail for reasons previously stated. However the following table summarizing the general results of the Twenty-second General Election held on April 10, 1946 is presented here for purposes of comparison.[8]

TABLE 1

Party	Number of Seats Obtained	Number of Candidates Advanced	Percentage of Successful Candidates	Percentage of National Vote	Percentage of Diet Seats Held
Liberal.........	141	482	29.3	24.4	30.4
Progressive.....	93	373	24.9	18.7	20.0
Socialist........	93	330	28.2	17.8	20.0
Communist......	5	142	3.5	3.8	1.1
Cooperative.....	14	93	15.1	3.2	3.0
Minor Party.....	38	566	7.1	11.7	8.2
Independents.....	80	795	10.1	20.4	17.3
TOTAL	464*	2781	....	100.0	100.0

*All election data presented in this table were compiled as of the election day. Changes in party affiliation following an election are not indicated in the data. In the 1946 election two seats were not filled at the regular general election. Accordingly, the results of this year are analyzed in terms of 464 seats, rather than 466.

The General Election of 1947

The 1947 House of Representatives election was held at the request of S.C.A.P. (Supreme Commander for the Allied Powers). Yoshida, who had been named chairman of the Liberal Party's Executive Committee and subsequently chosen as Premier shortly after the Party's founder and president, Hatoyama Ichiro, had been purged, dissolved the Diet on March 31 and set April 25, 1947 as the date of the election.

The Yoshida Cabinet had assumed office in May 1946. By the end of the year, however, the continuing food crisis and steadily rising inflation had made the Cabinet increasingly unpopular. Faced with these problems, as well as with growing Socialist opposition, Yoshida contemplated dissolving the Diet and calling for a new election. The rank and file of the Liberal and Progressive Parties who supported the coalition Cabinet, however, were unwilling to risk a new election.

Yoshida subsequently sought to pacify the Socialists by forming a three-party coalition of the Liberals, Progressives, and Socialists, but negotiations broke down over the left wing Socialist demands for a Socialist Premier and for the dismissal of Ishibashi Tanzan, the Minister of Finance. Following this failure, Yoshida reorganized the Cabinet without Socialist support. It was shortly after the Cabinet had been reorganized that S.C.A.P.'s request for a new election was made.

All of the political parties were divided by internal strife. The Progressive Party, which was participating in and supporting the Yoshida Cabinet, was rank with dissatisfaction, as evidenced by the drive by some of its membership to dissolve the Party and form a new one. The Democratic Party, the successor to the Progressive Party, was founded less than three weeks before the election and included all of the members of the Progressive Party, a few members of the People's Cooperative Party, a few independent Diet members, and some members from the Liberal Party.

It appears that many of the thirty-one recruits who joined with the Progressives to form the Democratic Party on March 31, 1947 were persuaded to do so not only because of available party funds, but also because many of them, coming from pre-war Minseito districts, felt their chances of reelection to be best served by the support of that party's post-war heir (the Democratic Party).[9]

The Liberal Party was struggling to maintain support for the Yoshida Cabinet and, at the same time, attempting to prevent the loss of its Diet support to the Democratic Party, while the Socialist Party was still faced with the unresolved differences between its left and right wings. It was against this background that the 1947 House of Representatives election was held.

General Survey of the 1947 Election Results

The following table summarizes the results of the Twenty-third General Election held on April 25, 1947.[10]

TABLE 2

Party	Number of Seats Obtained	Number of Candidates Advanced	Percentage of Successful Candidates	Percentage of National Vote	Percentage of Diet Seats Held
Liberal	131	324	40.4	26.6	28.1
Democratic	124	332	37.3	25.4	26.6
Socialist	143	281	50.9	26.2	30.7
Communist	4	120	3.3	3.6	0.9
People's Co-operative	31	110	28.2	7.1	6.7
Minor Party	20	149	13.4	5.0	4.3
Independents	13	251	5.2	6.1	2.8
TOTAL	466	1567	....	100.0	100.0

As the foregoing table indicates, the Socialist Party won the election, returning 143 members to the House, a gain of forty-eight seats over 1946. The Socialist margin of victory in the House, however, was a slim one. The Liberal Party returned 131 members, while the Democratic Party returned 124.

With political power so evenly balanced in the House, preparations for a four-party coalition, consisting of the Socialist, Democratic, Liberal, and People's Cooperative Parties, were started with a meeting of the Secretary-generals of the parties concerned. Agreement was reached on May 16 when the four parties issued a joint statement and took up the question of selecting a Premier. However, on May 19 Yoshida issued a statement calling on Katayama Tetsu, then president of the Socialist Party, to purge the leftist elements in the Socialist Party. Katayama could not and would not consent to such a demand, for it would have resulted in splitting his party. The Liberals thus withdrew from the negotiations. Subsequently, on May 23, the House of Representatives designated Katayama Tetsu

Premier, and a coalition Cabinet consisting of the Socialist, Democratic, and People's Cooperative Parties was formed. Although this Cabinet was the first Socialist-led Cabinet to be formed in Japan, it must be remembered that the leading position of the Socialists in the House was not so much the result of their increased parliamentary membership as of disunity among the conservative parties. The Liberal and Democratic Parties controlled 255 seats in the House and at any time could have upset the Katayama Cabinet.

Compared with 1946, the three major parties, Liberal, Democratic, and Socialist, gained in the percentage of total national vote received, and these gains were at the expense of independents and minor party candidates. The Socialist gain was the most substantial, 8.4 per cent. The Democrats followed with a gain of 6.7 per cent, while the Liberal Party gained the least, 2.2 per cent. However, the Liberals did retain a slight lead in percentage of national vote. The Communist Party declined only slightly from their 1946 percentage, a decline of 0.2 per cent of the popular vote. The People's Cooperative Party, on the other hand, increased their percentage of the national vote over their predecessor, the Cooperative Party, from 3.2 per cent in 1946 to 7.1 per cent in 1947. The most significant decline was in the ranks of the independent and minor party candidates. The number of independent and minor party candidates running for election was 1,361 in 1946, and 118 of these were elected. These figures had dropped to 400 and 38 respectively in 1947.

All parties except the People's Cooperative ran fewer candidates in 1947 than in 1946. Whereas in 1946 there were approximately six candidates for every seat to be filled, in 1947 there were only slightly more than three candidates per seat. The Liberal Party advanced 324 candidates, or an average of 2.8 per election district, the Democratic Party advanced 332 candidates, or an average of 2.9 per district, while the Socialist Party advanced a slightly smaller number of candidates, 281, or an average of 2.4 per district. From these figures, it would seem that the three major parties profited from their experience in the 1946 election and, at least partially, restricted the number of their candidates. The Liberal Party, in particular, drastically reduced the number of their candidates. The Party had put forward 482 candidates in 1946 but only 324 in 1947, a decrease of 158 candidates.

The fact that the Liberal Party received the highest percentage of the national vote and yet obtained twelve seats less than the Socialist Party is understood when we examine the percentage of successful candidates for the two parties. The Socialist Party returned 50.9 per cent of its candidates, while the Liberal Party was able to return only 40.4 per cent. The Socialist percentage is in no way remarkable when compared to similar figures for the pre-war conservative parties,[11] but it does indicate that the Socialists had far better results in manipulating their support in plural-member districts so as to obtain the best distribution of vote in terms of the members elected.

Urban-rural Analysis of the 1947 Election

Since the 1947 analysis is the first in a series of urban-rural voting analyses, it will serve as a basis; each succeeding analysis will be compared to the preceding one in order to describe trend. The 1947 group means are shown in Table 3.

Analysis of the Liberal Party Vote

No significant differences could be established between the three sample groups, Groups I, II, and III, in the analysis of the Liberal Party's vote in 1947. However, it was found that both Groups I and II were significantly different from Group IV. We find, then, that the Liberal Party received a greater percentage of the popular vote in communities with populations below 5,000, or what has been defined as rural Japan, than in urban centers with populations greater than 150,000. Although the exact percentage difference cannot be given, the sample of communities indicates that the Liberal Party received 7.6 per cent more of the popular vote in rural communities than in strictly urban centers of population. The Party also received a larger proportion of the popular vote in communities with populations of from 5,001-30,000 (semi-rural areas) than in the urban areas of the nation. The sample means indicate that this difference was 4.8 per cent.

TABLE 3

Group	Liberal Party Percentage	Conservative Block Percentage
Group I (rural)	31.5	52.5
Group II (semi-rural)	28.7	52.2
Group III (semi-urban)	24.6	49.9
Group IV (urban)	23.9	46.4
National Percentage*	26.6	52.0

*The figures in this row are the national percentages of the popular vote and are presented for comparison purposes.

Analysis of the Conservative Block Vote

No significant difference could be established between the three sample groups in the analysis of the Conservative Block's vote in the 1947 election, and only Group II could be proven significantly different from Group IV. However, since the percentage of the Conservative Block's vote was higher in Group I than in Group II, there is reason to believe that Group I would have proved significantly different from Group IV had the sample size in Group I been as large as that in Group II.

If we compare the means of the various groups of the Conservative Block with those of the Liberal Party, we find that although more people voted for the Conservative Block in rural than in urban Japan the percentage difference between the rural and urban groups was not as large as was the Liberal Party's percentage difference. This development was contrary to the hypothesis upon which the urban-rural analysis was predicated. That is, we would expect a greater difference between urban and rural voting to appear as a second conservative party's votes were added to the Liberal Party's.

These facts led to an investigation of the group means of the other member of the Conservative Block, the Democratic Party. The group means of the Democratic Party are as follows: Group I, 21 per cent; Group II, 23.5 per cent; Group III, 25.3 per cent; and Group IV, 22.5 per cent.

If we compare the trend of the Democratic Party's means with those of the Liberal Party, we find that, whereas the Liberals received their highest percentage of the popular vote in rural Japan, decreased in the next two categories, and received their lowest percentage of the vote in urban Japan, the Democratic Party received its lowest percentage in rural areas, its highest in the intermediate groups, and then declined in urban centers. It should also be noted that Democratic Party voting strength appears to have been more evenly distributed among the four groups than the Liberal Party's. This difference in trend is not offered as proof that such a trend would be found had it been possible to study the entire Japanese voting population. However, since such a difference in trend did exist within the sample being studied, a similar check was made upon the succeeding elections. The results of these checks will be included with each election analysis.

The General Election of 1949

The Katayama Cabinet had taken office on May 23, 1947. However, within six months the Socialists had outlived their newly found popularity. The Socialist-led Cabinet was faced with the problem of preserving the coalition upon which its Diet leadership rested. Katayama, then, was not free to carry out the Socialist program because of the restraints imposed on him by the Democratic and People's Cooperative Parties. The split between the left and right wing of the Party, rather than narrowing, widened once the Party had gained power. The antagonism between the left and right wing became conspicuous at the Party's Third National Convention held in January 1948. Although the offices of the Chairman of the Central Executive Committee and the Chief Secretary were both won by right wing members, Katayama Tetsu and Asanuma Inajiro respectively, the other offices of the Party were won by the leftists.

The extent of the split between the right and left can be best illustrated by a statement made by Suzuki Mosaburo, a left wing leader and Chairman of the Party's Political Affairs Investigation Committee. "It is almost shameful for us to walk along the streets in Tokyo with a Social Democratic Party badge on.... We demand the Katayama Cabinet carry out Socialist policies and no others. We shall never bolt the Social Democratic Party, which is our own. Let them (the right wing) bolt, if they do not like to stay with us."[12]

The expulsion from the Cabinet of the Minister of Agriculture and Forestry, Hirano Rikizo, led to a bolt of twenty-one right wing Socialist Diet members who later organized themselves as Reformed Socialists. On July 7, 1948 six left wing Diet members led by Kuroda Hisao were expelled by the Party's Executive Committee for voting against the 1948 government budget in opposition to the decision of the Party. The arrest of Nishio Suehiro in October, 1948 in connection with the Showa Denko Company scandal strengthened the influence of the left wing in the Party. This internal strife within the Socialist Party, as well as the Cabinet's inability to act effectively, led to the resignation of Katayama, February 10, 1948, and the downfall of Japan's first Socialist-led Cabinet. Following the resignation of Katayama, February 21 was set as the date for naming a new Premier.

The balance of power in the House was held by the Socialists, in particular by the left wing of the Party, for intra-party relations were so strained since the national convention and the resignation of the Katayama Cabinet that the right wing would probably have agreed to left wing desires in order to prevent further misunderstandings in the Party. When the election was held the Socialists gave their support to the Democratic Party President, Ashida Hitoshi, who won the election in the House of Representatives. However, in the House of Councilors Yoshida was chosen by a two-vote margin. In accordance with the provisions of the new Constitution, a joint conference was held and Ashida was chosen Premier.[13] Ashida subsequently formed a coalition Cabinet composed of the Democratic, Socialist, and People's Cooperative Parties which came into office on March 10, 1948.

The Ashida Cabinet also faced the difficulties of internal strife within the Democratic Party and the increasing estrangement between the Democrats and Socialists on questions of prices and wages and other economic matters. On October 7, 1948, slightly more than seven months after taking office, the Ashida Cabinet resigned.

In the meantime, the Liberal Party had reorganized (March 15, 1948) and changed its name to the Democratic Liberal Party. Yoshida was chosen President of the Party, while Shidehara was designated Chief Adviser. When the Ashida Cabinet resigned, the task of organizing the succeeding government fell upon the Democratic Liberal Party. On October 19, Yoshida succeeded in completing the formation of a new Cabinet which held office until the General Election for the House of Representatives on January 23, 1949.

General Survey of the 1949 Election Results

The following table summarizes the results of the Twenty-fourth General Election held on January 23, 1949.

TABLE 4

Party	Number of Seats Obtained	Number of Candidates Advanced	Percentage of Successful Candidates	Percentage of National Vote	Percentage of Diet Seats Held
Democratic Liberal	264	416	63.5	43.8	56.7
Democratic	69	210	32.9	15.8	14.8
Socialist	48	187	25.7	13.5	10.3
Communist	35	115	30.4	9.6	7.5
People's Co-operative	14	63	22.2	3.4	3.0
New Liberals	2	12	16.7	0.6	0.4
Minor Parties	22	147	15.0	6.7	4.7
Independents	12	214	5.6	6.6	2.6
TOTAL	466	1364	....	100.0	100.0

The Democratic Liberal Party won the election, returning 264 members to the House of Representatives, or 30 more members than the 234 required to control an absolute majority of votes in the House. This was the first post-war election in which a political party received an absolute majority of the House seats and, accordingly, Yoshida proceeded to form a cabinet which took office on February 16, 1949. Of the three major opposition parties, the Democrats received sixty-nine seats, the Socialists forty-eight seats, and the Communists thirty-five seats. The total combined seats of these three parties was 155 seats, a number too small to threaten the Democratic Liberal Party's parliamentary position.

The Democratic Liberal Party's success was striking in all respects when compared to the results of the 1947 election. The Party returned 264 of its candidates in 1949 as compared to 131 candidates returned in 1947, an increase of 133 House members. They received 43.8 per cent of the national vote in 1949 as compared to 26.6 per cent in 1947, or an increase of 17.2 per cent. The Party ran more candidates in 1949 than it did in 1947 and returned 63.5 per cent. The Democratic Liberal Party was the only party to increase the number of candidates put forward for election, 3.5 candidates per district as compared to 1947 when they advanced 2.8 candidates per election district.

The scope of the Democratic Liberal Party's victory is even more apparent when we look at the election statistics for the other parties concerned. The Democratic Party received only 15.8 per cent of the national vote and returned sixty-nine members to the House in 1949. As compared to 1947, this was a drop of 9.6 per cent in popular vote and fifty-five seats in the House. The Socialists obtained 13.5 per cent of the national vote and forty-eight House seats, a loss of 12.7 per cent in popular vote and ninety-five seats in the House. The Democratic Party returned only 32.9 per cent of its candidates, while the Socialists returned only 25.7 per cent.

The striking defeat of the Socialist Party was clearly indicated by the fact that among the Socialists who lost seats in the 1949 election were ex-Premier and Chairman Katayama Tetsu, ex-Labor Minister Kato Kanju, ex-Deputy Premier Nishio Suehiro, and ex-State Minister Nomizo Masaru. This serious loss of popular support can be traced directly to: (1) the disunity within the Party, (2) the Showa Denko scandal, and (3) the ineffectiveness of the Socialist-led government.

The People's Cooperative Party also suffered losses in this election. The Party received 3.4 per cent of the national vote and returned fourteen members to the House, a loss of a little more than one-half of its pre-election membership.

The Communist Party, on the other hand, made substantial gains in the 1949 election. The Communists received 9.6 per cent of the national vote and returned thirty-five members to the House of Representatives, or a gain of 6.0 per cent of the national vote and thirty-one seats in the House as compared to 1947. Undoubtedly, a large proportion of this increase in popular support was drawn from voters who had supported the Socialists in the 1947 election and who were subsequently disillusioned with the Party. However, the coincidence of the Communist victory in China and the Communist Party gains in Japan cannot be overlooked.

To summarize the results of the 1949 election, the Democratic Liberal Party won an overwhelming victory, returning 264 House members and obtaining absolute control over the Diet. All three parties, Democratic, Socialist, and People's Cooperative, which participated in the Katayama and the Ashida Cabinets suffered serious setbacks, while the Communist Party gained in terms of House seats and in percentage of the national vote.

Urban-rural Analysis of the 1949 Election

The 1949 means of the four groups are as follows:

TABLE 5

Group	Democratic Liberal Party Percentage	Conservative Block Percentage
Group I (rural)	47.9	65.4
Group II (semi-rural)	49.0	63.5
Group III (semi-urban)	44.3	59.4
Group IV (urban)	40.1	53.9
National Percentage	43.8	60.2

Analysis of the Democratic Liberal Party Vote

As in the 1947 election, no significant difference could be established between the three sample groups. However, the means of Group I, Group II, and Group III could be proven significantly higher than the mean of Group IV. The trend found in the means of the four strata in this election was not in accord with the original hypothesis that the percentage of the popular vote of the groups would decrease in size as the community size of the group increased. Although the sample means indicate that the Democratic Liberal Party received a larger percentage of the popular vote in the semi-rural group than they did in the strictly rural areas, the difference in percentages was slight, only 1.1 per cent. That this situation actually existed in the parent populations out of which the samples were drawn cannot be statistically demonstrated.

The means of all four groups in the 1949 election were significantly higher than the corresponding group means in 1947. It would appear that significant gains were registered at all population levels and that percentage-wise the gains were approximately the same. To determine the exact percentage of gain for the three sample groups was statistically impossible. However, in Group IV (the urban population), this gain was 16.2 per cent of the popular vote.

Analysis of the Conservative Block Vote

No significant difference could be established between the means of the three sample groups. However, the means of Groups I, II, and III were significantly higher than the mean of Group IV. The means of all four groups were significantly higher than the means of the corresponding groups in the 1947 election. The gain of 7.5 per cent in Group IV, the urban group, was the only gain that could be determined exactly. The fact that this increase is smaller than the increase of the Democratic Liberal Party in urban Japan was owing to the heavy losses suffered by the Democratic Party in this election. Large segments of previous Democratic Party voters shifted to the Democratic Liberal Party.

The group means of the Democratic Party in the 1949 election are as follows: Group I, 17.5 per cent; Group II, 14.5 per cent; Group III, 15.1 per cent; and Group IV, 13.8 per cent.

It should be noted that, contrary to the 1947 experience, the Democratic Party received a larger percentage of the popular vote in rural than in urban communities. However, in both the 1947 and 1949 elections the difference in the percentage of the vote between the urban and rural groups is not large.

To summarize briefly the results of the above investigation, we find that the analyses of the Democratic Liberal Party's and the Conservative Block's vote indicate that in 1949 there were at least two, if not more, patterns of voting behavior existing in Japan. The first pattern was found in communities with populations up to 150,000, and the second in communities with populations above 150,000. Both the Democratic Liberal Party and the Conservative Block received a higher proportion of the popular vote in communities less than 150,000 in population than they did in communities with populations over 150,000.

The General Election of 1952

The Democratic Liberal Party emerged from the 1949 election with an absolute majority of the seats in the Lower House, a position which would have allowed Yoshida to form Japan's first post-war non-coalition cabinet. However, immediately following their victory, the Democratic Liberal Party commenced activities which were aimed at the formation of a united conservative front. Inukai Ken, the President of the Democratic Party, was favorable to such a move and, as a result, the third Yoshida Cabinet, which was formed on February 16, 1949, included two members of the Democratic Party.

Toward the end of 1949 the Democratic Liberal Party began renewed activities directed at the merger of the Democratic Liberal and the Democratic Parties. This move had immediate effects on the Democratic Party. On November 20, 1949 Democratic Party State Minister Kimura resigned from his post. Two weeks later, on December 4, Inukai, together with twenty-three other Democratic Party members, made a formal proposal to join the Democratic Liberal Party. Inukai was not accepted, but the other members of this group were formally admitted to the Party on February 10, 1950. The other Democratic Party member serving in the Cabinet, Minister of Communications Inagaki, immediately resigned. On March 10, 1950, in preparation for a House of Councilors election, the Democratic Liberal Party was formally renamed the Liberal Party.

The Democratic Party, which had suffered a defeat in the 1949 election, returning only sixty-nine members to the Lower House, was dealt a serious blow by the disaffection of twenty-three of its members. The Party attempted to counter this setback by merging the Democratic and People's Cooperative Parties, forming the Progressive Party.

The Socialist Party split into two groups on October 5, 1951 over the issue of signing a unilateral peace treaty with the United States. The two wings pulled even further apart over the issue of rearmament. The dispute among the Socialists prevented them from offering a serious challenge to the Liberal Party's control over Japanese political life.

The signing of the Peace Treaty in San Francisco immediately brought forth demands for a new election which Yoshida, who controlled a majority of the seats in the Lower House, refused to recognize. He announced that a new election would not be held until his legal term expired in the spring of 1953. However, during the summer of 1952 a split developed in the Liberal Party which threatened to divide it into two camps. The political differences which developed between the so-called Yoshida and Hatoyama factions were primarily over the question of control and leadership of the Party.

During the Diet session in the early summer and continuing throughout the Diet recess in August of 1952, the Hatoyama clique joined with the opposition parties to demand an early dissolution of the House. However, the Hatoyama faction did vote with the Party to uphold the Cabinet under the assumption that Yoshida would call for a new election late in October or early November. Antagonism within the Party was intensified still more over the question of selecting a new Speaker of the House of Representatives. Yoshida, having given in to the Hatoyama group on the selection of a Speaker, suddenly announced the government's decision, on August 28, to dissolve the House and hold a new election on October 1, 1952. The opposition parties had not expected this move and were unprepared financially for the forthcoming election.

General Survey of the 1952 Election Results

The following table summarizes the results of the Twenty-fifth General Election held on October 1, 1952.

TABLE 6

Party	Number of Seats Obtained	Number of Candidates Advanced	Percentage of Successful Candidates	Percentage of National Vote	Percentage of Diet Seats Held
Liberals.........	241	475	50.7	48.0	51.7
Progressive.....	85	209	40.7	18.2	18.2
Right Socialist...	58	96	60.4	11.4	12.5
Left Socialist....	58	109	53.2	10.0	12.5
Communist......	...	107	....	2.5	....
Minor Party.....	17	80	21.3	3.2	3.6
Independents.....	7	168	4.2	6.7	1.5
TOTAL	466	1244	....	100.0	100.0

The Liberal Party was again returned as the majority political party in the House, although the number of the Party's members returned to the House was noticeably reduced. The Liberals returned 241 members to the Lower House, only seven seats over the 234 required for parliamentary control. On the other hand, their percentage of the total national vote increased over the period 1949 to 1952. In 1949 the Liberals received 43.8 per cent of the total national vote, while in 1952 they received 48.0 per cent, or an increase of 4.2 per cent. The Liberals put forward far too many candidates, thus splitting their vote in many instances and allowing opposition candidates to be elected to the House. The Liberals ran 475 candidates, or slightly more than one candidate for every Diet seat, as opposed to 416 candidates in the previous election. It would be safe to say that, had the Liberals advanced fewer candidates, they would have returned more members to the House. The excessive number of Liberal Party candidates was probably due to the Party's commitments to both incumbents and depurgees who were returning to the political scene.[14]

The Progressive Party fared slightly better in 1952 than in 1949, returning eighty-five members to the House and receiving 18.2 per cent of the popular vote as compared to sixty-nine members and 15.8 per cent in 1949. But, since the Progressive Party was formed by the merger of the Democratic and People's Cooperative Parties, and since the People's Cooperative Party polled 3.4 per cent of the national vote in 1949, it would seem that the Progressives actually lost 1.0 per cent of their popular support. The Progressives could have been more efficient in placing and limiting their candidates. They returned only 40.7 per cent of their 209 candidates, the lowest percentage of returned candidates for any of the major parties.

If the split in the Socialist Party is ignored for the moment, they received 21.4 per cent of the national vote, a gain of 7.9 per cent over 1949, which resulted in an appreciable improvement in their position in the Lower House. The Socialists' strength in the House increased from forty-eight seats in 1949 to 116 following the 1952 election. However, the split within the Socialist ranks effectively negated any improvement in their parliamentary position.

The Right-wing Socialists were slightly more successful in terms of popular vote than the Left-wing, obtaining 11.4 per cent of the national vote while the Left-wing received 10.0 per cent. Both wings returned fifty-eight members each to the House. Neither wing advanced an appreciable number of candidates: the Right-wing advanced ninety-six and the Left-wing advanced 109. Both were quite successful in returning members to the House; the Right-wing returned 60.4 per cent of its candidates and the Left-wing 53.2 per cent. The Left-wing made the most substantial gains of the two, undoubtedly because they received many, if not all, of the votes which the Communist Party lost. The Left-wing held only sixteen seats at the time the House was dissolved, while, following the election, the Party could claim fifty-eight seats, an increase of more than three and a half times their pre-election membership. On the other hand, the Right-wing held thirty seats prior to the election and, following the election, increased their representation to fifty-eight members.

The Communist Party, which had received 9.6 per cent of the popular vote and thirty-five seats in the House of Representatives in 1949, suffered a crushing defeat in 1952. The Party obtained only 2.5 per cent of the popular vote and lost its entire representation in the Diet. This loss of votes was almost equivalent to the entire gain of both wings of the Socialists. The Communists lost 7.1 per cent of the popular vote while the combined Socialist gain was 7.9 per cent.

It has been suggested that the Communist leadership, realizing they faced defeat in the forthcoming election, threw their votes to the Left-wing Socialists under the assumption that a good showing by the Left-wing would deepen the rift between the two Socialist groups. However, since there was a Communist running against a Left-wing Socialist in all but ten of the election districts in which the Left-wing Socialists advanced candidates, there seems to be little justification for the assumption. Although it has been estimated that a large percentage of the previous Communist strength turned to the Left-wing Socialists, a much more likely explanation of this phenomenon can be found in the Korean War and the new

Communist line developed in 1950. The new line made it clear that the "Japanese Communist party would support the Soviet Union and assist the North Korean forces by strikes and sabotage. At the same time it would make final preparations for the 'coming revolution in Japan.'"[15] The results of the Korean War and the tactics developed by the Japanese Communists to carry out the new line undoubtedly alienated a large number of Japanese who had seriously believed the Communists when they spoke of "achieving social justice and building a democratic Japan through a process of peaceful revolution."[16]

The 1952 election once more gave the Liberal Party a victory, tenuous though it was, and again demonstrated that Japan desired a conservative government. However, the election failed to provide a clear solution to the Liberal Party's most pressing problem, that of the split between the Hatoyama and Yoshida factions.

Urban-rural Analysis of the 1952 Election

The 1952 means of the four strata are as follows:

TABLE 7

Group	Liberal Party Percentage	Conservative Block Percentage
Group I (rural)	56.8	71.4
Group II (semi-rural)	51.4	70.6
Group III (semi-urban)	46.5	65.0
Group IV (urban)	38.7	55.9
National Percentage	48.0	66.2

In the analysis of the 1952 election, the Analysis of Variance indicated that there was a significant difference between the three sample groups. In subsequent testing between pairs of the sample groups, it was found that the mean of Group I could be proven significantly higher than the mean of Group III. Group II could not be statistically differentiated from either Group I or Group III. All three sample means could be proven significantly higher than the mean of Group IV.

Three voting patterns could be distinguished in 1952. The first was found in communities with populations below 5,000, or what has been labeled rural Japan. The second pattern was found in communities with populations of from 30,000 to 150,000, and the third was found in communities with populations above 150,000. Strictly rural communities gave a higher percentage of their popular support to the Liberal Party than did communities of 30,000 or more. In the urban areas of the nation the Liberal Party received its lowest percentage of the popular vote.

Only the means of the rural group and the urban group could be proven significantly different from the corresponding group means in 1949. The exact percentage gain in the rural group, of course, cannot be established. However, the increase as indicated by the sample mean was 8.9 per cent. The Liberal Party's strength declined slightly in the urban communities; the decline between 1949 and 1952 was 1.4 per cent. In the semi-rural and semi-urban groups the sample means indicate that there was an increase of slightly more than 2.0 per cent in Liberal Party popular vote. It would appear from the preceding figures that the Liberal Party gain in popular support was primarily drawn from rural communities.

The 1952 election witnessed an increased differentiation between the voting pattern of urban and rural Japan. The percentage difference between the means of the urban and rural groups in the 1952 election was 18.1 per cent as compared to 7.8 per cent in 1949. Statistical tests confirmed this widening of the gap between urban and rural voting. Another indication of this differentiation is found when the mean of the urban group is compared to the Liberal Party's percentage of the national vote. The Party in 1952 received 48.0 per cent of the total national vote, while in urban communities it received only 38.7 per cent of the popular vote. In other words, the Liberals obtained 9.3 per cent more of the popular vote in Japan as a whole than they did in urban communities. In 1949 this difference was 3.7 per cent and in 1947 it was only 2.7 per cent.

Analysis of the Conservative Block Vote

The statistical analysis of the Conservative Block's vote in 1952 indicated that there was a significant difference between the means of the three sample groups. In subsequent testing, it was found that the means of both Groups I and II could be proven significantly higher than the mean of Group III. However, no significant difference could be established at the five per cent level between the means of Groups I and II. Moreover, the means of all sample groups could be proven significantly higher than the mean of the urban group.

The means of Groups II, III, and IV could be proven significantly higher than the corresponding group means in the 1949 election. Again, only the gain in the urban group could be determined exactly. The Conservative Block's gain in this group, between the two elections, was 2.0 per cent of the popular vote. However, the Liberal Party vote in this group declined by 1.4 per cent. We can conclude that the Progressive Party increased its popular support in urban communities by 3.4 per cent.

If the percentage difference between the rural and urban groups of the Liberal Party and Conservative Block is compared, it is found that the difference in voting percentage between the Liberal Party's urban and rural groups was 18.1 per cent, while the Conservative Block's percentage difference was only 15.5. This, of course, is another indication that the voting strength of the Progressive Party was not following the same pattern as that of the Liberal Party. The group means of the Progressive Party are as follows: Group I, 14.6 per cent; Group II, 19.2 per cent; Group III, 18.5 per cent; and Group IV, 17.2 per cent. The Progressive Party, then, received its highest percentage of the popular vote in the semi-rural group, declined in the semi-urban and urban groups, and received its lowest percentage of the vote in the rural group. This pattern is quite similar to that developed in 1947.

To summarize the results of the analysis of the Conservative Block's vote, three patterns of voting behavior could be found, the first being in the rural and semi-rural groups, the second in the semi-urban group and the third in the urban group. The Conservative Block received its highest percentage of the popular vote in the rural and semi-rural communities, declined in the semi-urban communities, and received its lowest percentage in the large urban communities. However, the sample means of the Progressive Party in both the 1947 and 1952 elections cast serious doubt as to the Progressives' contribution to this trend.

The General Election of 1953

The April 19, 1953 House election was a direct outgrowth of the dissension within the Liberal Party caused by the return of Hatoyama Ichiro to the political scene. At the opening of the new Diet session following the 1952 election, a group of Liberal Party dissidents banded together to form the "League for Democratization of the Liberal Party." The League demanded that Yoshida reinstate Ishibashi Tanzan and Kono Ichiro, both Hatoyama supporters, who had been summarily ousted from the Party two days before the 1952 election, and also called for the transfer of leadership of the Party from Yoshida to Hatoyama. The League used Yoshida's dependence upon them for parliamentary support to pry concessions from him. In February of 1953 Yoshida, apparently fulfilling a promise to this group, appointed Miki Bukichi Chairman of the Party's Executive Board. Yoshida was also faced with difficulties within his own faction of the Party. His selection of Sato Eisaku as Secretary-General alienated Hirokawa Kozen, Agriculture and Forestry Minister. Until this time Hirokawa had been loyal to Yoshida, but following this appointment he joined forces with the anti-Yoshida dissidents.

The immediate cause of Yoshida's difficulties arose from his use of abrupt language in an exchange in the Diet. Yoshida immediately apologized but the opposition would not let the matter die. When the members of the Democratization League and the Hirokawa faction abstained from voting, the opposition succeeded in passing a resolution referring Yoshida's slip of the tongue to the House Disciplinary Committee. Yoshida met this attack by dismissing Hirokawa for breaking Party discipline. At the same time it was evident that Yoshida was not quite ready for an all-out fight, for he ignored the Democratization League's same infraction of Party discipline. Yoshida replaced dissident Liberal Party members in the Disciplinary Committee with his loyal followers, and in this manner was able to prevent action in the Committee.

The opposition parties, however, following extensive negotiation, agreed to bring a non-confidence vote in the Diet in March of 1953. The object of this move was to force Yoshida to resign without causing a new election. Yoshida at once let it be known that he would rather dissolve the Diet than resign. Both the Democratization League and the Hirokawa faction attempted to bargain with Yoshida, the price of support being the full reinstatement of Hirokawa. However, Yoshida would not compromise. Several hours before the non-confidence vote on March 14, Miki led twenty-one other Democratization League members out of the Liberal Party. The non-confidence motion was introduced as a joint opposition resolution and passed the House by a vote of 229 to 218. Immediately after the outcome was made known, the House Speaker announced that the House was dissolved and set the date of the Twenty-sixth General Election for April 19, 1953.

General Survey of the 1953 Election Results

The following table summarizes the results of the Twenty-sixth General Election held on April 19, 1953.

TABLE 8

Party	Number of Seats Obtained	Number of Candidates Advanced	Percentage of Successful Candidates	Percentage of National Vote	Percentage of Diet Seats Held
Yoshida Liberal..	199	316	63.0	38.9	42.7
Hatoyama Liberal	35	102	34.3	8.9	7.5
Progressive......	76	169	45.0	17.8	16.3
Right-wing Socialist.......	66	116	56.9	13.4	14.2
Left-wing Socialist.......	72	109	66.1	13.2	15.4
Communist.......	1	85	1.2	1.9	0.2
Minor Party.....	6	24	25.0	1.5	1.3
Independents.....	11	106	10.4	4.4	2.4
TOTAL	466	1027	....	100.0	100.0

The significance of the 1953 election was to be found in the victory of the Yoshida faction of the Liberal Party. The election, rather than being a contest over policy, was in reality a struggle for power within the Liberal Party. The scope of the Yoshida Liberals' victory over their rival, the Hatoyama branch, is evident when the election statistics of the two factions are compared. The Yoshida Liberals received 38.9 per cent of the popular vote and returned 199 members to the House, while the Hatoyama Liberals received only 8.9 per cent of the vote and returned thirty-five members. The Yoshida group returned 63.0 per cent of its 316 candidates put forward, while the Hatoyama faction returned but 34.3 per cent of its 102 candidates. The Yoshida Liberal Party was the only party which ran enough candidates to control a majority within the House. This fact, combined with the failure of any of the opposition groups to agree to a post-election coalition while the campaign was in progress, undoubtedly contributed to the Yoshida Liberals' victory. The return of the Hatoyama group to the Liberal Party was, of course, a recognition by the faction that they had lost the power struggle within the Party.

If the election statistics of the Yoshida and Hatoyama factions are considered collectively, the similarity of the 1952 and 1953 election results are at once evident. The Liberals received 48.0 per cent of the popular vote in 1952 and 241 House seats, while in 1953, collectively considered, they received 47.8 per cent of the vote and 234 seats. The Liberals' loss of 0.2 per cent of the popular vote and seven seats in the House was significant not in terms of the Liberals' loss in popularity but in the fact that although the Party was split it still was able to gather almost as much support as it did in 1952.

The Progressive Party received 17.8 per cent of the vote and returned seventy-six members to the House of Representatives, a loss of 0.4 per cent in popular vote and nine seats in the House as compared to 1952. Although the Progressive losses were minimal, three prominent members were not returned: Party Secretary-General Kiyose Ichiro, Kitamura Tokutaro, and Narahashi Wataru.

The left-of-center parties, especially the Left-wing Socialists, captured the seats lost by the conservatives. Although the Left-wing Socialists polled fewer popular votes (13.2 per cent) than did the Right-wing (13.4 per cent), they returned more members to the House. The Left-wing returned seventy-two members, the Right sixty-six. Both Socialist groups again demonstrated their ability to place their candidates strategically and thereby gain the maximum number of seats.

The Communist Party's percentage of the popular vote dropped to a post-war low, but they did manage to elect one candidate. There is some indication that the Communist Party threw its support to individual Left-wing Socialist candidates. In eight election districts where Left-wing Socialist candidates had been runners-up in 1952, the Communist candidate withdrew from the 1953 race shortly before the election. However, there seems to be no evidence that the two parties as a whole cooperated in the election; cooperation appears rather to have been only on an individual basis. The combined percentages of the Right- and Left-wing Socialists and the Communists was 28.5 per cent, an increase of 4.6 per cent over 1952. However, the largest proportion of this increase in strength was drawn from the losses suffered by minor party and independent candidates.

The 1953 election did not result in a meaningful political realignment. Its significance was to be found in the fact that for the fifth time in the post-war period the Japanese people went to the polls and returned a sizable conservative majority to the House of Representatives. The combined conservative parties retained a two-thirds control of the House. The election was also significant in that it very clearly indicated that the Liberal Party, at least for the time being, was to remain the dominant party within the Conservative Block.

Urban-rural Analysis of the 1953 Election

The 1953 means of the four strata are as follows:

TABLE 9

Group	Liberal Party Percentage*	Conservative Block Percentage
Group I (rural)............	57.1	72.4
Group II (semi-rural)......	50.6	68.9
Group III (semi-urban).....	46.8	63.1
Group IV (urban)..........	39.7	55.1
National Percentage........	47.8	65.6

*This column represents the combined percentages of the Yoshida and Hatoyama factions.

Analysis of the Liberal Party Vote

The Analysis of Variance as applied to the combined Liberal Party vote in 1953 indicated that there was a significant difference between the three sample groups. The mean of Group I could be proven significantly higher than the mean of Group III. Neither the means of Group I nor Group III could be proven significantly different from the mean of Group II. The means of all the sample groups could be proven significantly higher than the mean of Group IV.

The means of the corresponding sample groups of the 1952 and 1953 elections were quite close, the largest difference being a 0.8 per cent loss in the semi-rural group in 1953. The means, of course, are too close to establish statistically significant differences. However, the mean of the urban group was 1.0 per cent higher than its corresponding mean in 1952. Since in the nation as a whole the Liberal Party lost 0.2 per cent while a 1.0 per cent gain has been established in cities with populations of 150,000 and above, the Liberal Party must have lost votes in one or all of the sample groups. Viewed politically, no significance could be claimed for these small losses or gains in the urban-rural pattern. The percentage relationship between the rural and urban groups and the three voting patterns as established in the 1952 analysis were repeated in 1953.

Analysis of the Conservative Block Vote

The analysis of the Conservative Block vote in 1953 indicated a significant difference between the three sample means. The means of Groups I and II were significantly higher than the mean of Group III. The means of all three sample groups could be proven significantly higher than the mean of Group IV. No significant differences could be established between the corresponding sample groups of 1952 and 1953.

Again, as in the analysis of the Liberal Party vote, no political trend could be distinguished from the losses or gains for the Conservative Block from the 1952 election to the 1953 election. The voting pattern established in 1952 for the Conservative Block held true in 1953.

The trend found in the 1947 and 1952 elections for the Progressive Party remained the same in 1953. The group means for the Progressive Party are as follows: Group I, 15.3 per cent; Group II, 18.3 per cent; Group III, 16.3 per cent; and Group IV, 15.4 per cent. When these means are compared to the Progressives' 1952 means, it is found that the Progressives declined in all groups except the rural group where they made a slight increase. The Progressive loss in the urban group was 1.8 per cent, while in the nation as a whole they lost only 0.4 per cent of the popular vote.

The General Election of 1955

As a result of the 1953 General Election, the Yoshida wing of the Liberal Party returned 199 members to the House of Representatives, a number far short of the 234 seats necessary for effective control in the House. A temporary coalition of opposition parties would have had sufficient strength to prevent the organization of another Yoshida Cabinet. However, the refusal of the Right- and Left-wing Socialists to support the Progressive Party's President, Shigemitsu Mamoru, in his bid for the Premiership enabled Yoshida to form a cabinet for the fifth time.

The new government was in a precarious position, for its life depended upon the support of the conservative opposition within the Diet. In November 1953, Yoshida visited Hatoyama in an attempt to heal the breach that had split the Liberal Party. The immediate result of this visit was an announcement by Hatoyama stating that he would return to the Liberal Party but that he could not guarantee the return of those who had withdrawn from the Party with him. Hatoyama's return, however, resulted in bringing a number of the Liberal dissidents back to the Party.

Throughout 1954, political scandals spelled trouble for the Yoshida Cabinet. The opposition in the Diet furthered claims that members of the Yoshida administration had received money from government subsidized shipping concerns. Bitterness in the Diet was heightened by Yoshida's refusal to appear as a witness before a legislative committee that had reopened the shipping inquiry after the prosecuting authorities had dropped the case without bringing it to court. In November 1954, thirty-five members, including Hatoyama, bolted the Liberal Party following the expulsion from the Party of Ishibashi Tanzan and Kishi Nobusuke for breaking Party discipline.

On November 24, 1954, shortly after the bolt, the Japan Democratic Party was formally launched at Hibiya Public Hall in Tokyo. The new Party was composed of the members of the Progressive Party and the dissident Liberals. The distribution of strength in the House following the Party reorganization was as follows:[17]

Liberals	185
Democrats	120
Left-wing Socialists	72
Right-wing Socialists	61
Independents	9
Others	12
Vacancies	8

On December 7, 1954, faced with an impossible situation in the Diet, the Yoshida Cabinet submitted its resignation. The contest to succeed Yoshida took place between Hatoyama, the new President of the Democratic Party, and Ogata Taketora who had replaced Yoshida as the leader of the Liberal Party. Hatoyama obtained the support of the Socialists and was elected Premier by a vote of 257 to 191. As a price for support the Socialists obtained a guarantee from Hatoyama that a national election would be held by early March, 1955. The Diet was dissolved by the government on January 24, 1954, and February 27 was set as the date for the General Election.

General Survey of the 1955 Election Results

Two salient facts emerged from the 1955 election data. The first was the previously mentioned shift of power within the Conservative Block. The second was the increase in left-of-center representation in the House. The conservative political forces lost little over-all strength. However, conservative losses following the election were significant in that the combined left-of-center representation in the House control more than one-third of the seats. The left-of-center representation can now effectively block any move to amend the Constitution.[18]

The following table summarizes the results of the Twenty-seventh General Election held on February 27, 1955.

TABLE 10

Party	Number of Seats Obtained	Number of Candidates Advanced	Percentage of Successful Candidates	Percentage of National Vote	Percentage of Diet Seats Held
Liberal	112	248	45.2	26.6	23.8
Democratic	185	286	64.7	36.6	39.8
Right-wing Socialist	67	122	50.8	13.8	14.3
Left-wing Socialist	89	121	73.6	15.4	19.1
Communist	2	60	3.3	2.0	0.4
Minor Party	6	53	11.3	2.4	1.2
Independents	6	127	4.7	3.3	1.4
TOTAL	467	1017	....	100.0	100.0

The 1955 election resulted in a major redistribution of power within the conservative political forces with the Democratic Party replacing the Liberal Party as the dominant political group within the House. The decline of the Liberal Party was striking in all aspects. The number of Liberal Party candidates returned to the House was the smallest since the formation of the Party. The Liberals' percentage of the total national vote was approximately the same as the percentage in 1947. However, the Party returned fewer candidates in 1955 than it did in 1947. In fact, the Liberals' percentage of returned candidates was the lowest of any of the major parties with the Liberals returning only 45.2 per cent of their candidates.

The Democratic Party, of course, replaced the Liberal Party as the leading party in the House. The Democrats increased their representation from 120 members following their organization in 1954 to 185 members after the election. The Party received 36.6 per cent of the popular vote and returned 64.7 per cent of its candidates.

The Right-wing Socialists remained quite stable when we compare the 1953 and 1955 election results. The Right wing obtained 13.4 per cent of the popular vote in 1953 and returned sixty-six members to the House. The Party in 1955 increased its representation in the House by one seat and increased its percentage of the popular vote by only 0.4 per cent. The Left-wing Socialists, on the other hand, made substantial gains in 1955. The Party increased its percentage of the popular vote by 2.2 per cent and was able to increase its representation in the House by seventeen seats. The Left wing was very successful in placing its candidates, returning 73.6 per cent of them.

The Communists polled almost the same percentage of votes as they did in 1953, although they did increase their representation by one seat in the House.

Urban-rural Analysis of the 1955 Election

The 1955 means of the four strata are as follows:

TABLE 11

Group	Liberal Party Percentage 1955	(1947)	Conservative Block Percentage 1955
Group I (rural)...............	31.2	(31.5)	69.6
Group II (semi-rural)...........	30.2	(28.7)	68.6
Group III (semi-urban)..........	25.3	(24.6)	60.2
Group IV (urban)..............	22.9	(23.6)	55.1
National Percentage	26.6	(26.6)	63.2

Analysis of the Liberal Party Vote

In the analysis of the Liberal Party's urban-rural voting strength no significant differences could be established between the three sample groups. However, both Groups I and II could be proven significantly different from Group IV.

The Liberal Party sustained a heavy loss of voting support at all levels of population. However, the Party suffered significantly heavier losses in rural communities than in urban communities. The Liberal Party's percentage of the popular vote declined by 25.9 per cent in the rural group while the decline in the urban group was only 16.9 per cent. An explanation for this pattern of losses emerges if we glance back at the previous urban-rural distributions of Liberal Party support. We find that from 1949 to 1955 the percentage of Liberal Party vote in urban communities has been stable. The Liberal Party's percentage of the popular vote in the urban group was 40.1 per cent in 1949, 38.7 per cent in 1952, and 39.7 per cent in 1953. At the same time, the sample means indicate that the Liberal Party increased its strength in the rural group in each of the three elections. It would appear, then, that when a heavy loss of voting strength did occur, the Liberals in rural Japan lost not only what they had gained in the 1949 upsurge but also all subsequent gains. In fact, we find a very strong similarity between the Liberal Party voting pattern in 1947 and 1953. The 1947 group means have been presented to make comparison possible.

Analysis of the Conservative Block Vote

The analysis of the Conservative Block's vote in 1955 indicated that there was a significant difference between the three sample groups. Subsequent testing indicated that Groups I and II were significantly different from Group III. All three sample groups were significantly different from Group IV.

The 1955 Conservative Block's pattern of voting strength was similar to the 1953 and 1952 patterns. In the nation as a whole the Conservative Block lost 2.4 per cent of its popular support between 1953 and 1955. However, in the urban group the conservative strength remained the same as in 1953 and 1955, i.e., 55.1 per cent of the vote. Losses of conservative strength, then, must have been in one or more of the other groups. The distribution of these losses, however, cannot be determined statistically.

The Democratic Party's group means in 1955 are as follows: Group I, 38.4 per cent; Group II, 38.4 per cent; Group III, 34.9 per cent; and Group IV, 32.1 per cent.

The Democratic Party's distribution of urban-rural voting strength more closely resembles the urban-rural distribution which we had originally anticipated than did the Party's distribution in 1947, 1952, and 1953.

Conclusions

Geographical

In order to investigate the geographical distribution of the Liberal Party's and the Conservative Block's support, the 1947-55 average percentage of Liberal Party and Conservative Block vote was obtained for each election district. These percentages were then ranked in ascending order of strength. That is, the election district in which the Liberal Party received its lowest average percentage of the popular vote was ranked No. 1, while the district where the Party received its highest average percentage of the popular vote was ranked No. 117. Lists of the ranked election districts are appended.

In order to facilitate geographical analysis, the ranked districts were then divided into five groups. Districts of rank 98-117 were considered areas of primary strength, ranks 79-97 areas of secondary strength, ranks 1-20 areas of primary weakness, and ranks 21-39 areas of secondary weakness. Ranks 40-96 were considered neutral areas. The geographical location of the districts comprising the preceding categories for the Liberal Party is shown in Figure I, and for the Conservative Block in Figure II. It must be remembered in evaluating the data presented that we are dealing with a relative scale. Districts are considered areas of strength or weakness only in terms of the performance of other districts and are not evaluated by an external standard.

An examination of the districts of strength on the two maps reveals certain characteristics which a majority of them held in common. The districts are predominantly rural, agricultural areas. The districts tend to be located in areas of relatively low population density. Notably absent from the groups of primary and secondary strength are the large number of districts comprising the Tokyo-Yokohama, Osaka-Kobe, and the Nagoya complexes which are some of the most highly industrialized areas of Japan and, hence, are among the most densely populated areas of the nation. It should be noted that many of the districts in Tokyo and Osaka, as well as the districts comprising Yokohama and Kobe, fall in the weak group.

It is apparent that Liberal Party strongholds were more numerous in northern Japan than elsewhere. Of the thirty-nine districts included in the combined strong categories, eighteen were located in the Tohoku and Kanto regions. The Liberals were also fairly strong in Chugoku and Shikoku. The Liberals were consistently weak in Hokkaido, Kinki, and Kyushu.

The regional distribution of Liberal Party areas of strength and weakness is shown in Table 12.

A comparison of Liberal Party strongholds with those of the pre-war Seiyukai indicates that there was at least some continuity between Liberal and Seiyukai areas of electoral strength. Nine of the twenty districts considered as Liberal Party districts of primary strength have been identified in a previous study as pre-war Seiyukai strongholds.[19] Only two Minseito districts are included in the present group of primary strength.

Conservative Block strength is more evenly distributed throughout Japan than was Liberal Party strength. The Hokkaido and Kinki regions are the only large areas of appreciable Conservative weakness. The regional distribution of the Conservative Block's areas of strength and weakness is shown in Table 13.

TABLE 12

Region	Total Number of Districts in Region	Number of Districts in Combined Weak Group	Number of Districts in Combined Strong Group
Hokkaido	5	3	1
Tohoku	13	3	8
Kanto including Tokyo and Yokohama	25	7	10
(Tokyo I-VII and Yokohama)	8	4	0)
Chubu	24	8	9
Kinki including Osaka and Kobe	18	10	1
(Osaka I-V and Kobe)	6	3	1)
Chugoku	9	1	4
Shikoku	7	1	3
Kyushu	16	6	3

TABLE 13

Region	Total Number of Districts in Region	Number of Districts in Combined Weak Group	Number of Districts in Combined Strong Group
Hokkaido	5	3	0
Tohoku	13	2	6
Kanto including Tokyo and Yokohama	25	10	9
(Tokyo I-VII and Yokohama)	8	6	0)
Chubu	24	6	9
Kinki including Osaka and Kobe	18	11	3
(Osaka I-V and Kobe)	6	5	0)
Chugoku	9	3	2
Shikoku	7	0	2
Kyushu	16	4	8

While it is apparent that the Conservative Block does not possess unified territorial support analogous to the "Solid South" in the United States, the Conservative Block support has been so strong and so widely dispersed that, with the exception of the largest cities and a few election districts, it would be appropriate to consider all of Japan as an area of conservative strength. In fact, there were only ten election districts in which the average percentage of the Conservative Block vote fell below 50.0 per cent. Of these ten districts, five are strictly urban districts and three are dominated by mining communities.

The results of the elections studied have indicated one weakness in the Conservative Block's electoral record which appears to be directly correlated to the plural member district system, and that is the conservatives' inability to manipulate its support with sufficient effectiveness to return a maximum number of candidates to the House. In 1955, for instance, the Conservatives on an average needed 78,739 votes to return a candidate to the House, while the Socialists needed only 69,314. The Conservatives, then, wasted approximately 9,000 votes for each candidate returned.

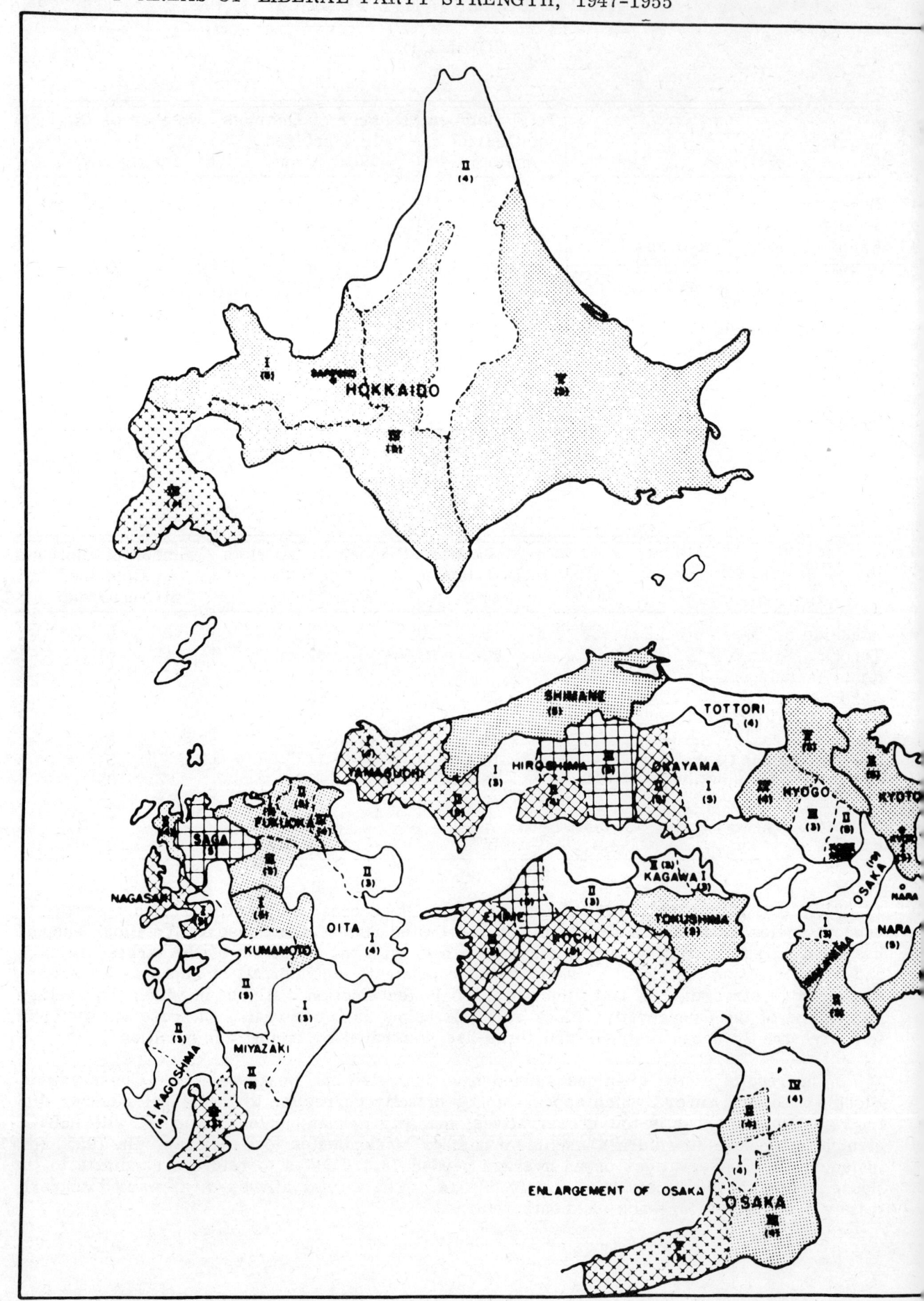

FIGURE I—AREAS OF LIBERAL PARTY STRENGTH, 1947-1955

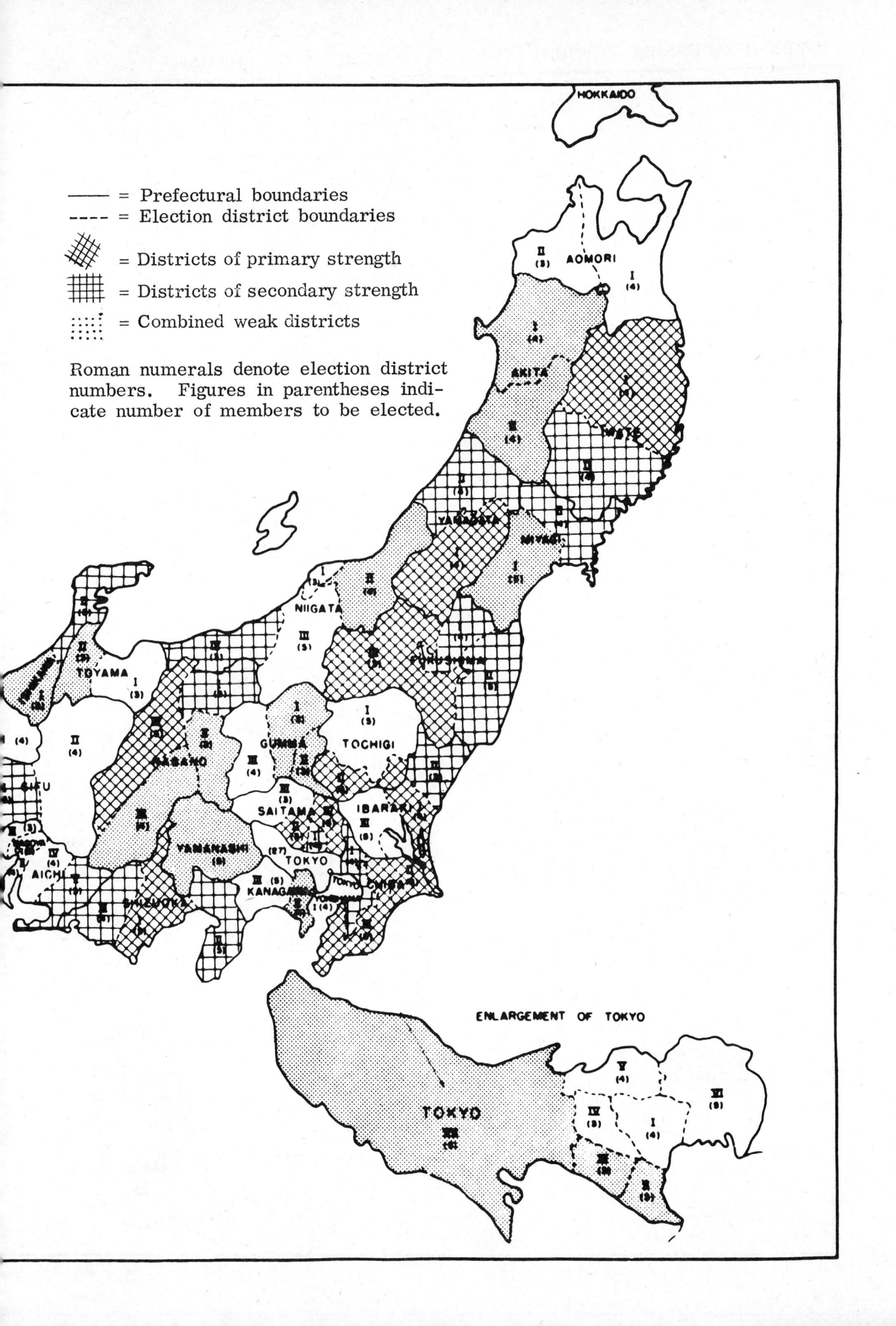

—— = Prefectural boundaries
---- = Election district boundaries
▧ = Districts of primary strength
▦ = Districts of secondary strength
⋮⋮⋮ = Combined weak districts

Roman numerals denote election district numbers. Figures in parentheses indicate number of members to be elected.

ENLARGEMENT OF TOKYO

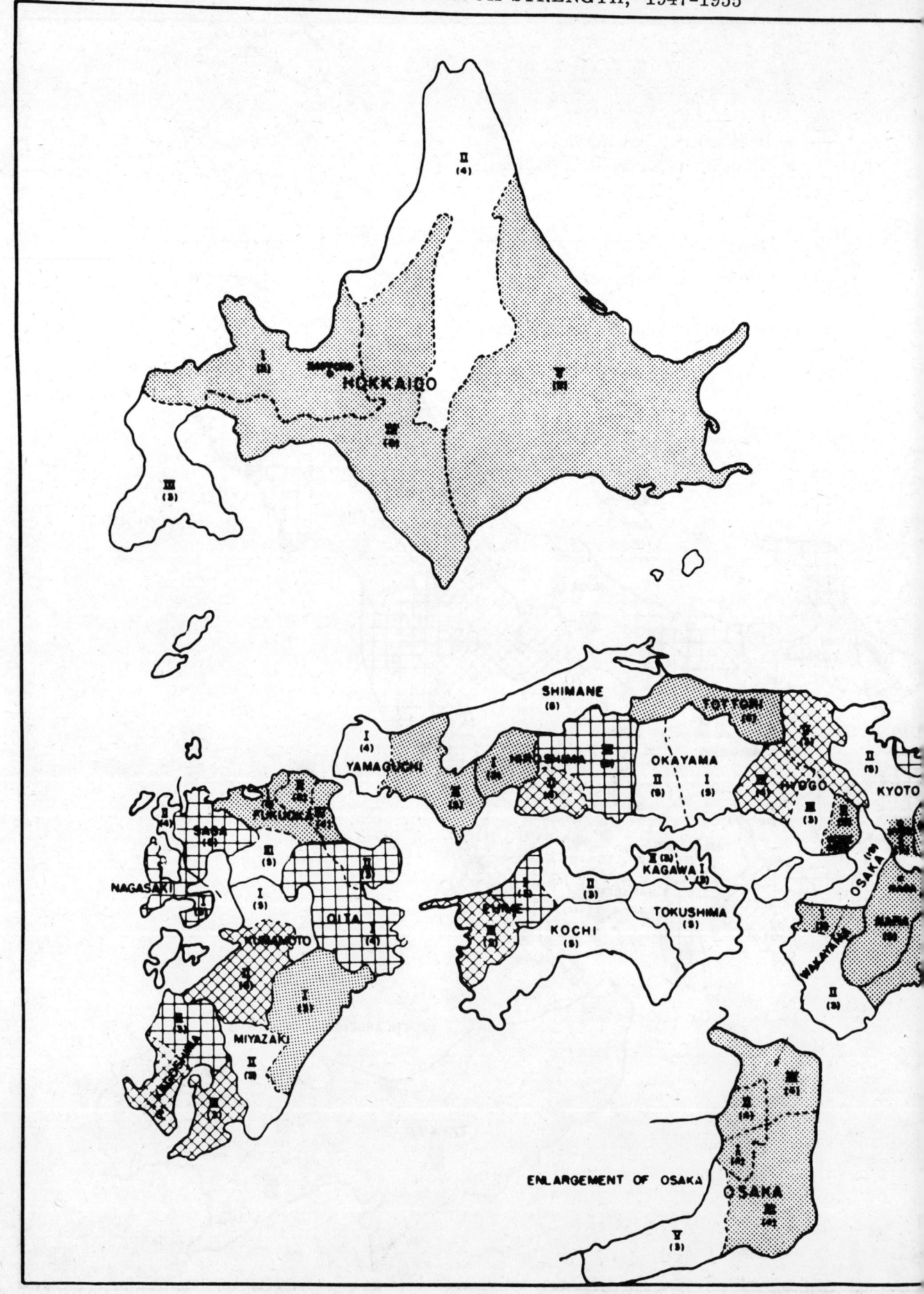

FIGURE II—AREAS OF CONSERVATIVE BLOCK STRENGTH, 1947-1955

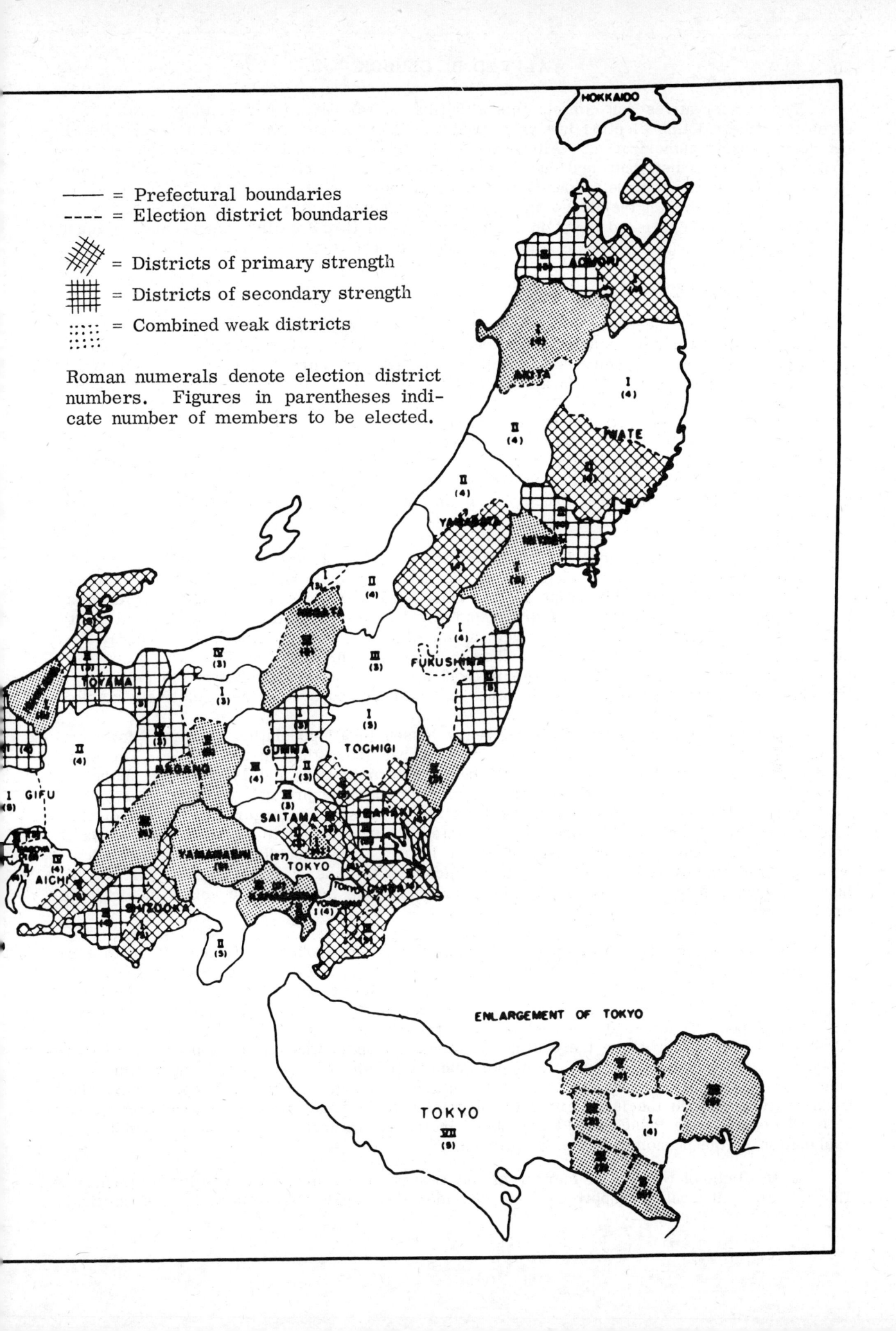

— = Prefectural boundaries
---- = Election district boundaries
▨ = Districts of primary strength
▦ = Districts of secondary strength
⋯ = Combined weak districts

Roman numerals denote election district numbers. Figures in parentheses indicate number of members to be elected.

ENLARGEMENT OF TOKYO

The Conservatives can correct this situation in two ways. First, they could strengthen the existing election law under which candidates can run under a party title without central party authorization. Alternatively, in order to isolate opposition strength, they could attempt to redistribute and decrease the size of the election districts. The Conservatives are apparently seriously considering this second alternative in order to decrease Socialist membership in the House and thereby do away with Socialist control of the amendment process. There is no doubt in the author's mind that Socialist representation can be drastically cut through the use of a gerrymandering process.

Urban-rural Analysis

The results of the preceding urban-rural analyses of Liberal Party strength indicate that the hypothesis upon which this study was based is valid. Granting the assumption that population size of a community is in itself an adequate measure of the degree of urbanization of a community, then we can accept the fact that as the degree of urbanization increases the proportion of the Liberal Party vote within the community decreases. A similar relationship has been demonstrated for the conservative forces as a whole. However, as has been indicated previously, the contribution of the Progressive Party to this trend is seriously in question. In three of the four elections preceding the 1955 election, the Progressives obtained their highest percentage of the group vote in the semi-rural and semi-urban groups rather than in the rural group where the Liberal Party obtained their highest percentage.

The graphic presentation (Figure III) of the urban-rural analysis for the years 1947-55 is included to illustrate the development of the urban-rural voting pattern. The outstanding fact which emerges from this graph is that until 1955 there was an increasing differentiation between the voting behavior of urban and rural Japan in relation to the Liberal Party and the Conservative Block. The source of this differentiation in relation to Liberal Party strength appears to be in rural rather than in urban Japan. For the Liberals' gains in popular support following their upsurge in 1949 appear to have been restricted primarily to the rural group while their support in other population groups remained relatively stable.

In 1955 the Liberal Party suffered heavy losses in all population groups. However, Liberal losses were significantly heavier in the rural group than in the urban. The similarity of the Liberal Party's urban-rural voting pattern in 1947 and 1955 led the author to the conclusion that the 1955 urban-rural distribution was the product of a hard core of Liberal Party strength. In rural Japan the Liberals simply had a larger number of voters to lose before they reached this core of party voters. This is not to say that Liberal Party voters in 1955 were motivated solely by Party loyalty. Undoubtedly, voter identification with specific candidates contributed in large measure to Liberal Party support. There have been, however, indications that party identification among the Japanese voting public is increasing.[20]

The strength of the Conservative Block increased in Groups I, II, and III up to and including the 1952 election. In Group IV, the urban group, following substantial gains in 1949, the Block's support appears to have achieved relative stability. In fact, the behavior of the urban group is rather difficult to explain. Since the 1952 election the Conservative Block has lost 3.0 per cent of the total popular vote in the nation as a whole. However, in the urban group the decline in popular support was only 0.8 per cent. Admittedly, a 3 per cent drop in popular support cannot be viewed as a significant decline in conservative strength. However, the very small percentage of popular support which the Conservatives lost in the large cities is surprising for we had anticipated that a large segment of conservative losses would have been in the urban centers. At the present time no explanation of the phenomenon can be offered.

In the light of the recent merger of the Liberal and Democratic Parties following the 1955 election, it would be appropriate to consider the Conservative Block as one political

FIGURE III

LIBERAL PARTY—CONSERVATIVE BLOCK
URBAN-RURAL VOTING DISTRIBUTION

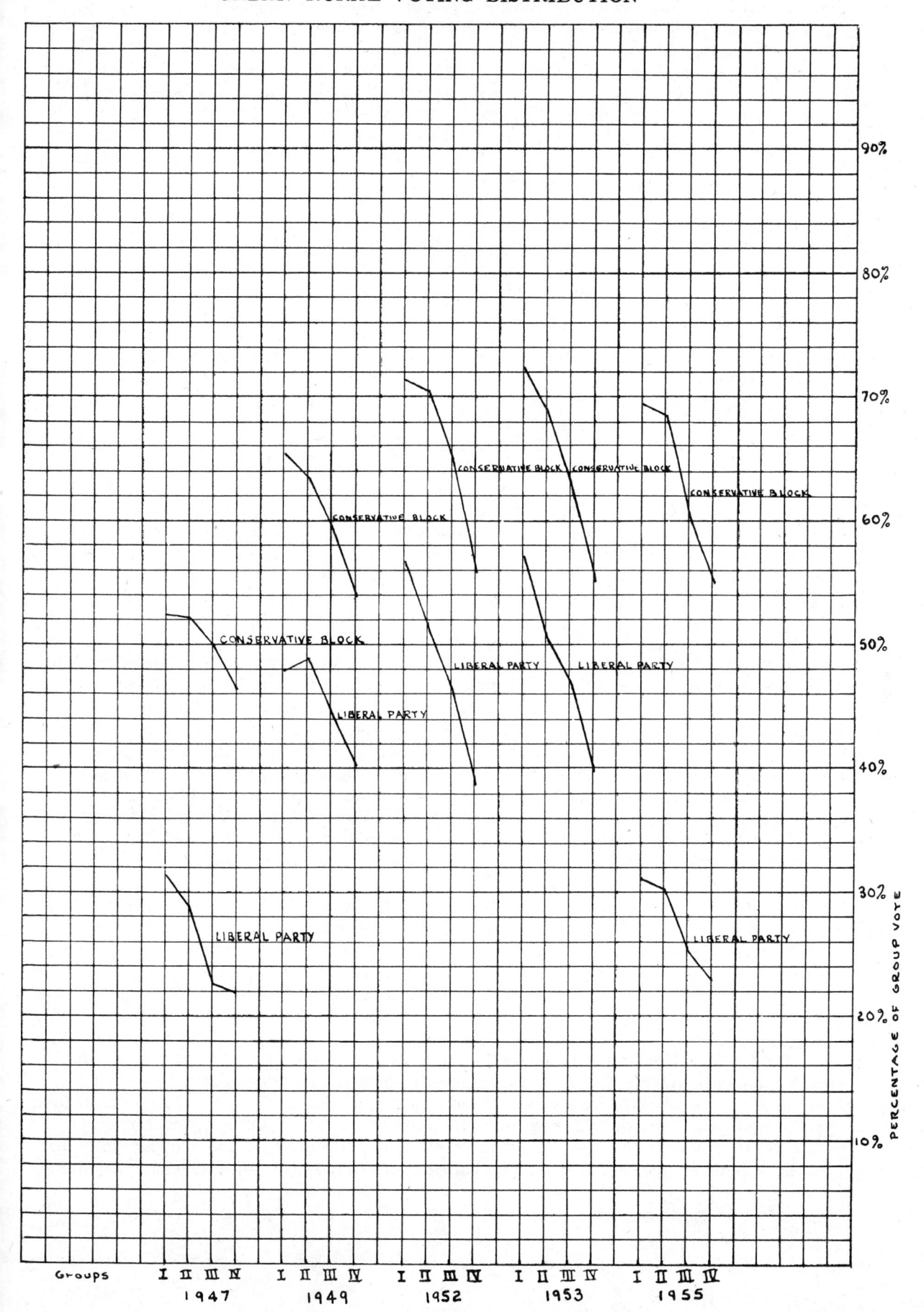

unit. The results of the urban-rural analyses leave little area for disagreement as to the strength of Japan's conservative forces. Barring an unforeseen military or economic crisis, the author cannot foresee a broad enough shift of electoral support to remove the control of political power from the hands of the conservative political elements. The fact that in 1955 the conservative candidates, collectively, received approximately 70.0 per cent of the popular vote in the rural and semi-rural groups, which include approximately 60.0 per cent of the Japanese people, is evidence enough of the strength of the conservative political forces. Even in the large centers of urban population, which by implication from the preceding analyses are the areas of greatest left-of-center support, the conservative candidates received 55.0 per cent of the popular vote. In view of these statistics, further evidence of conservative strength seems unnecessary.

Since the mergers within both the Socialist and Conservative forces, there has been increased reference to the emergence of a two-party system in Japan. In the author's opinion, however, the recent merger, rather than leading to the development of a meaningful two-party system, has produced a conservative party whose legislative position can hardly be challenged.

The factors underlying the existence of the observed urban-rural pattern cannot, of course, be isolated by means of an analysis of election data. However, some areas for further study may be tentatively indicated.

The Japanese conservative political forces have been extremely hesitant to organize as mass parties. Although they have been utilizing Western electioneering techniques, it is fairly safe to assume that the conservatives, especially in rural Japan, have been depending heavily on traditional Japanese election devices; for example, the conservatives have depended on prestige candidates and the influence of local personalities to secure votes. To what extent, then, are traditional techniques effective at the various levels of urbanization? It can be assumed that these techniques will lose some of their effectiveness as the degree of urbanization of a community increases. However, our lack of information vis-à-vis this form of political action makes an accurate judgment impossible at this time.

A second matter which could be investigated is the relationship of the Japanese family system to urban-rural voting behavior. Although quantitative data as to the strength or weakness of the family system are not available, the few qualitative assessments which have been made indicate that the system is losing strength. The point which is of interest here is that this deterioration process is proceeding at different rates over the urban-rural continuum; the process has been accelerated in urban Japan while the pace has been much slower in the rural areas. That the family system is a conductor of conservative social, economic, and political behavior needs no verification. The nature of the relationship between the urban-rural voting patterns as established in this study and the unequal deterioration of the family system is an obvious, although difficult, research problem.

Third, the land reform program carried out under the auspices of the Supreme Commander for the Allied Powers undoubtedly contributed in some measure to the observed voting patterns. The peasant in possession of his own land under reasonably secure economic conditions is notably conservative in his political outlook and, accordingly, there would be a tendency on his part to identify his own interests with those of the conservative political forces.

The political motivations of the tenant farmer, on the other hand, are not as clear, for although the tenants' desire for land is axiomatic, there are reasonable doubts as to whether they would identify this desire with conservative political groups. The land reform program carried out early in the Occupation alleviated, to a large extent, the tenant problem in the Japanese countryside. Although the program presented an ideal opportunity for the study of the effect of land reform on the political predisposition of the tenant farmer, unfortunately, the opportunity was passed by. Again qualitative observations have indicated that the land reform program did strengthen the support of the conservatives in the countryside. All indications are that the percentage of tenants among the peasantry is again slowly rising. This increase in the number of tenant farmers presents an opportunity to study the effects of land reform in reverse. If, as is claimed, the land reform program increased conservative support in the countryside, the increase in the number of tenants should produce a reverse effect.

Other possible research areas could be mentioned, but it would seem more helpful to repeat that considering our almost complete lack of knowledge about Japanese political dynamics, any material put forward must, of necessity, be in the form of hypothesis. The factors underlying the observed voting patterns can be investigated only by means of intensive field work directed at causal relationships. The author does feel, however, that the present method of study provides an analytical tool which permits investigation over a considerable time span, an opportunity which is rarely available to the field worker.

NOTES

1. Japan, Office of the Prime Minister, Bureau of Statistics, Population Census of 1950, Tōkyō, 1950, Vol. 1. Vol. 1 is printed in both Japanese and English.

2. Occupation statistics for individual communities were available for eight prefectures: Fukushima, Toyama, Fukui, Yamanashi, Shizuoka, Wakayama, Tottori, and Shimane. In a limited survey of these prefectures, it was found that in communities with a population of 5,000 and below almost the total labor force was employed in primary production, e.g., agriculture, fishing, and forestry; while in communities with populations of 150,000 and above almost the entire labor force was engaged in secondary occupations, such as manufacturing, and tertiary occupations, i.e., distribution and services. In Groups II and III it was found that as the size of the community increased, the per cent of the labor force engaged in primary industries decreased.

3. Nihon, Shūgiin Jimukyoku 日本衆議院事務局 (Japan, House of Representatives, Secretariat), Shūgiin giin sō-senkyo ichiran 衆議院議員総選挙一覧 (Summary of the General Election of Members of the House of Representatives), Tōkyō, 1947, 1949, 1952, 1953, and 1955.

4. For the complete text of the 1945 law see: Nihon, Zenkoku Senkyo Kanri I-in Kai, 日本全国選挙管理委員會 (Japan, National Election Management Commission), Shūgiin giin senkyo-hō enkaku, 衆議院議員選挙法沿革 (History of the Law for Election of the House of Representatives), Tōkyō, 1948.

5. Okinawa is excluded from this count.

6. Kenneth E. Colton, "Pre-war Political Influences in Post-war Conservative Parties," The American Political Science Review, Vol. XLII, October 1948, p. 948.

7. For a text of the 1947 law see: Japan, National Election Management Commission, Law and Ordinance for the Election of Members of the House of Representatives, Tokyo, 1949. Text in both Japanese and English.

8. Information for this summary has been compiled from: Department of State, Office of Research and Intelligence, Analysis of the 1946 Japanese General Election, Washington, 1946.

9. Colton, op. cit., p. 952.

10. All information in this and subsequent tables, unless otherwise noted, is derived from the Shūgiin giin sō-senkyō ichiran, (op. cit.), 1947, 1949, 1952, 1953, and 1955.

11. In the 1930 election, the Minseito returned 76.9 per cent of its candidates while in 1932 it returned 86.8 per cent of its candidates. See: Robert E. Ward, Party Government in Japan, Its Development and Electoral Record, 1928-37. University of California, 1948. Unpublished doctoral dissertation.

12. Yukichi Kuroki, "Reshaping of Japanese Political Parties," Contemporary Japan, Vol. XVI, October-December 1947, p. 465.

13. Chapter V, Article 67 of the Constitution provides that "if the House of Representatives and the House of Councilors disagree and if a joint committee of both Houses, provided for by law, cannot reach an agreement, or the House of Councilors fails to make designation within ten days, exclusive of the period of recess, after the House of Representatives has made designation, the decision of the House of Representatives shall be the decision of the House."

14. This was the first post-war election in which depurgees ran in sizable numbers. Out of a total of 321 depurgees who were candidates, 132 were elected. The Liberal Party elected 76 depurgees to the Lower House. This represents 31.5 per cent of the Liberal's membership in the House.

15. Rodger Swearingen and Paul Langer, Red Flag in Japan, Cambridge, 1952, p. 241.

16. Ibid., p. 135.

17. Embassy of Japan, Information Section, Japan Information, Washington, Vol. I, No. 10, January 17, 1955.

18. Article 96 of the Constitution states "Amendments to the Constitution shall be initiated by the Diet, through a concurring vote of two-thirds or more of all members of each House...."

19. For a discussion of Seiyukai and Minseito strongholds see: Ward, Party Government in Japan, op. cit.

20. Douglas H. Mendel, Political Behavior in Post-treaty Japan, University of Michigan, 1954. Unpublished doctoral dissertation.

TABLE 14

LIBERAL PARTY COMBINED RANK

Ranked in Ascending Order of Strength
(Average Percentage 1947-1955)

Rank	Prefecture	District	Percentage	Region
1	Gumma	1	15.9	Kanto
2	Ishikawa	1	19.3	Chubu
3	Fukuoka	2	19.7	Kyushu
4	Hokkaido	4	20.0	Hokkaido
5	Niigata	2	23.4	Chubu
6	Kyoto	1	24.9	Kinki
7	Kanazawa	1	25.0	Kanto
8	Hokkaido	5	25.8	Hokkaido
9	Kyoto	2	26.4	Kinki
10	Kumamoto	1	26.5	Kyushu
11	Kanazawa	2	26.6	Kanto
12	Akita	1	26.7	Tohoku
13	Nagano	3	26.8	Chubu
14	Fukuoka	1	26.8	Kyushu
15	Mie	2	27.7	Kinki
16	Hyogo	4	27.8	Kinki
17	Yamanashi	1	29.0	Chubu
18	Tokyo	3	29.5	Kanto
19	Toyama	2	29.5	Chubu
20	Hyogo	1	29.6	Kinki
21	Fukuoka	4	30.0	Kyushu
22	Shimane	1	30.1	Chugoku
23	Tokushima	1	30.9	Shikoku
24	Osaka	2	31.2	Kinki
25	Aichi	1	31.3	Chubu
26	Gumma	2	31.4	Kanto
27	Wakayama	2	31.7	Kinki
28	Fukuoka	3	31.9	Kyushu
29	Mie	1	31.9	Kinki
30	Aichi	3	31.9	Chubu
31	Miyagi	1	32.0	Tohoku
32	Osaka	3	32.5	Kinki
33	Hyogo	5	32.6	Kinki
34	Akita	2	32.7	Tohoku
35	Nagano	2	32.7	Chubu
36	Tokyo	7	33.0	Kanto
37	Hokkaido	1	33.1	Hokkaido
38	Tokyo	2	33.1	Kanto
39	Nagasaki	2	33.2	Kyushu
40	Osaka	1	33.3	Kinki
41	Tokyo	6	33.6	Kanto
42	Tokyo	5	33.7	Kanto
43	Shiga	1	33.8	Kinki
44	Ehime	2	34.1	Shikoku
45	Gumma	3	34.7	Kanto
46	Hyogo	2	34.8	Kinki

TABLE 14 (Continued)

Rank	Prefecture	District	Percentage	Region
47	Aichi	2	34.8	Chubu
48	Kagawa	2	35.1	Shikoku
49	Hiroshima	1	35.3	Chugoku
50	Kagawa	1	36.3	Shikoku
51	Aomori	2	36.4	Tohoku
52	Hokkaido	2	36.5	Hokkaido
53	Tottori	1	37.0	Chugoku
54	Tokyo	1	37.1	Kanto
55	Osaka	4	37.4	Kinki
56	Niigata	3	37.5	Chubu
57	Tochigi	1	38.2	Kanto
58	Toyama	1	38.3	Chubu
59	Tokyo	4	38.9	Kanto
60	Oita	1	39.2	Kyushu
61	Yamaguchi	2	39.2	Chugoku
62	Oita	2	39.7	Kyushu
63	Miyazaki	2	39.9	Kyushu
64	Hyogo	3	39.9	Kinki
65	Kagoshima	2	40.1	Kyushu
66	Gifu	2	40.4	Chubu
67	Aomori	1	40.7	Tohoku
68	Nara	1	40.9	Kinki
69	Aichi	4	41.1	Chubu
70	Wakayama	1	41.1	Kinki
71	Kagoshima	1	41.2	Kyushu
72	Ibaraki	3	41.7	Tohoku
73	Okayama	1	42.0	Chugoku
74	Kanazawa	3	42.2	Kanto
75	Fukui	1	42.6	Chubu
76	Niigata	1	42.9	Chubu
77	Miyazaki	1	43.2	Kyushu
78	Kumamoto	2	43.2	Kyushu
79	Ishikawa	2	43.6	Chubu
80	Fukushima	1	43.6	Tohoku
81	Ehime	1	43.6	Shikoku
82	Yamagata	2	43.8	Tohoku
83	Shizuoka	2	44.1	Chubu
84	Saitama	1	44.2	Kanto
85	Saga	1	45.0	Kyushu
86	Nagano	1	45.5	Chubu
87	Ibaraki	2	45.5	Kanto
88	Chiba	1	45.9	Kanto
89	Hiroshima	3	46.7	Chugoku
90	Aichi	5	46.8	Chubu
91	Saitama	3	47.0	Kanto
92	Shizuoka	3	47.2	Chubu
93	Miyagi	2	47.6	Tohoku
94	Gifu	1	47.9	Chubu
95	Niigata	4	48.0	Chubu
96	Fukushima	2	48.2	Tohoku
97	Iwate	2	48.3	Tohoku

TABLE 14 (Continued)

Rank	Prefecture	District	Percentage	Region
98	Ibaraki	1	49.3	Kanto
99	Okayama	2	49.2	Chugoku
100	Fukushima	3	49.6	Tohoku
101	Yamaguchi	1	49.7	Chugoku
102	Chiba	3	50.6	Kanto
103	Kochi	1	50.6	Shikoku
104	Tochigi	2	50.8	Kanto
105	Nagano	4	51.9	Chubu
106	Iwate	1	53.2	Tohoku
107	Nagasaki	1	53.6	Kyushu
108	Osaka	5	54.1	Kinki
109	Hokkaido	3	55.3	Hokkaido
110	Chiba	2	55.6	Kanto
111	Ehime	3	56.5	Shikoku
112	Yamagata	1	58.3	Tohoku
113	Shizuoka	1	60.3	Chubu
114	Kagoshima	3	61.6	Kyushu
115	Saitama	4	61.8	Kanto
116	Saitama	2	62.5	Kanto
117	Hiroshima	2	62.7	Chugoku

TABLE 15

CONSERVATIVE BLOCK COMBINED RANK

Ranked in Ascending Order of Strength
(Average Percentage 1947-1955)

Rank	Prefecture	District	Percentage	Region
1	Hokkaido	4	31.5	Hokkaido
2	Tokyo	3	38.7	Kanto
3	Fukuoka	2	39.4	Kyushu
4	Fukuoka	4	41.5	Kyushu
5	Osaka	2	45.1	Kinki
6	Fukuoka	1	45.6	Kyushu
7	Hyogo	1	46.2	Kinki
8	Tokyo	2	46.4	Kanto
9	Miyagi	1	46.6	Tohoku
10	Kanazawa	1	48.2	Kanto
11	Osaka	1	50.5	Kinki
12	Kanazawa	2	50.5	Kanto
13	Hokkaido	5	50.9	Hokkaido
14	Kyoto	1	51.0	Kinki
15	Tokyo	4	51.4	Kanto
16	Yamanashi	1	51.5	Chubu
17	Aichi	1	51.9	Chubu
18	Osaka	3	52.1	Kinki
19	Akita	1	52.4	Tohoku

TABLE 15 (Continued)

Rank	Prefecture	District	Percentage	Region
20	Yamaguchi	2	52.7	Chugoku
21	Kanazawa	3	53.1	Kanto
22	Osaka	4	53.6	Kinki
23	Shiga	1	53.6	Kinki
24	Hokkaido	1	53.6	Hokkaido
25	Ishikawa	1	54.1	Chubu
26	Tokyo	5	54.2	Kanto
27	Tokyo	6	54.7	Kanto
28	Hiroshima	1	54.9	Chugoku
29	Nagano	3	55.1	Chubu
30	Mie	2	55.4	Kinki
31	Niigata	3	55.4	Chubu
32	Ibaraki	2	55.6	Kanto
33	Saitama	1	56.0	Kanto
34	Tottori	1	56.3	Chugoku
35	Wakayama	1	56.9	Kinki
36	Hyogo	2	57.2	Kinki
37	Nagano	2	57.5	Chubu
38	Miyazaki	1	57.5	Kyushu
39	Nara	1	57.6	Kinki
40	Wakayama	2	57.8	Kinki
41	Fukuoka	3	57.8	Kyushu
42	Yamaguchi	1	57.9	Chugoku
43	Nagano	1	58.2	Chubu
44	Kyoto	2	58.7	Kinki
45	Tokyo	7	58.9	Kanto
46	Tokyo	1	59.6	Kanto
47	Shizuoka	2	59.8	Chubu
48	Gifu	1	60.2	Chubu
49	Akita	2	61.1	Tohoku
50	Osaka	5	61.3	Kinki
51	Fukushima	3	61.3	Tohoku
52	Tochigi	1	61.4	Kanto
53	Okayama	2	61.7	Chugoku
54	Kagawa	1	61.8	Shikoku
55	Gumma	2	62.0	Kanto
56	Shimane	1	62.0	Chugoku
57	Tokushima	1	62.3	Shikoku
58	Gifu	2	62.5	Chubu
59	Hyogo	3	62.6	Kinki
60	Kumamoto	1	62.9	Kyushu
61	Gumma	3	63.0	Kanto
62	Fukushima	1	63.0	Tohoku
63	Hokkaido	2	63.3	Hokkaido
64	Miyazaki	2	63.4	Kyushu
65	Aichi	4	63.4	Chubu
66	Niigata	1	63.4	Chubu
67	Iwate	1	63.5	Tohoku
68	Okayama	1	63.6	Chugoku
69	Niigata	2	64.0	Chubu
70	Nagasaki	2	64.7	Kyushu

TABLE 15 (Continued)

Rank	Prefecture	District	Percentage	Region
71	Hokkaido	3	65.0	Hokkaido
72	Kochi	1	65.2	Shikoku
73	Saitama	3	65.4	Kanto
74	Ehime	2	66.0	Shikoku
75	Yamagata	2	66.0	Tohoku
76	Niigata	4	66.1	Chubu
77	Kagawa	2	66.2	Shikoku
78	Aichi	2	66.3	Chubu
79	Nagasaki	1	66.6	Kyushu
80	Shizuoka	3	66.7	Chubu
81	Toyama	1	66.9	Chubu
82	Oita	1	66.9	Kyushu
83	Fukushima	2	67.1	Tohoku
84	Saga	1	67.1	Kyushu
85	Kagoshima	2	67.2	Kyushu
86	Aichi	3	67.3	Chubu
87	Gumma	1	67.9	Kanto
88	Aomori	2	68.0	Tohoku
89	Nagano	4	68.7	Chubu
90	Fukui	1	68.9	Chubu
91	Mie	1	69.4	Kinki
92	Ibaraki	3	69.5	Kanto
93	Hiroshima	3	69.6	Chugoku
94	Miyagi	2	69.7	Tohoku
95	Ehime	1	70.0	Shikoku
96	Toyama	2	70.4	Chubu
97	Oita	2	70.4	Kyushu
98	Shizuoka	1	71.3	Chubu
99	Chiba	1	72.2	Kanto
100	Tochigi	2	72.4	Kanto
101	Iwate	2	73.2	Tohoku
102	Yamagata	1	73.6	Tohoku
103	Hyogo	4	73.7	Kinki
104	Hiroshima	2	74.5	Chugoku
105	Saitama	2	74.7	Kanto
106	Kumamoto	2	74.9	Kyushu
107	Saitama	4	75.3	Kanto
108	Aichi	5	75.4	Chubu
109	Ehime	3	76.3	Shikoku
110	Hyogo	5	77.4	Kinki
111	Kagoshima	3	77.6	Kyushu
112	Aomori	1	78.4	Tohoku
113	Kagoshima	1	79.4	Kyushu
114	Ibaraki	1	80.0	Kanto
115	Chiba	2	81.2	Kanto
116	Chiba	3	83.1	Kanto
117	Ishikawa	2	85.7	Chubu

THE ISSUE OF SAKHALIN IN RUSSO-JAPANESE RELATIONS

William C. Amidon

Introduction

Throughout the modern period of contacts between Japan and the West, Sakhalin has been an important and controversial part of Japan's northern boundary. Although it has figured prominently in most of the boundary agreements signed between Japan and Russia, no well defined and lasting settlement has ever been reached. Ownership of the island has passed back and forth between these two powers whenever one has been able to assert sufficient pressure on the other. At times, when both have been equally strong or well prepared, the island has been held jointly or divided between them. These successive transfers of title have drastically altered the national and racial composition of the population and have confused and distorted the economic growth of Sakhalin. When viewed in connection with the expansionist desires of both Russia and Japan, the national and economic problems which these transfers brought about have served to make Sakhalin a central point of controversy whenever a Russo-Japanese boundary is discussed.

The most recent change in title came after World War II. Prior to the war Sakhalin was divided between Russia and Japan at the fiftieth parallel. The U.S.S.R. held the northern half while Japan held South Sakhalin or Karafuto. As a result of agreements signed between the Allies at Yalta, Russian forces occupied South Sakhalin at the end of the war in the Pacific. The Yalta agreements had promised South Sakhalin along with other concessions, such as the Kuriles, to the Soviet Union in exchange for Russia's agreement to enter the war against Japan.[1] Acting on the basis of this agreement, the Soviet Union set about assimilating South Sakhalin; as early as November, 1946 it was proclaimed a voting district within the Russian Soviet Federated Socialist Republic.

The process of assimilation proceeded in the post-war years, but no further agreements were signed to legalize these Russian moves. Instead, as time went on, opposition from the Western nations led by the United States and from Japan became more pronounced. The United States viewed the acquisition of South Sakhalin by Russia at the conclusion of World War II as a step toward further communist expansion in the Pacific area, and this action was therefore condemned widely in the United States. The Senate specifically claimed that its approval of the San Francisco Peace Treaty did not "diminish or prejudice, in favor of the Soviet Union, the right, title and interest of Japan or the Allied powers, as defined in such treaty, in and to Sakhalin and its adjacent islands...."[2] Although American opposition to the transfer of South Sakhalin has not progressed farther than public criticism, it has probably been significant in encouraging the Japanese government's persistence in discussing the Sakhalin question prior to reaching a general agreement with the Soviet Union.

In raising the question of Russia's right to South Sakhalin, the Japanese have focused their attention on two main arguments.[3] The first of these states that Japan has an historical right to Sakhalin, based on prior exploration and settlement of the island. Secondly they contend that it was Japan who was most responsible for building Sakhalin economically and that any settlement which would take South Sakhalin out of the Japanese economy permanently would do great harm to Japan. Following these arguments the Japanese have pressed Russian negotiators to make a favorable settlement on the Sakhalin question. In all probability such arguments will have little effect on negotiations between Russia and Japan, for the soundness of the logic or the honesty of such claims would seem to weigh lightly in the power-conscious world of the twentieth century.

To understand the nature of the disagreement one must study the historical process which has brought about the present controversy and evaluate the importance of Sakhalin to both powers. Then, if Sakhalin can be placed in its true perspective within the framework of Russian and Japanese national aspirations, it may be possible to find in the claims and counterclaims of the two countries some meaning that will help to explain the nature of the present settlement.

The island is located north of Japan between the Sea of Okhotsk and the Sea of Japan,[4] extending north and south for more than six hundred miles. It has a total area of approximately 29,700 square miles; the southern half, Karafuto, is 13,934 square miles in area. In the south it is separated from Japan by only twenty-five miles at the La Perouse Strait. The distance between Sakhalin and the Amur delta region in the northwest is even less, measuring only eight miles at one point. Thus the closeness of Sakhalin to both Russian Eastern Asia and Japan has made it a natural corridor between the two nations. The value of this corridor to the two countries has been enhanced and the conflict for control sharpened by Japan's early refusal to carry on direct intercourse with the Russians and the latters' insistence on forging ahead in their attempts to bring it about.

The population of Sakhalin has changed erratically several times during the past one hundred years. This has been due primarily to the colonization policies of Japan and Russia, both of which have tried with varying success to move large groups of their nationals into the island. By 1900 the colonization efforts which Russia had begun about the middle of the previous century had increased the population from 7,000 to approximately 30,000. Of these over half were convicted criminals who had been deported from European Russia or Siberia. In 1907, the population had again decreased to only 7,000. The huge outflow of people had resulted from the repatriation of the convicts from the southern half of Sakhalin which had passed into Japanese hands as a result of the peace treaty of 1905. By 1930 there had been another huge increase in the island's population. The northern or Russian half of the island was reported to have in excess of 50,000 inhabitants while the southern half boasted a population of nearly 340,000. In the 1940's the Russian government reported that the population in North Sakhalin had doubled, bringing the total in their area up to 100,000. The Japanese published no figures for that period. Recent figures claim that the population has grown to 500,000 since World War II; however the lack of a reliable census for the island, coupled with the problems created by Soviet immigration and Japanese repatriation, has made it difficult to establish more than a rough approximation of the present population.

Agriculture on Sakhalin has been limited by the severe climate. In North Sakhalin there has been a recent emphasis on dairy farming and the growing of fodder grasses. A few vegetables and some grain crops are raised in the area, but they are of minor importance. In the milder climate of South Sakhalin sugar beets, leguminous crops, oats, barley, wheat, and rice make up the bulk of the agricultural production.

The major industries on Sakhalin include lumbering, herring fishing, oil production and coal mining. There has been some shipbuilding in recent years and a considerable increase in the amount of small industry on the island. However the major portion of the industrial effort is still directed toward the exploitation of Sakhalin's natural resources: the forests, fishing grounds, and coal and petroleum deposits.

The Historical Development of Sakhalin as an Issue in Russo-Japanese Relations

It was not until the seventeenth century that the Japanese and Russian exploration and settlement of the Sakhalin area began. The first contact of these two nations in the north came as a result of the great eastward movement of Russian explorers and adventurers in that century. In 1638 the first of these men arrived, having traveled an overland route from Russia. The second adventurer to make his way into the northern Pacific region was the Cossack Dejneff, who came instead by a sea route. He sailed from the Kolyma River through the Behring Strait and on to Anadyr.[5] Although this voyage proved the possibility of sailing the northern route to the Far East, it was not until modern times that the Russians again used it.

These early explorers had opened the way to further Russian expansion into the Far East, but neither appears to have actually brought Russia into direct contact with Japan. It was not until 1697 that a genuine contact was established. In that year the Russian explorer Atlassov met a Japanese fisherman named Debune, whose boat had been blown off course, forcing him to land on Kamchatka.[6] Debune's fabulous stories of the great wealth of Japan so impressed Atlassov that he began preparing operations directed at Japan even though the conquest of Kamchatka had not yet been completed. He first dispatched a subordinate to pillage the Kurile Islands. He then sent a petition to Tsar Peter the Great, asking for permission to launch an immediate attack upon Japan. The tsar however withheld permission for such a venture; instead his reply ordered that Debune be transported to Moscow. In 1702 Debune was given an audience with the tsar and was questioned at length about his country. Impressed with the need for learning more about Japan, Peter commissioned Debune to teach Japanese to a number of Russian scholars and military officers. Although he was only a common seaman and hardly qualified to teach Japanese, Debune was retained in a post at the Academy of Science until his death in 1736.[7]

Apparently the tsar installed Debune at the Academy of Science preparatory to the dispatch of a major expedition to the East, for soon after he sent a party, headed by Ivan Petrovitch Kosirewski, to survey the area north of Japan. Kosirewski was instructed to find out to what government the inhabitants owed allegiance. In case they had no sovereign, he was to claim the land for Russia and collect tribute. With reference to Japan he was to try to discover what sort of weapons the Japanese used and how they waged war. If the Japanese appeared willing to conduct commercial relations with Russia, he was also to find out what items they would be willing to trade.[8] Kosirewski's expedition was only able to proceed against a few of the smaller Kurile Islands. He spent three summers in exploring the region, but could collect only scant information about the area. This failure appears to have been caused mainly by dissensions which arose within the party and by the duplicity of Kosirewski, who was later discharged from government service because of the secret plundering he had carried on during this assignment. The only material gain which the government received from these journeys appears to have been a chart which Kosirewski was able to make with the aid of some Kurile islanders. The chart showed Hokkaido and thirty-two of the northern islands. The natives also pointed out the location of the city of Matsumae, but they warned that it was heavily guarded and advised against a Russian attempt to proceed against it. The chart and a report were passed on to the governor of Yakutsk. They apparently were never used, however, for Peter the Great died in 1725, before he could perfect his plans for expansion into the Far East. The years following his death were marked by internal turmoil, and the government displayed little interest in activities in the East.

The Japanese also were late arriving in the Sakhalin area. An extensive trade had been carried on between the Yezo (Hokkaido) Ainu and the natives of Sakhalin since the latter part of the fifteenth century; however no effort to establish a systematic government of the island appears to have been attempted prior to the seventeenth century.[9] The Kakizaki clan had been enfeoffed in Yezo in 1582 or 1590 in a grant from Toyotomi Hideyoshi, but little was done to develop Sakhalin until late in the following century. On the contrary, every effort was made to limit migration to the island. The Kakizaki, who changed their name to Matsumae in 1603, at first had attempted to foster the growth of their new domain by throwing it open to immigration from Japan. Later, however, they established a policy of limiting this immigration as much as possible and restricting new settlers to an area in southwest Hokkaido. Their purpose in curtailing the amount of movement into the frontier area seems to have been twofold. First they hoped to curb the growing contact between the native Ainu people and the Japanese. To develop the fisheries and fur trade, which constituted the real wealth of the area, it was necessary only to allow a number of traders and merchants to travel in the northern regions. Further troublesome encroachment upon the Ainu territory seemed unnecessary. A second and perhaps more significant reason for limiting immigration was the scarcity of food in the area. The staple food, rice, had to be imported from Japan and paid for by the trading income of the Matsumae retainers. It was thought that an increase in the population would bring with it an increase in the price of rice; consequently the Matsumae took steps to limit immigration and thereby protect the interests of their retainers.[10]

In 1672 the Matsumae established the first permanent Japanese settlement on Sakhalin at Kushnukotan.[11] From this point onward it seems fairly safe to say that the Japanese were carrying on a systematic effort through local Matsumae lords to establish control of Sakhalin. Parties under the direction of Shirobei Atsuya and Seizayemon Takahashi were dispatched to establish fishing stations and settlements for the Matsumae, and in 1700 the island was listed in the clan register of the Matsumae as Karafuto Island with a reported twenty-two villages or stations. However even these repeated efforts to build a Japanese community on Sakhalin had only a small degree of success. The fishing stations established by Shirobei Atsuya in 1679 had to be abolished in 1684, and by 1806 it appears that the garrison which the Matsumae had placed on the island had been withdrawn to Soya.[12] Although the Japanese have listed these efforts to colonize and administer Sakhalin as definite evidence of their long-established rights to the island, it appears that until the end of the seventeenth century these efforts did not reach a stage that would provide a substantial basis for possession. One Japanese historian has admitted that prior ownership was not "very distinct."[13]

The same period that saw these Japanese claims to Sakhalin and the adjoining areas becoming firmly established also witnessed Russia's growing interest in the Far East, even though after the death of Peter the Great in 1725, the Russian government displayed no official interest. Desires for empire gave way to desires for profit, and the leadership of Russian expansion passed from commissioned government agents into the hands of merchants and traders. The islands to the north of Japan were rich in beavers and sea otters, providing a highly lucrative and appealing trade to the merchants and adventurers who had traveled to the East. The yearly migrations of these animals to the south furnished a primary impetus for Russian expansion into the area off Japan's northern coast.[14] Thus the eighteenth century saw Russia and Japan brought into closer contact through the efforts of Russian traders.

It was during the same period that the first official Russian landing was made on Japanese soil. Martin Spanberg, a member of Vitus Behring's scientific expedition, was commissioned to explore the area south of Kamchatka to Japan. After preparing three boats he set out in 1738 to explore the area. He spent the remainder of the favorable months of that year sailing throughout the Kurile Islands. In 1739 he returned with a fleet of four ships and sailed south to the Japanese coast somewhere in the vicinity of Mutsu province.[15] Although Spanberg is said to have been the first Russian to look upon Japanese soil, the credit for the first landing belongs to another member of his party, Captain William Walton. Captain Walton's ship, the St. Gabriel, became separated from the others during a storm, and he was forced to land at a Japanese city to replenish his supplies. From the description given, the landing seems to have been made at Kochi on Tosa Bay.[16] Captain Walton was well received by the Japanese and was able to procure the needed supplies; however he feared that the Japanese would try to capture the ship so he set sail as quickly as possible.

By the end of the eighteenth century, many of the merchants engaged in the Far Eastern trade were becoming discouraged. The trade, although it had initially been quite promising, had really proved increasingly precarious. So great were the losses of some merchants such as Lebedev Lastochin that it became virtually impossible toward the end of the century to interest private individuals in undertaking any trading ventures in the Far East. From this time on it was necessary for the government itself to sponsor further trade and expansion in that area.

The government's efforts took the form of a series of semi-official attempts by merchants and provincial governors to open direct communications with Japan. Although the government at St. Petersburg still did not display any overt interest in Japan, it is quite probable that these efforts made by the governors and merchants in the Far East represented the official Russian policy to the extent that one existed. The Manchu government had been quite effective in opposing further Russian expansion and exploration into China. As a consequence, in the second half of the eighteenth century, Russian undertakings in the Far East had to be concentrated upon Japan.[17]

In September, 1792 Russia made its first attempt to open direct communications with Japan. Captain Adam Laxman sailed from the Russian post at Okhotsk, carrying as a pretext two Japanese seamen who had been shipwrecked in Russian waters. On October 9, 1792 he docked his ship, the Ekaterina, in the harbor of Nemuro on the northeast coast of Hokkaido. The real reason for the voyage was contained in a request for trade which he presented to the local official. Unable to act upon Laxman's request, the official passed the news of his arrival on to the government at Edo. On June 4, 1793 Laxman's ship was allowed to proceed to Hakodate where he was to meet with the shogun's officials. Two envoys, Ishikawa and Murakami, were sent to Matsumae and there received Laxman's petition. The Russian state paper was returned without a specific reply; instead Laxman was informed that Nagasaki was the only place where foreigners could conduct business in Japan; neither trade nor negotiation could be allowed in the north. With this they gave Laxman a permit for one vessel to visit Nagasaki. Feeling that nothing more could be accomplished, Laxman withdrew and sailed back to Okhotsk.

Although Laxman had received permission to send a ship to Nagasaki, Russia made no effort to do so until 1804. There were several possible reasons why the Russians were slow to take advantage of the Japanese permit. First of all it appears that the government still did not share the views of some of the more enthusiastic traders. Excerpts from the correspondence of Catherine II indicate that she shared little interest in ventures in the Far East.[18] Secondly the feeling of insecurity which attended the French Revolution made it necessary for the European monarchs to concentrate on their internal affairs. In Russia this appears to have stifled the growing interest evidenced by Laxman's mission. This was also a period in which the clashes between the Indians and Russians in North America tended to restrict operations all along the Russian frontier. These became so violent at times that they even stopped transactions of the Russian-American Company, the foremost protagonist of Russian expansion in the North Pacific.

While the emphasis in Russian activity had switched from the Northern Islands to Japan proper in this period, there seems to have been little slackening in the efforts of the Russian traders to gain control of Sakhalin and the Kuriles. In 1780 two Russian ships were reported to have entered Karafuto, and in 1789 another party landed in order to survey the island and make presents to the natives.[19] The traders were slowly gaining a familiarity with the area and were expanding their trade with the natives.

In 1804 Nicolai Rezanov was appointed Ambassador Plenipotentiary to Japan. As a director of the Russian-American Company, Rezanov had a personal interest in the success of the mission.[20] His company needed Japanese ports for winter anchorage. Also, if it were possible to procure food in Japan, much of the difficulty of establishing colonies in North America could be overcome. The tremendous cost of transporting food overland from Irkutsk to Okhotsk and then transferring it to vessels for further shipment had been a deciding factor in the poor condition of the colonies in Alaska and the Aleutian Islands. Besides, his instructions ordered him to determine whether Sakhalin belonged to China or Japan, and some sources state that he was to annex Sakhalin for the Russian-American Company.[21]

The Nadezhda, carrying Rezanov and Captain Krusenstern, dropped anchor off Nagasaki on September 6, 1804. The permit which had been given to Captain Laxman a decade earlier was presented to the Japanese officials along with Rezanov's credentials. The credentials were accepted, but Rezanov was told that he must wait outside the harbor for a reply from Edo. Only after seventy-six days was the ship allowed to enter the harbor, and it was not until Rezanov became ill that the Japanese allowed him to come ashore. Even then they prepared only a small shack and restricted the Russians' movement around it.[22] The negotiations between Rezanov and the shogun's officials were carried on for six months, but without result. During these negotiations Rezanov was opposed by the Dutch in Nagasaki and a number of the shogun's advisors. The main objections were that the opening of the country would mean an "influx of Christianity and an outflow of gold."[23] The Dutch were undoubtedly jealous of the monopoly of Japanese trade which they had held throughout the Tokugawa period, and were encouraging opposition to the Russian mission in order to protect their own position.

In March, 1805, having had no luck in his efforts to negotiate a trade agreement with the Japanese, Rezanov left Nagasaki to carry out the second part of his instructions, the investigation of the Sakhalin area. He sailed north along the coast of Honshu and Hokkaido to the La Perouse Strait. When he reached Sakhalin, he investigated Aniwa Bay and the eastern side of the island up to the forty-eighth parallel. Following this survey Rezanov reported that the occupation of Sakhalin could and should be undertaken in the near future. This was seconded by Krusenstern who noted that "control over Aniwa can be gained without any resistance and the bay can be easily held since there are no troops either in the northern part of Ezo or on Sakhalin."[24] In consequence of his failure to reach an agreement with the government at Nagasaki, Rezanov became more and more interested in projects directed at the Northern Islands. In his report he stated that the failure at Nagasaki should be followed by a more gradual approach to the opening of trade, starting first with Sakhalin and Hokkaido and then working south.

Rezanov himself set out to initiate this plan the following year when he ordered two of his captains, Nicholas Kvostov and Gavrilo Davidov to sail to the Kuriles and Sakhalin. He explained his plan in a report to Tsar Alexander I:

> I do not suppose that Your Highness would charge me with a crime when with my worthy coworkers, such as Khvostoff and Davidoff...., I should next year go down to the shores of Japan to destroy their settlement of Matsuma (sic), to drive them out from Sakhalin, and to spread terror on the shores so that by taking away, in the meantime, their fishing areas, and thereby depriving 200,000 of their men of subsistence, the sooner to compel them to open up trade with us....[25]

Rezanov, receiving no reply from the tsar, decided to go on his own. He instructed the two young naval officers, Kvostov and Davidov, first to reconnoiter the Kurile Islands to the south. They were then to proceed to Sakhalin, wipe out the Japanese installations there and place the natives under the "protection" of the tsar. It was further ordered that they should make prisoner a number of Japanese, and should take them to Okhotsk where they were to be maintained with the best care possible. After one year they were to be returned to Japan to spread the news of the good treatment one might expect from the Russians. Rezanov's subsequent actions seem to indicate that he did not feel quite safe in initiating a venture of this importance without further authority. Prior to the beginning of the expedition he issued a set of conflicting orders and then left Okhotsk before Kvostov and Davidov could question him as to his real intentions.[26] Apparently this second set of instructions was no more than a form of protection for himself, for in a letter to the Minister of Commerce, Rumiantsev, he outlined his plan and described in detail the capabilities of Lieutenant Kvostov.[27]

Though not quite sure of what Rezanov's real intentions were, Kvostov and Davidov decided to follow the original instructions. In September, 1806 they sailed to Aniwa Bay. The village and fishing station at Kushnukotan were looted and burned. On a copper plate which he left nailed to a nearby torii, Kvostov warned the Japanese that further refusal to trade with Russia would bring about similar devastation of northern Japan. After declaring Sakhalin a possession of the tsar, the two naval officers sailed off to carry out similar raids along the coast and on Etorofu.

The result of these persistent Russian efforts was the awakening of the bakufu to the need for improving the defenses in the north. The first step toward strengthening the frontier region was taken in 1780 when the Tokugawa government sent a mission to the Kuriles to investigate the reports of Russian activity in that area. A second mission was sent to Sakhalin in 1785 for a similar purpose.[28] As a result of these investigations, in 1797 the Matsumae were made to entrust the northern part of Yezo and the adjacent islands to the bakufu for a period of seven years. The administration of this area was placed in the hands of a commission appointed by the shogun. In 1805 another mission, led by Kinshiro Toyama and Sadayu Muragaki, was sent to investigate the state of affairs in Sakhalin.[29] On the return of the mission it was decided that the northern area could best be defended if the whole of the Matsumae territory were to be absorbed by the bakufu. In March, 1805 the Matsumae were dispossessed, receiving in compensation an eighteen thousand koku grant on Honshu. (Land holdings during this period were measured in terms of the yearly rice production. 1 koku = 5.1 American bushels.) The areas on Sakhalin that had been directly controlled by the Matsumae were then placed under the supervision of bakufu agents, and the remainder of the island was leased to contractors.[30] Two Hakodate bugyo, Toda and Habuto, were placed in charge of the administration of Sakhalin; however the work of these two men was cut short by the Russian raids of 1806. Holding themselves responsible for the ease with which the Russians entered Etorofu and Sakhalin, they resigned, thus setting back the progress which had been made in the north. These first few steps which the bakufu took to protect their interests in the Northern Islands were mostly ineffectual and seem to indicate that they had only a very slight understanding of the purpose or the resolve of these merchants and explorers to the north.

Not all Japanese, however, were unaware of the threat which this Russian activity presented. Typical of the small group of men who were strongly opposed to Russian designs in the north was Toshiaki Honda (1774-1821). To him Japan's future lay in its ability to stop the Russian advance and to assert its own power over the North Pacific area. One of his schemes to bring this about called for moving the capital from central Japan to the southern part of Kamchatka. A strongly fortified city would be built near the forty-sixth or forty-seventh parallel on Sakhalin as well. This would place Kamchatka and Sakhalin in the very center of Japan's military and political control, thereby providing an excellent base for defense and expansion in the north.[31] Though Honda had come to grips with a problem which most of his contemporaries could not even see, the solution he devised shows how clouded was the Japanese understanding of the outside world. Honda was considered an acute thinker for his time, but even he could fall into the grave error of assuming that because his two projected cities in the north would be at the same latitudes as London and Paris, they could be expected to have the same advantages and prosperity as these two European capitals. The foremost difficulty which the Japanese faced in erecting a defense in the north was their own inadequate understanding of what the land in that area was really like.

The Russian raids of 1806 moved the Tokugawa government to action. The severity of the winter that year had slowed communications so that it was not until March, 1807, that the news was carried to Matsumae.[32] The bakufu did not hear of the attacks until April. They immediately set out to implement the defense preparations which had been begun under the direction of Toda and Habuto, but the delays of the preceding winter and spring had already made it too late to prevent another raid on Etorofu.[33] In the face of these continuing raids and the hopeless condition of the defenses in the north, the bakufu overruled an attempt by the Matsumae to take a force to Sakhalin. Instead they ordered that all men who were stationed there should be brought back to defend Soya on the north coast of Hokkaido.

Having rejected the Matsumae's appeal to meet the Russians squarely, the Edo government decided instead to build a stronger foundation for Japan's defense by learning more about the area to the north. As a first step toward gaining a better knowledge of the extent and nature of their northern possessions, the bakufu commissioned Mamiya Rinso to explore and report on Sakhalin and the adjoining area. Rinso, who had been greatly influenced by another geographer of this region, Ino Tadataka—he had been the first to map Hokkaido scientifically—set out in the spring of 1808 to map Sakhalin. That summer while mapping the east coast of the island, he discovered that Sakhalin was not part of the Asiatic continent, as had been believed earlier. He spent the winter of 1808 alone on Sakhalin, and then in the spring of 1809 he crossed the narrow straits to the continent where he explored the Amur delta and traveled up the river as far as the Chinese settlement of Delen. Later that year he returned to Japan and there dictated his findings in a report to the government. The discovery that Sakhalin was actually an island and not part of the continent was a milestone in the exploration of the island. However the Tokugawa government made little use of this knowledge. The information was not passed on to Europe, and not until 1849 was Sakhalin generally known to be an island.[34] As soon as negotiations were begun between Russia and Japan, however, the work of Rinso began to assume an important place in the Japanese arguments that it was they who were first in Sakhalin and had first explored it.

The distrust and fear of Russia which had been growing in Japan was increased a hundredfold by the raids of 1806 and 1807. The whole country was placed in readiness for another attack. Couriers were kept traveling continuously from Edo to Yezo and the roads were reported to be filled with troops.[35] This excitement and preparation continued until May, 1811 when Captain Golovnin, who was surveying the Kuriles, was captured and sent to prison at Hakodate. The captain was held responsible for what had occurred in 1806 and 1807. Captain Rikord who had accompanied Golovnin to the Kuriles, but who had not been captured, returned to Japan in 1812 to negotiate Golovnin's release. The result of preliminary talks was a Japanese agreement to release Golovnin if Rikord could obtain a disavowal by the Russian government of the Kvostov and Davidov raids. Rikord was able to get a declaration from the governor of Kamchatka explaining that the government had no knowledge of these actions and expressing the deep regret of the Russian government. In October, 1813 Golovnin was released after two years of imprisonment. The Japanese took advantage of Golovnin's release to send a note to the Russian government, expressing in the strongest terms their opposition to further intercourse between the two nations.[36] The letter said in part:

> In our country the Christian religion is strictly prohibited, and European vessels are not suffered to enter any Japanese harbor except Nagasaki. This law does not extend to Russian vessels only. This year it has not been enforced, because we wished to communicate with your countrymen; but all that may henceforth present themselves will be driven back by cannon balls. Bear in mind this declaration, and you should experience a misfortune in consequence of your disregard of it.

And in reply to Rikord's request for trade, the letter continued, "From the repeated solicitations which you have hitherto made to us, you evidently imagine that the customs of our country resemble those of your own; but you are very wrong in thinking so. In the future, therefore, it will be better to say no more about a commercial connection." With this the Japanese hoped they had settled the issue of Russian contacts in the north. For the next thirty years their hopes seemed justified, for no consistent efforts were made to renew intercourse with Japan.

Prior to 1825 the Russian motives in trying to open relations with Japan had been primarily economic.[37] In the main these efforts had been carried out by merchants and traders in the hope of facilitating the growth of commerce in the North Pacific. The Russian government had granted some financial assistance for these ventures and had even appointed an official envoy, but the government had never shown a particular interest in Japan itself. During the reign of Tsar Nicholas I (1825-1855), however, the central government began to display a desire to take an active part in these relations. The reasons behind the change in Russian attitude seem to have been both personal and national. Probably the most important factor in this growing interest was a fear of other Western powers. It was not until the United States, France, and England had begun to firmly establish their interest in China, that Russia became interested in Japan.[38] Japan was considered to be strategically important if Russia were to stem the advance of other European powers—especially Great Britain—and were to continue her own expansion to the East.

A second reason for this new interest in Japan was the growing need for a year-round supply point in the Far East. Russia's growing involvement in the maritime trade in the Pacific area made it necessary to acquire coaling and supply stations for the increased shipping. This need was greatly accentuated by the outbreak of the Crimean War in Europe. Without such stations it was feared that the Russian fleet in the Far East would be at the mercy of British marauders.

Another factor in Russia's newly begun efforts to force a quick opening of Japan seems to have been the aggressive character of Tsar Nicholas I himself and his agent in the Far East, Nicholas Muraviev. Both the tsar and Muraviev were greatly opposed to the activities of Great Britain in China, and both felt that steps should be taken to further the interests of Russia at the expense of the British. To them the purpose of Russian expansion was to enhance the grandeur of the Russian Empire. They embodied what has been described as the "official philosophy" of the nineteenth century which "made the Russian autocrat an instrument of divine power leading Russia toward victories and greatness."[39]

The extension of the central government's interest to the Far East brought with it a desire to acquire Sakhalin. In 1849 Captain Nevelskoy, an assistant to Nicholas Muraviev, circumnavigated Sakhalin, and for the first time Russia learned that it was an island. During his exploration of Sakhalin, Nevelskoy became convinced that it would be a valuable addition to the Russian Empire. He noted that its position opposite the mouth of the Amur and its ice-free approaches from the south made it strategically important to any further expansion. It was at this time that Muraviev too was calling for the occupation of Sakhalin. Muraviev, who was violently opposed to Great Britain, was fearful of British interest in Sakhalin and the Amur. In 1848 he reported to the tsar that he felt there might be an effort by British ships to occupy Sakhalin the following spring. A second report of this nature was again made in 1849. In order to curb British advances in the North Pacific area, Muraviev would have brought about a close alliance between Russia and the North American states, and as part of the same plan he felt they "must gain control of Sakhalin and the estuary of the Amur River."[40] Consequently in 1852 and 1853 Nevelskoy and his aides renewed exploration and embarked on a plan for the colonization of Sakhalin. In April, 1853 the tsar ordered the Russian-American Company to take over the island and "not to tolerate any alien settlements of Sakhalin." On August 31, 1853 this order was carried out when a force of sixty men was landed at Kushnukotan. Forts were built there, and big guns were emplaced to provide for coastal defense.[41]

At the same time that these efforts were being made to establish Russian control over the Northern Islands, the Russian government was also attempting to open direct negotiations with the Japanese. As early as 1843 Tsar Nicholas I had planned to send a mission to Japan.[42] However financial and diplomatic difficulties delayed its sailing. In June, 1851 a similar mission, under the supervision of Commodore Aulich, was announced by the United States. This moved the Russian government to action. Fearing to wait any longer the tsar decided to organize a Russian mission and precede the Americans.

In the spring of 1852, the directors of the Russian-American Company ordered Captain Lindenberg to prepare the armed merchant ship, Prince Menchikoff, and then to proceed to Japan.[43] After making rapid preparations, Lindenberg left New Archangel in May and sailed to Japan, arriving at Shimoda in July. In organizing his mission Lindenberg decided to take along several shipwrecked Japanese as a partial pretext for the trip. Upon meeting with the Japanese at Shimoda, he found them strongly opposed to the opening of trade relations. They even refused to accept the shipwrecked sailors which he had brought along as a goodwill gesture. Unable to evoke any favorable response from the Japanese, Lindenberg was forced to quit Shimoda without gaining any results from his negotiations.

The failure of Lindenberg did not end Russian efforts to force the Japanese to open formal relations. On August 21, 1853 Admiral Efimii Vasilevich Putiatin arrived at Nagasaki with a fleet of four Russian men-of-war.[44] Putiatin carried a dispatch from the Russian foreign minister, Count Nesselrode, which called for the delimitation of the Japanese border in the north and the opening of one or two ports to Russian vessels and trade. The Japanese officials at Nagasaki received the letter and sent it on to Edo with a request for instructions. The bakufu replied by sending two commissioners to Nagasaki to negotiate with Putiatin. The two men, Mananori Tsutsui, a high official in the shogun's court, and Seibo Kawaji, the minister of finance, were instructed to use the recent death of the shogun as a pretext for not taking any immediate action. With respect to the opening of ports, they were to refuse any Russian offers, using ancestral law as their reason. Some negotiation did take place concerning the delimitation of the border in Sakhalin however. The letter from Count Nesselrode had noted that there were only a few Japanese living in Sakhalin, but that there were a number of natives on the island. He therefore requested the Japanese to transfer the sole ruling power over Sakhalin to Russia, so that the inhabitants, both Japanese and native, could enjoy the privileges of Russian subjects.[45] In reply to this request Tsutsui and Kawaji stated that the Japanese government would dispatch a commission to the north to investigate the border question. In a counter proposal, the Japanese did suggest that the island might be divided between Russia and Japan at the fiftieth degree parallel.[46] Putiatin however insisted that all of Sakhalin should belong to the tsar. The negotiations remained stalemated at this point, for Putiatin, hearing of the outbreak of the Crimean War, decided that he should proceed to Shanghai. On November 23, 1853 the Russian fleet sailed from Nagasaki, having first warned the Japanese that they would soon return, and in the event that they were not met by the Japanese plenipotentiaries or a definite reply to Count Nesselrode's letter, they would sail on to Edo.

The Russian demand for a definite border settlement stirred a controversy within Japan about what should be done. In the government itself there was no solid agreement. Some of the most zealous patriots insisted that Sakhalin had been the possession of Japan since the days of the first emperor, Jimmu Tenno, and could not be given up. A group of academicians who studied the Dutch maps at the Asakura observatory decided that the island should be divided at the fiftieth parallel—or approximately in half. Higher government officials who reviewed this decision felt that the Dutch maps were in error, and they set the line at the fifty-fifth parallel. In order to settle the controversy over the border issue a meeting of daimyo was called. Within this group there was also a disagreement as to the border formula which should be presented to Russia. One group felt that Sakhalin should be yielded to the Russians in order to avoid a conflict. The majority of the support for this plan came from the Sendai clan who were hoping to gain large profits from trade with Russia.[47] Their strongest opponents were the Mito branch of the Tokugawa family, who were opposed to giving up any claims to the Northern Islands. Fortunately there was no need for this council to reach an immediate decision, for the outbreak of the Crimean War temporarily relieved the pressure which Russia had been applying.

Putiatin, who had sailed for the Chinese coast in November of 1853, returned to Nagasaki in January of 1854. Neither that trip nor a second in April, 1854 yielded any new results. In June he sailed to Sakhalin where he instructed a subordinate, Lieutenant Possiet, to write to Tsutsui and Kawaji and inform them that after removing the garrison from Aniwa Bay he would sail for Osaka. The letter also stated that since negotiations had been conducted with the United States, it was now felt that Japan and Russia would be able to settle their border problems with no difficulty. In the meantime Russian forces would be temporarily removed from South Sakhalin.

On November 8, 1854 after an eight-day stopover at Hakodate, Putiatin sailed into Osaka Bay to resume negotiations. Word was sent to Edo that the Russians had arrived to meet with the plenipotentiaries. The shogunate replied that a conference could not be allowed at Osaka since the port was not open to foreigners; instead the Russians should go to Shimoda, one of the ports that had been opened to the United States. They would be preceded by Tsutsui, Kawaji and other Japanese officials. Putiatin, deciding that it would be best to comply with the request, proceeded to Shimoda on December 4, 1854.[48]

The negotiations now took a more serious turn, owing largely to a more favorable attitude on the part of the Japanese. There seem to have been several reasons behind this Japanese change. Perhaps the most important was the recognition by the Japanese that it would be necessary for them to open formal relations with the Russians, a fact attested to by the treaties which had already been signed with the United States and Great Britain. Another reason seems to have been the threatening tone which Admiral Putiatin had assumed during the course of the negotiations. And finally it was feared that a refusal to come to agreement might bring about an extension of Russian attacks on Japanese possessions in the north.

The result of the negotiations was the Treaty of Shimoda (February 7, 1855). The treaty pledged "continuous peace and sincere friendship between Russia and Japan" and opened three Japanese ports to Russian vessels. The Russian desire to open the door of Japan had been fulfilled, but the status of Sakhalin and the northern boundary still remained in doubt. Article II of the treaty stipulated that "the boundaries between Russia and Japan will pass between the islands of Iturup (Etorofu) and Urup (Uruppu)," thus giving Russia title to the northern Kuriles.[49] However, the article further stated, "As regards the island Krafto (Kurafuto-Sakhalin), it remains unpartitioned between Russia and Japan, as has been (the case) to this time." Though the establishment of a firm and agreeable boundary had been one of the most important points in Count Nesselrode's instructions, the year-long negotiations had failed to bring it about. The Japanese, who were divided on the issue of Sakhalin, had proposed a partition of the island at the fiftieth parallel, but Putiatin had had to refuse, for both the tsar and Muraviev had remained adamant in their desire to control Sakhalin. Thus Sakhalin continued to remain a point of contention between Russia and Japan, with both sides continuing their policies of colonization as before.

Determined to secure the cession of Sakhalin, Count Muraviev sailed to Japan himself.[50] In August, 1859 he arrived at Yokohama with a fleet of seven ships. Caught in the growing tide of anti-foreignism that was sweeping Japan in the last days of the shogunate, his mission was ruined on the opening day of the negotiations when three of his men were attacked by a group of ronin in a Kanagawa market place and literally cut to pieces. Though there was a public apology, the murderers were not punished. Instead, the governor, who was presumably disgraced by this attack, was later appointed—but refused—as an envoy to St. Petersburg. Under the circumstances Muraviev saw little hope for his plan of gaining clear title to Sakhalin. After waiting for the Japanese to carry out the light demands which had been made for the murder of his men, he sailed from Yokohama without continuing the negotiations.

The period between 1862 and 1875 saw a series of attempts by the Japanese and Russian governments to solve the problem which Sakhalin had raised. The first came in 1862 when Shimotsuke Takenouchi and Iwami Matsudaira went to St. Petersburg to ask for a postponement of the opening of the treaty ports at Niigata and Hyogo. While in St. Petersburg they extended their negotiations to the question of the boundary in Sakhalin. A series of talks between the two Japanese envoys and Lieutenant General Ignatiev, chief of the Asiatic Bureau, continued throughout the summer. Both sides claimed the island as their own. During the negotiations Ignatiev offered to divide Sakhalin at the forty-seventh or forty-eighth parallel where there were rivers and mountains that would make a clear line of demarcation.[51] The Japanese envoys however had specific instructions to cede nothing south of the fiftieth parallel.[52] Before the mission left St. Petersburg it was decided that field teams would be sent to Sakhalin to study the terrain and arrive at a decision. The meeting in Sakhalin never came about, for the bakufu, which was bending under the weight of the Shimonoseki indemnity and the opposition of the other clans, was unable to meet its obligation.

In 1864 Yamato Koide made a new attempt to reach an agreement over Sakhalin. Arriving in St. Petersburg he tried to reopen the discussion of 1862, but Prince Gorchakov, who was currently in charge of foreign affairs, refused to negotiate, claiming that the bakufu had not lived up to its obligations. Koide was forced to return home empty-handed.

Again, in 1866, Koide returned to St. Petersburg to settle the problem. This time Koide and Kawachi Ishikawa called upon Stremonkhov of the Asiatic Department of the Foreign Ministry. Referring to the provisional agreement of 1862, they asked for a division of Sakhalin. At this point Stremonkhov countered by offering Japan the northern Kuriles and fishing rights off Sakhalin for cession of the whole island. When the Japanese proved unwilling or unable to accept this offer, he proposed as a final alternative the joint possession and colonization of Sakhalin. Soon, after further discussion, it became evident that little could be accomplished in the form of a permanent boundary settlement, and on March 18, 1867 the Russian and Japanese representatives signed a group of "Temporary Regulations Relative to the Island of Sakhalin."[53] The provisions of this convention stated that the island would be "common possession" of both, each having the right to found colonies and trading posts.

The condominium which the convention of 1867 established was of the weakest sort and appeared doomed to failure from the beginning. In order to gain as much land as possible under the agreement, Russia soon inaugurated a policy of transferring convicts to the island. Early in 1870 the United States became apprehensive about the growing controversy, and offered the mediation of the President. Minister De Long of the United States requested a complete list of the Japanese claims to Sakhalin in preparation for the possible mediation. The mediation offer was favorably received in Tokyo, and on March 1, 1870 the Japanese government presented a list of proposals to the United States for study.[54] This list included a request for the division of Sakhalin at the fiftieth parallel, the opening of Aniwa Bay as an "open port," and the promise to respect property cultivated by nationals of either country beyond the boundary upon the payment of ground rent to the proper authorities. On March 26, 1870 this was augmented by a comprehensive written history of the controversy. Plans were brought to an abrupt end, however, when the Russian government informed the United States that it could not accept its offer of mediation. Direct Russo-Japanese negotiations were resumed.

Between 1870 and 1873 Count Taneomi Soyejima made several attempts to effect a settlement of the boundary. Soyejima was personally convinced that Sakhalin was quite valuable, so after becoming minister of foreign affairs, he developed a plan for the purchase of South Sakhalin similar to the United States' purchase of Alaska. In a conference with the Russian chargé d'affaires in Tokyo, he proposed that Japan purchase Sakhalin south of the fiftieth parallel for two million yen, but the offer was rejected. Thereupon Soyejima made an alternative offer of ceding the whole of Sakhalin in return for a Russian cession of the islands of Urup, Kunashiri, and Iturup. This was to be made conditional upon a Russian promise to allow the passage of Japanese troops through Sakhalin in the event of a war with a continental power. Before the negotiations could be completed, Soyejima had been replaced as foreign minister and a new government policy with respect to Sakhalin had been introduced.[55] The basis of the policy change was the "Kuroda Memorial" which maintained that Sakhalin was "worthless" because of the barrenness of its soil and the extreme cold. It was further felt that continued possession of part of Sakhalin by Japan would merely add to the troubles between that country and Russia.

In 1874 Takeaki Enomoto was appointed Envoy Extraordinary and Minister Plenipotentiary to St. Petersburg, to arrange a final settlement of the Sakhalin question. He was instructed to find a natural boundary between Russian and Japanese territories in Sakhalin if that were possible. If Russia should claim the whole island, however, he might cede it in return for a Russian recognition of Japan's sovereignty over the Kuriles. After a relatively short period of negotiation a treaty of mutual cession was signed at St. Petersburg by Enomoto and Prince Alexander Gorchakov.[56] The treaty provided that Japan cede the whole of Sakhalin to Russia in exchange for which the Russian government was to cede the Kurile Islands to Japan. Each party also promised to pay the other for all non-movable property, such as public buildings, barracks, and fortifications, which it received as a consequence of the mutual cession. Besides, Russia agreed to let Japanese ships use the port of Korsakov (Kushnukotan), exempt from harbor dues and customs duties for ten years and also allowed Japanese vessels the right to trade along the Okhotsk and on the Kamchatka coast.

Despite the "Kuroda Memorial" it appears that Russia got the better bargain; there was little comparison between the economic potentialities of the Kuriles and Sakhalin. Signing of the agreement at this time cannot be entirely explained by reference to Sakhalin's "worthless" nature. Japan's willingness to accept second best in these negotiations seems to be based on several other factors as well. One of the most important considerations was the defense of the home islands. The recent movement of a Russian force to South Sakhalin was feared to be a sign that Russia had designs on Hokkaido too. In order to forestall any Russian movement in this direction it was deemed necessary to improve Russo-Japanese relations as soon as possible. Besides, the Japanese were already involved with China over the Formosan problem and were unwilling to be confronted with two enemies at one time. A further factor may have been the feeling of doubt which the Japanese had about their own military capabilities. Japan had recently undergone a revolution and was still suffering from a degree of internal strife; it seemed foolhardy to risk defeat or embarrassment at the hands of so worthy an adversary as Russia. Along with these practical considerations, there was also a certain positive appeal which the treaty held for the Japanese. This was the period in which Japan's government was doing everything possible to free itself from the unequal treaties of the previous generation. The possibility of negotiating a treaty with Russia on equal terms made the agreement far more palatable to those Japanese who were so deeply concerned with the relative position of Japan in world relations.[57]

The period between 1875 and 1905 was one of comparatively friendly relations between Russia and Japan. The disagreements which did arise were restricted mostly to Korea and Manchuria and had little immediate effect upon the frontier to the north of Japan. Russia used this period to develop Sakhalin into a gigantic prison. The economy of the island, which consisted primarily of coal mining, lumbering, and road building, suffered greatly from the exclusive use of prison labor. The island saw little progress during these years;

by 1900 the population was still under 30,000, and this consisted mainly of prisoners and their families.

Though the question of Sakhalin had seemed to be a closed matter after the settlement of 1875, it once more became a major issue in Russo-Japanese relations with the outbreak of war in 1904. The war had developed mainly from the conflicting desires of both Russia and Japan for a Far Eastern Empire. The weakness which beset China and Korea at the turn of the century made it seem urgent for both powers to move as quickly as possible if they were to fulfill their ambitions. Japan's victory over China in 1895 had established her on the continent and had opened the way for her Empire. The railroad agreement which Russia signed with China in 1896 set her directly in the path of the Japanese goal, a position which Russia was quick to reinforce during the Boxer Rebellion.

Armed with an alliance with Great Britain, Japan in 1902 and 1903 set out to extend her influence in Korea and at the same time restrict Russian expansion through a series of agreements. The immediate pretexts for the war resulted from Russia's refusal to live up to these agreements and from "the aggressive and erratic policy carried out by the Russian officials and adventurers in both Manchuria and Korea."[58] The fighting was marked by a series of Japanese victories; however both sides were so worn down by the encounter that an offer of good offices by President Theodore Roosevelt was received with a degree of relief by both Russia and Japan. After the battle of Mukden, which was certainly a Japanese victory, General Kodama went to Tokyo in March, 1905 to demand that the war be concluded. Later, he was joined in these demands by Admiral Yamamoto. Members of the general staff became so insistent in their claims that the war was becoming militarily impossible that it required some urging on the part of the Japanese government to persuade the army to occupy Sakhalin as a diplomatic advantage at the peace conference.[59]

To effect the occupation of Sakhalin, a Japanese force was landed on the island on July 7, 1905. On the first of August the Russian army capitulated, and by the end of that month the whole island was in Japanese hands. Military operations on the island were much smaller in size and of less importance than those in Manchuria. Neither Japan nor Russia committed a major force to the battle in Sakhalin.

The peace conference which was called by President Roosevelt convened at Portsmouth, New Hampshire on August 9, 1905. The Russian negotiators included Count Witte, Russia's foremost diplomat, and Baron Rosen, the former Ambassador to Tokyo. Representing Japan at the conference were Baron Komura, the Minister of Foreign Affairs during the war, and Takahira, the Japanese Minister to the United States.

During the negotiations, the question of Sakhalin presented one of the most difficult issues to be settled. As part of their preliminary proposals, the Japanese demanded that Russia cede the whole island of Sakhalin.[60] Count Witte rejected en bloc the original conditions set forth by the Japanese. He said that the tsar would never agree to the cession of Sakhalin, the payment of a war indemnity, the surrender of Russian warships, or the limitation of Russian naval forces in the Far East. Faced with this strong Russian resistance, the Japanese were willing to yield somewhat from their original demands, and by August 21 agreement was reached on everything but the indemnity question and the cession of Sakhalin.

On August 23 Witte received a communication from the tsar, instructing him to offer Japan South Sakhalin with the understanding that Russia would buy back the northern half. The Japanese then countered this offer by saying they would relinquish the indemnity if Russia were to cede all of Sakhalin to Japan. At this point the Russian attitude stiffened perceptibly. The tsar stated to Witte that his final offer would be to cede the southern half of Sakhalin if Russia could keep possession of the northern half. The Japanese finally accepted the Russian offer to bisect the island at the fiftieth parallel, and the completed form of the treaty provided for the cession of the southern half of Sakhalin to Japan and included no provision for an indemnity.

There was a great deal of bitterness in Japan over the terms of the agreement.[61] It had been hoped that the whole of Sakhalin would be given to Japan as a prize at the peace table. When it was learned that only half of the island was to be ceded by Russia, there was a widespread feeling of disappointment and dissatisfaction. The lack of any form of indemnity also provoked a loud protest, as did the failure to enforce a reduction of Russian naval strength in the Far East.

On the surface it is difficult to understand how Russia could have won such a decided victory at the conference table. Even President Roosevelt admitted he was sure that Russia would have to back down on the question of Sakhalin and the indemnity and that after the agreement was made he still felt that Japan had relinquished more than was necessary when she returned North Sakhalin without some form of compensation. However the Russian negotiators did have two distinct advantages in the discussions. First they were aware of the critical condition of Japan's economy, and they knew that this was exerting considerable pressure on the Japanese government. Secondly, the Russian armies in the Far East had never been completely defeated, and during the span of the peace negotiations the forces commanded by General Kuropatkin were constantly being strengthened. Thus they could afford to wait out the Japanese on each point, for every day of debate made their position more favorable in the Far East.

The years 1907 to 1917 marked a reversal in the tendencies of the previous period and witnessed a growth of friendliness between Russia and Japan. The Russo-Japanese war settled Russia's designs to create a monopoly in Korea and Manchuria. Following the Treaty of Portsmouth, the Russian government turned instead to strengthening its position in Mongolia, leaving the Japanese free to develop their interests in Korea and South Manchuria.[62] In the treaties of 1907, 1910, 1912 Russia and Japan guaranteed each other's rights with respect to Manchuria and Mongolia. These treaties were especially important to Russia. Chinese efforts to strengthen their position in Mongolia had made it imperative that Russia have a free hand in that area. To allow the Chinese to carry out their intentions would mean a stronger power would be placed on the Russian border and would limit Russia's chances to get closer to the great centers of Chinese life. Both of these possibilities were in direct conflict with Russian ideas of expansion in Asia.

On July 3, 1916 the political rapprochement between Japan and Russia culminated in a treaty of alliance. The treaty was directed at a third party which was probably Germany and Austria. During the negotiations a German newspaper and the New York Times carried frequent rumors to the effect that Russia would trade North Sakhalin.[63] The island apparently was to be traded for Japanese arms which the Russians needed so badly. Although the treaty made no mention of any such deal, the possibility of a trade continued to be discussed. During January and February of 1917 a series of conferences was carried on between Russia and Japan in an effort to get more direct Japanese aid in Europe. The Russian negotiator, General Dessino, offered the cession of North Sakhalin to Japan in return for a Japanese agreement to send a force of 500,000 troops to Europe. The Japanese, however, felt they should get more. General Inagaki, who was representing Japan, suggested that control of the Chinese Eastern Railway as far as Harbin and the dismantlement of the fort and naval base at Vladivostok should also be conditions of such an agreement.[64] Faced with such harsh Japanese demands, Russia withdrew the offer.

The spirit of friendliness which had pervaded Russo-Japanese relations in the years between 1905 and the first World War disappeared soon after the war. Russia, which had been defeated by Germany in the war and then wracked by a gigantic social revolution, was straining every effort to regain its balance and restore order within its borders. The difficulty of this task made it virtually impossible for Russia to provide an adequate defense against foreign incursions after the war. The Japanese were quick to take advantage of Russia's weakness to further their hopes for a Far Eastern Empire. Their movement was primarily in two directions. First, they used the Siberian intervention, a joint allied venture into Eastern Siberia, to expand to the north on the continent. Then, taking as pretext the cruelties perpetrated by a group of Bolshevik guerrillas in Nikolaevsk, where approximately seven hundred Japanese were killed, they also occupied northern Sakhalin. Behind these Japanese movements there appears to have been a hope that they could gain control of all the areas surrounding the Japan Sea and thereby create a new "Inland Sea."[65] If this were possible, then it was felt that Japan would be assured of markets and sources of raw materials to maintain her industries, especially those which had skyrocketed during World War I and were in danger of collapse without some sort of artificial support.

The United States, which had led the opposition to Japan's misuse of the Siberian intervention, also raised strong objections to the occupation of northern Sakhalin. A series of strong notes was sent by Bainbridge Colby and Charles Evans Hughes, American Secretaries of State, deploring Japanese activities in that area. On May 31, 1921 Secretary Colby advised the Japanese, "The Government of the United States can neither now or hereafter recognize as valid any claims or titles arising out of the present occupation and control, and cannot acquiesce in any action taken by the Government of Japan which might impair existing treaty rights, or the political or territorial integrity of Russia."[66] Baron Shidehara denied that his country wished "to take advantage of the present helpless conditions of Russia for prosecuting selfish designs." In reply to Secretary of State Hughes' questions about Sakhalin, he stated, "Military occupation of the Russian Province of Sakhalin is only a temporary measure and will come to an end as soon as satisfactory settlement of the question shall have been arranged with an orderly Russian Government."[67]

Japanese activity in Sakhalin gave little indication that it was only a temporary occupation. On the contrary, there appears to have been a fairly elaborate plan for exploitation of this territory on a permanent basis.[68] The whole approach to Sakhalin differed from that in Siberia where there had been a period of piecemeal grabbing by the Japanese. Rather than allowing this sort of activity, the Japanese administration set out to integrate the economy of North Sakhalin into the Empire. A company was organized to build a railroad on the northern part of the island. The various industrial projects there were to be integrated into a syndicate of five Japanese firms. The right to develop coal mines was handed over to the Mitsubishi family. A survey was made of the oil resources of the island and exploitation was begun. The Japanese intention to continue these operations revealed itself further in their failure to withdraw from the island during the general evacuation of the Russian Far East in 1922. In June of that year the Japanese government informed the United States Department of State that it would remove its forces from the Russian Far East by October. However, the pledge did not apply to Sakhalin; by November 14, 1922 all Japanese troops had been moved from Russian soil—with the exception of Sakhalin. The United States protested but the Japanese made no move to withdraw.

While the Japanese were taking steps to stabilize their position in North Sakhalin, a series of conferences took place between Japan and the Far Eastern Republic to determine the legal status of that island. The Far Eastern Republic had grown out of the turmoil which attended the Soviet Revolution in Siberia. Though not officially a part of the new Soviet government in Russia, it was closely allied to that regime and had fallen heir to its responsibilities in the Far East. One of these was the ownership of North Sakhalin. In August, 1921 representatives of the Far Eastern Republic met with a Japanese mission at Dairen to negotiate the removal of Japanese forces from Asia. In October the Japanese representative, Matsushima, presented a set of twenty demands which were to be complied with as conditions for the withdrawal. They included a provision for "the transfer to Japan (as compensation for the Nikolaevsk incident) of all of North Sakhalin on the basis of an eighty-year lease."[69] It was further stipulated that the evacuation of North Sakhalin would take place only after the lease had been agreed upon. Other provisions called for the demolition of all coastal fortifications at Vladivostok as well as those along the Korean border, the destruction of Russia's naval forces in the Pacific waters, and a guarantee to Japan of complete freedom to navigate the Amur River. Jurin, the representative from the Far Eastern Republic, felt that the Japanese conditions were far too harsh. Since there seemed to be little chance of a settlement on these terms, the conference dissolved in April, 1922 with no results.

The failure to settle the Sakhalin issue at Dairen led Japan and the Far Eastern Republic to arrange a second conference later that year. On September 4, 1922 Tsuneo Matsudaira, the director of the European and American Departments of the Japanese Foreign Ministry, and Foreign Minister Janson of the Far Eastern Republic met at Changchun to arrange for the evacuation of North Sakhalin and decide upon a settlement of the Nikolaevsk affair. The conference had been convened as the result of a Japanese note of July 19, 1922 which had expressed Japan's willingness to discuss the Sakhalin issue. When the conference met, however, the Japanese position had changed little from that expressed at Dairen. Although there was a fairly wide feeling in Japan against the continuance of the "expensive and unprofitable ventures in Eastern Asia," the business community was still very much interested in the resources of Sakhalin.[70] In view of this strong feeling, the government continued pressing for extensive economic privileges in return for North Sakhalin. The Far Eastern Republic, which had been assured of favorable United States backing, refused to grant these privileges, and the conference ended November 3, 1922 with no prospect of agreement in sight.[71]

By 1923 the changing fortunes of Japan and Russia had begun to alter the terms of negotiation. Russia was no longer fighting to maintain its borders in Europe and Central Asia. The opposition which the new regime had faced following the revolution had been virtually destroyed, and in the period between 1923 and 1925 the Soviet Union was approaching the peak of its diplomatic success, receiving the recognition of one great power after another. At the same time Japan's position was growing comparatively weaker. The agreements signed at the Washington Conference in 1922 had been a great blow to Japanese pride and had set back the plans for expansion temporarily. Difficulties at home, such as the earthquake, had also made a reappraisal of Japan's foreign relations necessary. In 1923 it became evident that a settlement of the Sakhalin issue would have to be made soon.

The Japanese first tried to buy North Sakhalin from Russia. In unofficial talks with Adolf Joffe, the Soviet representative in the Far East, the Japanese government offered to pay 150 million yen for the purchase of North Sakhalin. Joffe replied that the Soviet Union would demand one billion gold rubles in payment for the island. The price was far too much for the Japanese, and the talks were broken off with no results.

The poor outcome of these meetings convinced the Japanese that they should discontinue the informal conversations in favor of formal negotiations which might produce a more rapid settlement of the problem. As time progressed a quick settlement seemed more and more appealing and a meeting was arranged in Peking between Lev Karakhan and Kenkichi Yoshizawa. On January 20, 1925 after a series of meetings the settlement was at last signed.

The agreement for the return of North Sakhalin contained a main treaty and two separate protocols.[72] The main treaty was quite general in scope and dealt primarily with the broader issues of Russo-Japanese understanding. It pledged that both parties would abstain from interfering in the affairs of the other, and in accordance with the Treaty of Portsmouth it also recognized Japanese fishing rights in principle. The two protocols dealt more specifically with the disposition of North Sakhalin. In the first of these Japan pledged the evacuation of North Sakhalin by the end of May, 1925. The second protocol settled Japanese economic privileges on the island, which were to last for forty-five years, and were in the form of concessions to Japanese industrial and mining firms. They stipulated that Japan was to receive fifty per cent of the oil lands in North Sakhalin against the payment of five to fifteen per cent of their yearly output. Further concessions were given with respect to the operation of coal mines. In return for the latter the Japanese firms were to pay from five to eight per cent of their yearly output. The conclusion of the negotiations opened the way for a fairly large number of other concessions to Japan, but not all of these were connected directly with the price that the Soviet Union had to pay for Japan's evacuation. Most of the concessions, such as the right to develop gold mines in Kamchatka or exploit the lumber resources of the Maritime Province, were actually part of the over-all "New Economic Policy" (N.E.P.), which the Soviets had inaugurated in the 1920's, and were granted to stimulate the investment of foreign capital. These were mostly eliminated by 1930 and did not continue to provide a point of conflict as did those in North Sakhalin. The settlement of 1925 brought about the end of a period in which Japan was able to press its designs upon a weakened Russia and extend its frontier beyond the dividing line in Sakhalin to control the whole island. By 1925 Russia had recovered from the wounds of World War I and the internal strife of the revolution and was able to roll the Japanese back once again to the fiftieth parallel.

During the period which followed, from 1925 to 1939, the expressions of amity which Japan and Russia had declared in their treaty became more and more meaningless, and relations began to deteriorate. The first five years of the period, however, remained peaceful and constructive; the basic conflicts of Russian and Japanese interests in the Far East were subordinated by both powers to a temporary desire for peace. In 1930 Molotov reported to the Fifth Congress of the Soviets that "not a single political conflict is recorded between the Soviet Union and Japan during the years which elapsed since the signing of the treaty (of 1925)."[73]

The main reason for the peaceful atmosphere which marked these years seems to have been the Soviet Union's intense desire to have peace while building up its economy. During the early years of the first Five-Year Plan, Russia needed peace to make it work. O. Hoetzch wrote of these years:

> Anyone who, like myself, was in Russia in 1929, and saw the extent to which the mobilization of Bluecher's army in the conflict with China over the Manchurian frontier disturbed the "Plan" and everything which depends on it, knows as well as the rulers in the Kremlin, that the U.S.S.R. could not bear the extraordinarily intensive effort demanded by a war, in what is called the decisive year of the Five-Year Plan.[74]

A second reason for the Soviet Union's interest in maintaining friendly relations with Japan was Stalin's personal desire to use Japan as a wedge between the United States and Great Britain. Although Stalin was aware of the designs which Japan had on Northeastern Asia, it appears that his dislike and distrust of the two great Western Powers outweighed his fear of Japanese aggression. Probably the only way in which Russia could have safely countered Japanese moves into this area would have been to accept British and American offers of conciliation and mediation. Stalin, however, viewed the United States and Great Britain as the purest embodiments of capitalism and he could not bring himself around ideologically to accept their aid.[75] Furthermore, he felt that Western intervention in Manchuria would probably lead to some form of international control—a situation which would hamper Russia's plans for expansion even more than if the area were under Japan's control. With this possibility in mind Stalin conceived a plan of maintaining friendly relations with Japan while waiting for the war which he was sure would develop between the United States on one side and Great Britain and Japan on the other. Once its position in the Far East was assured by such a war, the Soviet Union could then time its own moves effectively.

Sakhalin during this period was politically quiet but growing economically. Japanese industries were formed in both North and South Sakhalin, and oil and coal production grew rapidly. In December, 1925 The North Sakhalin Petroleum Company and the North Sakhalin Mining Company were established. The two firms had been formed in accordance with the agreements of 1925 and were founded with an initial capital of ten million yen each. Under the direction of these companies the production of oil and coal was expanded considerably in the five years between 1925 and 1930. Oil production which was estimated at 14,000 tons annually in 1925 rose to 194,000 tons in 1930. A similar expansion was made in coal mining. In 1925 the coal output was only 850 tons. By 1930 the yearly production had become 150,000 tons.[76] The advances made by these concessions firms in North Sakhalin were more than matched by developments in the southern half of the island. By the early 1930's the population of South Sakhalin had grown to more than 300,000 and the economy of the Japanese half of the island grew apace, providing a large percentage of Japan's badly needed wood pulp and fishery products.

From 1930 onward Russo-Japanese relations became more strained. The feeling of friendliness which had marked the previous five years disappeared as Russian and Japanese interests came more and more into conflict. A major clash between the two powers was averted however by an active Russian policy of appeasement with respect to Japanese activities. Though the Japanese had become more bold and threatening in their attitude toward Russia and the Far East in general, the Soviet government remained convinced that its own interests could be best served by avoiding conflicts until it could complete the build-up of its economy. In 1931 the Russian leaders initiated this policy by taking a stand of complete neutrality with respect to Manchuria, thereby virtually allowing the Japanese a free hand in what would normally be considered an area of Russian interest. In 1932 they attempted to further this program by concluding a new fisheries agreement which extended a number of concessions to the wishes of Japanese industry.

This policy of appeasement culminated in a Russo-Japanese economic agreement in 1936. Litvinov, "Stalin's technician for foreign policy,"[77] felt that Japan should be given no possible pretext for an attack on Russian possessions in the Far East. In order to guard against a Japanese charge that Russia was failing to fulfill previous obligations, he was careful not to allow the agreements of 1925 to expire. Even though Litvinov was aware that Japan was conducting anti-communist negotiations with Germany and Italy, he proceeded with his own plans to renew the fisheries and concessions agreements of 1925. In October, 1936 an agreement was signed which provided for a five-year extension of the North Sakhalin Petroleum Company's lease. Before further agreement could be reached, however, Germany and Japan concluded the "Anti-Communist Pact" on November 25, 1936. Bernard Pares has noted that the "Anti-Communist Pact had little to do with Communism, for the three contracting Powers had all fiercely suppressed it within their own borders, but it had everything to do with territory...it was equally a threat against two Empires, the Russian and the British."[78] This meaning was evidently not missed by Litvinov. Although negotiations for the fisheries agreement had already been completed prior to the announcement of the pact, Litvinov refused to sign the eight-year renewal. He was not moved completely from his plan of appeasement, however, for on December 28, 1936 he did agree to renew the lapsing fishing agreement for one year, and when it expired he extended it for another year.

While the Soviet Union was continuing its policy of appeasement, Japan was becoming more demanding in its dealings with Russia and other foreign powers. The Japanese had regained a feeling of strength, having overcome the difficulties which had confronted them during the 1920's. The Sino-Soviet conflict of 1929 had revealed the actual positions and strengths of the major powers and had assured the Japanese that they could proceed with their plans for expansion in the Far East with little fear of interference. The war had once again proven China's impotence. The revolution and the establishment of the Republic had not added significantly to China's strength; instead it had temporarily weakened the country and seemed to make Japanese designs on North China more likely than ever to succeed. The war had also shown Russia's opposition to interference by the Western Powers. The Soviet Union seemed far more willing to accede to Japanese demands than to look to Britain and the United States for aid. No less important was the fact that both Britain and the United States had shown themselves quite reluctant to resort to arms in the face of combined Russo-Japanese opposition. With each of the powers thus canceling out areas of resistance, either by their own weakness or unwillingness to combine and act, the Japanese felt free to begin a serious implementation of their program for a Far Eastern Empire. On July 7, 1937 Japan launched a full-scale attack upon North China.

As Japan's attitude grew more aggressive, the Soviet Union continued to try to appease the Japanese demands while promoting the hoped-for conflict between Japan and the Western Powers. In 1933 Karl Haushofer reported in the Berliner Borsenzeitung that Russia was preparing to sell North Sakhalin to the United States and that the United States Navy was to visit Vladivostok.[79] The subsequent negotiations between the Soviet Union and the United States failed to bring about any such agreement; however the circulation of such rumors seems to indicate the Russian leaders still hoped that they could successfully resist Japan through indirect methods. Whether North Sakhalin had actually been offered to the United States and turned down by President Roosevelt is questionable. It seems unlikely in view of Russia's previous attitude toward American interference. Perhaps a more reasonable explanation would be that the mention of such deals was intended primarily to build distrust between the United States and Japan, not to effect a change in Russian territory.

After the Japanese invasion of China in 1937 there was a noticeable stiffening in the Soviet attitude toward Japan. By committing a large force in China, Japan had greatly eased the pressure on Russia in the north, and as the danger lessened the Soviet leaders became more and more unwilling to acquiesce to Japanese wishes. During this period Russia's major policy in the Far East was directed toward aiding China. On August 21, 1937, six weeks after the outbreak of the Sino-Japanese war, the Soviet Union concluded a non-aggression pact with the Chinese government at Nanking.[80] The treaty was a "cautious document" that obligated neither party greatly. Its real significance seemed to lie in its effect on Chinese morale. It was part of an effort to buoy up the hard-pressed Chinese. Arms and other material aid were sent through Siberia to China. With these, Russia hoped to keep the Chinese resisting Japan as long as possible without direct intervention. So long as Japan could be tied down in China the Soviet Far East appeared safe from attack.

A change in Russia's attitude toward North Sakhalin became apparent during the period. Severe criticism was raised concerning practically every aspect of the concessions' operations.[81] The Soviet government accused the coal and oil companies operating in North Sakhalin of violating a multiplicity of fire and safety regulations. They also claimed that the ratio of Japanese workers there was too high. Although the ratio had been set at one to three, the Japanese employees had grown to exceed forty per cent. Another difficulty arose over the building of pipelines in North Sakhalin. The Russian authorities accused the Japanese of projecting lines from the oil fields without preliminary approval, and the Japanese countered that the Soviet officials were too slow in granting permits. A further charge was leveled at the Japanese government when Moscow declared that the building of fortifications on South Sakhalin was contrary to previous agreement and should be stopped. Finally, a number of Japanese were arrested in the Russian area, and operations were begun to close down the Japanese consulates.

The mounting friction between the Japanese on North Sakhalin and the Soviet authorities led the Tokyo government to communicate directly with the Russian government at Moscow. In April, 1939 a detailed memorandum was submitted to the Soviet Union, outlining the disagreements in North Sakhalin. The note expressed concern that the continuance of the disagreements would make normal economic activity there impossible. When the Soviet government took no immediate action, a second note was delivered on July 16, demanding a reply by July 18. The Narkomindel returned the note immediately, and the Japanese envoy was told that it could not be accepted because the time limit appeared to make it an ultimatum. The following week the Foreign Commissariat presented a detailed reply to the first Japanese note, renewing the charges which it had made on the concessionaires and the Japanese government.

These tensions were eased slightly in 1939 after the signing of the Berlin-Moscow Pact, but relations improved for only a short time—especially with respect to North Sakhalin. The main reason for the temporary improvement seems to lie in the fact that the Nazi-Soviet agreement had left Japan alone. In the face of worsening relations with Germany the Japanese felt that they could not hope to push their demands on Russia too far.[82]

By 1940 the relative positions of Russia and Japan had once more changed greatly. The Japanese decision to strike to the south at China in 1937 had eased Soviet fears that they would be forced to fight Japan in Eastern Siberia. The Berlin-Moscow Pact of the previous year had bolstered Russian confidence even more. After 1940 the Soviet Union no longer had to move as cautiously in the Far East as it did in the 1930's. Instead, it began to assert more strongly its own demands upon Japan and the other nations in that area. The response to the growing strength of the U.S.S.R. in Asia was mixed and half-hearted. To China and some of the Western Powers, Russia seemed to be a formidable ally, and therefore its growing opposition to Japan was looked upon with favor, even though communist expansion was still viewed as a menace. In Japan resistance to the new Soviet attitude did not reach serious proportions, for the events of 1940 made a war with Great Britain and a conquest of Southeast Asia and the South Pacific area much more alluring. It was seen that the neutrality of Russia would have to be a prerequisite for any Japanese attack to the south, so the Tokyo government refrained from doing anything which would antagonize Moscow. Such resistance as there was reached its peak before the final military decisions were made and then quieted quickly as Japan turned instead to insure a Russo-Japanese peace.

The new situation which arose in 1940 led the Soviet Union to adopt an intensive campaign for the closing of Japanese concessions in North Sakhalin. The Russian government viewed the presence of Japanese nationals in these concessions as a hindrance to the building of an adequate defense of the Soviet Far East. As long as these Japanese remained, it would be impossible to have any "naval secrets." From this period on the Russian government insisted that the cancellation of the concessions must be the condition for any new Russo-Japanese settlement.

The imminence of war in the Pacific moved the Japanese to open formal negotiations with the Soviet Union in 1940. The biggest problem which Japan would have to overcome before it could strike at the British possessions in the Far East was to make sure that Russia would remain neutral. Realizing this, the Tokyo government was eager to conclude a treaty of non-aggression with Russia. It also hoped that it could clear up the Sakhalin question, and at the same time get clear access to the natural resources of the island. In recent years the deteriorating condition of Russo-Japanese relations had made the concessions in North Sakhalin practically valueless. As a result of the pressure applied by the growing opposition of Russia, one of the coal companies had been forced to close down in 1937, while the other had cut its production to a minimum.[83] The Japanese estimated that coal production fell from a peak of 240,000 tons in 1935 to only 5,000 tones in 1943.[84] Though the oil companies had fared better, they too had suffered a huge decrease in production. In the same period oil output dropped from more than 190,000 tons annually to approximately 16,000 tons. Since the continuance of the concessions under these circumstances could mean little to the Japanese, it was decided that an effort should be made to buy the island either by paying cash or even abolishing fishing rights in Russian waters if that were the price asked. Stalin, however, considered the sale of North Sakhalin completely out of the question. Molotov, who was representing Russia in the talks, was adamant in maintaining that the Soviet condition for any agreement with the Japanese was the cancellation of the concessions in North Sakhalin. Molotov even carried this over into his talks with von Ribbentrop about a Four Power Pact. After returning from the meeting in Berlin in November, 1940, he outlined for von Ribbentrop the conditions which the U.S.S.R. would demand if it were to join such a coalition. One of these proposals was that Japan be made to close the concessions.

In April, 1941 Foreign Minister Yosuke Matsuoka went to Moscow in a new attempt to conclude a non-aggression pact with Russia. Matsuoka, who had not been informed of the impending German invasion of Russia, called for a comprehensive non-aggression treaty. Stalin countered by proposing a plain treaty of neutrality. His only condition was that the coal and oil concessions in North Sakhalin be abolished. Matsuoka at first refused to accept the condition, but when he finally became convinced that Russia's neutrality could not be assured without acceding to Stalin's demands, he agreed to cancel the concessions. In a secret letter he stated that "he would do his best to bring about the elimination of the Japanese concession in North Sakhalin."[85] Later he confirmed that the decision to abolish the concessions would be made no later than six months after the signing of the Moscow Treaty.

On April 13, 1941 the Neutrality Pact between the U.S.S.R. and Japan was signed. The Japanese, however, did not live up to the secret agreement concerning North Sakhalin. The setbacks which Russia suffered during the first six months of its war with Germany gave Japan the opportunity to back out of the agreement without fear of Soviet reprisal. In February, 1942, four months after the Japanese were supposed to have withdrawn from North Sakhalin, the Vice-Minister of Foreign Affairs told a committee of the Diet that Japan would not give up her rights in northern Sakhalin and that "Russia's attitude will change with the international situation."[86] The Russian attitude did not change even though the German attack prevented any movement to force Japan's compliance with the agreement. During the negotiations for the renewal of the fisheries agreement in March, 1942 the Soviet government renewed its insistence that Matsuoka's promise be fulfilled, and on the first anniversary of the Neutrality Pact, Pravda carried an article discussing Russo-Japanese relations with special emphasis on the Neutrality Pact itself. Within the article was a thinly veiled threat that must have been quite understandable to the Japanese leaders who knew about the secret agreement. The article concluded, "In order for the pact to continue in existence, Japan must show the same attitude toward treaties as does the Soviet Union. It is essential to carry out signed treaties and agreements taken upon oneself most strictly and unwaveringly...."[87]

So long as the war progressed well for the Axis, Japan continued to ignore its pledge to abolish the concessions. By the second half of 1943, however, the Axis position had begun to deteriorate considerably, and once again Russia's neutrality became important to Japan. By October of 1943, the situation had changed so greatly that the Cabinet decided to reopen negotiations with Russia with a view to settling the concessions issue. The conferences which followed resulted in the exchange of several protocols on March 30, 1944 concerning the disposition of North Sakhalin.[88] In the two weeks prior to the conclusion of the agreements, Japan had closed down the concessions and handed them over to Soviet authorities, thus ending the Japanese hold on the Russian land. According to the agreement Japan transferred "to the Union of the Soviet Socialist Republic all rights to the Japanese oil and coal concessions in Northern Sakhalin." In return for this the Soviet Union promised to pay Japan five million rubles. Russia was also to supply the Japanese government "on the usual commercial terms fifty thousand metric tons of oil extracted at the Okha oil fields in the course of five consecutive years" dating from the end of the "present war."

At the same time that this agreement was reached, it was decided that the Japanese government should close down its consulates in Alexandrovsk and Okha. The Soviet policy of clearing North Sakhalin of Japanese nationals had succeeded, though it had taken a great war and a major change in the international positions of the two countries to bring it about. As a reciprocal gesture for the Japanese withdrawal, the Soviet consulates on Hokkaido and at Tsuroka were likewise removed.

The conclusion of World War II brought with it another change in the status of Sakhalin. As a result of the Allied victory in the Pacific, the U.S.S.R. occupied the southern half of the island. As late as the middle of 1945 there had been some doubt that the Soviet Union would enter the war against Japan. The Japanese were so unsure of the Russian attitude that they requested Soviet mediation with the Allies. This proposal would have given the Soviet Union an opportunity to press demands on Japan without becoming involved in a war, and the Japanese felt that the Soviet leaders would grasp such a chance in the light of the long and bitter struggle and the tremendous losses that the Russo-German war had brought. In this respect, however, Tokyo was wrong, for though some of the Soviet plans in the Far East could be achieved without the use of arms, Stalin's dreams for Russian hegemony of all Asia could be assured only in the wake of a military or semi-military operation.

The agreement which brought Soviet troops into South Sakhalin was signed at Yalta on February 11, 1945. At the meeting between the "Big Three," Winston Churchill, Franklin Roosevelt, and Joseph Stalin, the Russian government promised that "in two or three months after the war in Europe has terminated the Soviet Union shall enter into the war against Japan on the side of the Allies...."[89] The negotiations which had led up to this agreement were marked with concern about whether Russia would actually enter the war in the Pacific. Stalin had listed several conditions which would have to be fulfilled before he could consider fighting Japan; one of these was the return of South Sakhalin to the U.S.S.R. The British and American desire to see Russia in the war prompted them to acquiesce. The text of the agreement stated that "the former rights of Russia violated by the treacherous attack of Japan in 1904 shall be restored, viz: (A) The southern part of Sakhalin as well as the islands adjacent to it shall be returned to the Soviet Union.... The heads of the three great powers have agreed that these claims of the Soviet Union should be unquestionably satisfied after Japan has been defeated."[90] Thus, the Russian government once more was able to recover the whole of Sakhalin. The agreement which the Allies signed at Yalta gave Russia the backing which it needed to assert its power in the southern half of the island, and as soon as the war ended, Russian forces moved into the area.

The parties involved in the transfer of South Sakhalin to Russian control viewed its undertaking with varied reactions and emotions. Following the signing of the Yalta Pact, the United States completely reversed its attitude toward the cession of South Sakhalin. The initial official attitude was expressed at Yalta by President Roosevelt. Roosevelt apparently did not feel that he should haggle over the cession of South Sakhalin and the Kuriles. He is reported to have said that "he felt there would be no difficulty whatsoever in regard to the southern half of Sakhalin and the Kurile Islands going to Russia at the end of the war."[91]

Soon after the war, however, feeling in the United States rose against the transfer. Typical of the more vocal opponents of the Yalta agreement was Senator William Jenner. In April, 1951 Senator Jenner verbally attacked John Foster Dulles on the grounds that he was designing a peace treaty that would legalize the Soviet occupation of South Sakhalin and the Kuriles. He claimed that Mr. Dulles was trying to give "permanent title" to Sakhalin and the Kuriles to the U.S.S.R. In response to such charges, Mr. Dulles stated in a meeting of the Senate Foreign Relations Committee that the treaty did not confirm the transfer of South Sakhalin and the Kuriles to Russia. Instead, he claimed, the Japanese Peace Treaty actually reversed the agreement at Yalta in that it left open the question of ownership for future settlement. Later, before the same committee, Dulles stated that approval of the peace treaty by the Senate would represent a "formal repudiation" of those acts at Yalta which pertained to South Sakhalin and the Kuriles.[92]

The United States Senate went one step farther than this "formal repudiation." When ratifying the Japanese Peace Treaty it tacked on an interpretative statement which spelled out in the plainest terms its disapproval of the transfer to Russia of Japanese territory. The statement said:

> As part of such advice and consent (to ratification), the Senate states that nothing the treaty contains is deemed to diminish or prejudice, in favor of the Soviet Union, the right, title and interest of Japan or the Allied powers, as defined in such treaty, in and to Sakhalin and its adjacent islands, the Kurile Islands, the Habomai Islands, the island of Shikotan or any other territory, rights or interests possessed by Japan on December 7, 1941, or to confer any right, title or benefit therein or thereto on to Soviet Union.[93]

Thus, within six years after the signing of the agreement at Yalta the United States had raised strong objections to the Soviet Union's occupation of South Sakhalin. American feeling had expressed itself in opposition to the present settlement which left Russia—without sanction of a formal agreement—in complete control of the whole island.

The Soviet attitude toward the agreements at Yalta was one of complete acceptance. The securing of South Sakhalin represented the fulfillment of a long cherished plan. The official Soviet view had been for some time that South Sakhalin already belonged to the U.S.S.R. In October, 1940, when General Yoshitsugu Tatekawa made a call on V. M. Molotov to arrange a non-aggression pact with the Soviet Union, he was informed: "We cannot conclude a non-aggression pact as long as Japan continues to hold in her custody Russian soil."[94] At this Tatekawa broke off negotiations because he suspected "with reason" that Molotov was going to demand the return of South Sakhalin.

The acquisition of South Sakhalin had also been a pet project of Joseph Stalin. The Russian Premier viewed it as an important step toward extending communist influence into the Pacific area. When combined with the northern half of the island in one political unit it could provide a base well suited to the control of the North Pacific sea lanes as well as a sturdy wall across the approaches to the Amur. On September 2, 1945, the day Japan signed the terms of surrender, Stalin made a speech in Moscow in which he said, "From now on, South Sakhalin and the Kurile Islands will serve as a means of direct communication of the Soviet Union with the ocean and a base for the defense of our country against Japanese aggression."[95] On February 3, 1946 these declarations were reiterated in even stronger terms. In a broadcast dealing with military preparedness, Radio Moscow announced that the Kurile Islands and South Sakhalin "will no longer bar the Soviet Union from the Pacific Ocean.... All this is naturally a source of gratification to people in this country, and so is the communist party's intention, proclaimed in the election manifesto, to make the Soviet armed forces still stronger and the Soviet frontiers invulnerable."[96] The occupation of South Sakhalin was accepted in Russia as a basic and justified step toward building their post-war world.

The Japanese attitude toward the loss of the island was not officially formed until 1949. Beginning in that year, the Japanese government has consistently held that it is not obligated to respect the agreements made at Yalta. They feel that their acceptance of the terms of surrender bound them only to the conditions expressed at Cairo and Potsdam, and cannot be construed as a blank check for Russian encroachment. Furthermore, the Ministry of Foreign Affairs has taken the position that the legal right to Sakhalin should be Japan's on the basis of prior settlement and exploration.[97] It contends that the early trade carried on between Japan and the natives in that area, the pioneer settlement of Japanese themselves on the island, and the extensive explorations of the geographer, Mamiya Rinso, substantiate the claim. In an effort to gain public and international approval of their demands, they have also asserted that the permanent separation of South Sakhalin from Japan would be a great detriment to the recovery of Japan's economy—an argument that would be of particular importance in gaining United States assistance.

From 1945 to 1955 relations between Japan and Russia were conducted on an informal basis through the agencies of occupation and the unofficial Soviet Mission in Japan. During the period of occupation Russia was represented in Japan by its member of the Allied Council. In this capacity, Generals Derevyanko and Kislenko maintained fairly close contact with the Japanese government—at Japan's expense. After the occupation the Russian staff in Japan remained, forming the nucleus of the "unofficial mission" which was to carry on negotiations until 1955.

During these years the disposition of South Sakhalin was not touched upon officially, mainly because of Russia's refusal to take an active part in forming the San Francisco Peace Treaty. There was some success in dealing with the problems of repatriation and trade, but none of the agreements in these fields seem to bring closer the settlement of the Sakhalin question. The issue raised by the Soviet Union's refusal to carry out its repatriation obligations has been a continuing sore spot in Russo-Japanese relations. In the Potsdam Declaration the Allies had pledged that "the Japanese military forces, after being completely disarmed, shall be permitted to return to their homes with the opportunity to lead peaceful and productive lives."[98] However, from the surrender in September, 1945 until December of 1946, the Soviet authorities in Russian-occupied areas made no move to repatriate any of the 1.3 million Japanese under their control. On December 14, 1946 an agreement was signed in Tokyo under which the Soviets promised to return 50,000 Japanese every month. Although the Supreme Commander for the Allied Powers set up more than adequate transportation for the repatriates, the Soviet authorities were extremely lax in fulfilling the agreement. By May, 1949 only 900,000 Japanese had been returned, leaving approximately 240,000 in Soviet territory. The next six years saw a slackening in Russian efforts to complete the repatriation and a growing determination in Japan to bring it to a close. In 1955, ten years after the surrender, the Tokyo government still claimed there were 10,000 Japanese nationals in Soviet hands.[99]

Trade arrangements between Japan and Russia were also conducted in a rather haphazard manner after the war. Until the summer of 1954 trade between these two countries was conducted on the basis of several short-term agreements. During the summer of that year a Soviet trade mission visited Tokyo with a view to establishing a more solid commercial relationship. As a result of the negotiations carried on between the Soviet mission and a group of Japanese representatives, trade contracts were signed with five large Japanese firms. The terms of the contracts provided for a twenty million dollar expansion in Russo-Japanese trade for the following two years. The results of these agreements were not so great as expected, however. Japanese sources indicate that the contracts amounted to only eight million dollars in goods between the summer of 1954 and February, 1955, and of this only two million were Japanese exports. Although no great benefits accrued to either country, the move toward normalization which these trade negotiations had brought seems to have provided a step toward the next stage in Russo-Japanese negotiations.

This most recent stage in Russo-Japanese relations began in January, 1955 when I. A. Dominitsky, head of the unofficial Soviet mission in Japan, presented Premier Hatoyama with a proposal to open formal negotiations with Russia. Although neither side would give any details concerning the exact nature of the unsigned, undated note, Dominitsky was reported by Kyodo News Service to have referred to it as a "peace overture."[100] On February 5, 1955 the Japanese government, through Renzo Sawada, its unofficial observer at the United Nations, notified the Soviet Union of its acceptance of the Soviet proposal to discuss normalization of relations between the two countries. The Japanese hoped that the negotiations would cover four major problems which had previously blocked an amicable Russo-Japanese settlement. These included the admission of Japan to the United Nations—which Russia consistently vetoed—the return of Soviet-occupied Japanese territory, the repatriation of Japanese prisoners of war, and the settlement of economic questions such as trade relations.

After several months of debate as to where the talks should be held, negotiations were finally begun in London on June 1, 1955. The Soviet Union was represented by Jacob A. Malik, the Ambassador to Britain; representing Japan was Shunichi Matsumoto, the former Japanese Ambassador to the British capital. Prior to the opening of the negotiations, Premier Hatoyama is reported to have said that he felt Russia might offer the return of South Sakhalin and the Kuriles to Japan in exchange for a pledge that they would never be used as bases by the United States or any other power.[101] On June 6 Premier Hatoyama stated further that Japan would ask for the return of the Kurile Islands and the southern half of Sakhalin in the peace treaty negotiations. To this, Foreign Minister Mamoru Shigemitsu added that if Japan were to regain these islands, Tokyo would oppose the building of United States bases there. These early days of the negotiations were marked by Japanese hopes for the return of their territory.

On June 14, 1955, at the formal meeting, Ambassador Malik presented a list of proposals for a neutrality pact between Japan and the Soviet Union. The pact was to cover eight points.[102] These were: (1) The waters between Japan and Korea as well as the Japanese inland seaways should be barred to all foreign military craft except those of the Soviet Union and Communist China. (2) Japan should not enter into any alliance or military coalitions directed against any power that fought against Japan in World War II. (3) Both Russia and Japan should pledge mutual non-aggression and non-interference in each other's domestic affairs. (4) Japan should relinquish all claims to the Kurile Islands, South Sakhalin, and the Habomais and Shikotan Island. (5) Both sides should renounce claims for war reparations and damage. (6) There should be long-range plans for cultural exchanges. (7) The Soviet Union should support Japan's admission to the United Nations. (8) Lastly, tariff arrangements, including the "most favored nation," and a fishing agreement should be made, pending the conclusion of a formal commerce pact.

Japanese officials were shocked at the harshness of the proposed terms. Russia's part in initiating negotiations had led the government in Tokyo to expect a far more favorable settlement. Especially objectionable were the maritime provisions. If put into effect they would give the Soviet Union virtual military control of Hokkaido and prevent the use of United States warships in the event of a new war in Korea. Besides, since Japan had no effective navy, it would make Soviet naval forces dominant in Japanese home waters. A second major objection to the Russian proposals was that they contained no mention of a territorial settlement, and this had been one point on which Japanese officials had been virtually certain there would be some Soviet compromise. Nor had there been a mention of repatriates. The Japanese government felt that "the repatriation of Japanese nationals still detained in Soviet territory is a question which should be settled before anything else... [that] all these unfortunate compatriots be sent home immediately and that details regarding those whose fate is unknown be fully disclosed."[103] Without some provisions for settlement of the repatriation and territorial problems the Japanese were reluctant to negotiate. In the light of these omissions and the impossible Russian maritime demands, the Japanese mission raised the strongest objections, and the negotiations became deadlocked on the Russian proposals.

Negotiations remained at a standstill until August, 1955 when Ambassador Malik was called to the meeting of the United Nations General Assembly. They were not renewed until January 17, 1956. During the interval between the two series of meetings there were a number of important statements concerning the possibility that the two parties might withdraw from their stalemated positions of the previous autumn. On August 19 Asahi Newspaper reported that Japan would drop her demand for territorial rights to South Sakhalin and the Kuriles in an effort to minimize the differences which had arisen during the talks in London.[104] The paper also said that the Tokyo government would insist upon the sovereignty over Iturup, Kunashiri, and the other smaller islands in the southern Kuriles plus Shikotan and Habomai Islands. On the following day the Japanese Foreign Office denied this report saying that "the new policy of the Government is as previously decided."

However, in September a Foreign Office spokesman said that Japan had proposed during the negotiations in August that the Soviet Union return the southern Kuriles and that the status of South Sakhalin and the northern Kurile Islands be decided at an international conference, but that Russia had rejected the idea.

During the period between the conferences, the Russian government also took some steps to improve the possibilities for a settlement. On September 12, 1955 The Nippon Times carried a report that the Soviet Union had offered the return of Shikotan and Habomai Islands to Japan on the condition that they were to be left unfortified. The offer was refused by the Japanese envoy, Matsumoto, on the grounds that Japan could accept no conditions. On September 21 Morito Morishima, a member of a Japanese delegation visiting the U.S.S.R., reported that he had been told by Nikita S. Khrushchev, the Communist Party Secretary, that the Soviet Union would not return South Sakhalin and the Kurile Islands; however, they might be prepared to make minor territorial concessions "in order to normalize relations with the Japanese."[105]

In January, 1956 the Soviet Union attempted to bypass Japanese demands and the negotiations in London and gain a quick peace settlement. The Japanese Foreign Office announced that it had received an informal proposal, through the Soviet mission in Tokyo, suggesting that the state of war be terminated. The Foreign Office said that Russia could proceed "unilaterally" and declare the war over if it wished; however this would in no way affect either the question of diplomatic relations or the questions which Japan had raised at the peace negotiations in London.[106]

Having been refused in their attempts to gain a simple termination of war, the Soviet leaders once more turned their interest upon the meetings in London. On February 10, 1956 Jacob Malik made an official offer to return Shikotan and the Habomai Islands—both of which had been mentioned unofficially and in rumors since the meetings of the previous August. Malik suggested a plan under which the islands would simply be handed over to the Japanese. A map and protocol defining the settlement would then be attached to the forthcoming peace treaty. Matsumoto asked him to produce the planned protocol and map, and when he failed to do so, the Japanese envoy "rejected the offer as a basis for debate."[107]

Thus Russia and Japan had once more reached a stalemate. The negotiations continued, but at the end of February, 1956 there was little indication of what these negotiations might achieve—if anything. The meetings which had been carried on since January of the previous year had netted little in the way of a final settlement of the continuing problems between Russia and Japan. The only tangible results of the conferences were a preamble, last clause, and one other minor clause of a proposed twelve-point peace treaty.

The future status of Sakhalin remained to be settled. Both Russia and Japan continue to claim title to the southern half of the island. Japan renounced her title to Southern Sakhalin in Article 2, paragraph (c) of the San Francisco Peace Treaty, but the Japanese contend that this should not give the right of occupation to the Soviet Union. A Japan Information bulletin has outlined its country's position:

> Japan promised the signatories to waive title to Southern Sakhalin and the Kurile Islands; (this) is practically the sole internationally recognized commitment pertaining to the status of these two areas. However, in view of the fact that the Soviets refused to sign the San Francisco Treaty, its provisions do not apply in the case of the Soviet Union.[108]

At present, however, the U.S.S.R. has de facto possession of the island and has given no indication in negotiations or in its official pronouncements that it will give up South Sakhalin. In view of all the claims and counterclaims it appears that neither party will surrender its title to Sakhalin without other major concessions. Whether this is true or not is difficult to ascertain. The question will probably not be answered until the settlement is actually made, or a way has been found to measure the real significance of Sakhalin to Russia and Japan.

An Evaluation of the Strategic and Economic Importance of Sakhalin

When attempting to determine the importance of Sakhalin to Russia and Japan, two major considerations seem to be most prominent. These are its strategic importance and the value of the island to each country's economy. In statements since World War II, the Soviet Union has placed most of its emphasis on the strategic value of the island while the Japanese have consistently referred to the place which Sakhalin could and should have in the economy of Japan. However neither country has omitted consideration of the other element in its arguments. It would seem probable that a fair understanding of the relative importance of Sakhalin to Russia and Japan might be gained from studying these two aspects of the controversy.

Although the Japanese in the years before World War II placed a great deal of emphasis on the economic importance of their colonies, W. W. Lockwood maintains that the chief significance of the area lay in the strategic realm. "It gave the Japanese government political control over enlarged food resources, created a ring of defensive barriers around the home islands, and afforded a series of steppingstones for further imperialist expansion in the Far East."[109] With Japan on the move to create an empire, these strategic considerations probably were the most important to the Japanese leaders, and little weight should be given to their professions of economic need.

Today, however, the situation seems to be quite different. The time is wrong for Japan to build an empire. First of all, since its devastating defeat in World War II, it no longer possesses the resources upon which to start a new building program. Encumbered by shortages of capital and material, the Japanese would have great difficulty if they attempted to force their wishes upon another party on the basis of their own prestige. The suggestion has been made that Japan might circumvent the difficulties stemming from its lack of resources by becoming the central power in a new third-force movement in Asia. This seems an unlikely prospect in the near future, for during World War II Japan lost many of the allies on whom it would have to depend for such a venture. Until more friendly relations can be established between Japan and its former enemies in the Far East there is little chance for a third force attempt that would include Japan. Besides, the great powers—primarily the U.S.S.R. and United States—are far too interested in developments in Asia and the Pacific to allow the Japanese a free hand there. In view of the difficulties which Japan at present faces with respect to building a new empire, there is little likelihood that any serious attempts will be taken in that direction. If this is so then part of the strategic value of former possessions such as South Sakhalin can no longer be considered important. With no imperial design, it virtually goes without saying that Japan will certainly have no need for "steppingstones."

There is another aspect of the strategic value of Sakhalin to Japan. That is, does the island provide a defensive perimeter in the north? Situated less than ten miles from the Amur delta, Sakhalin could be used as a base for blocking the Amur River and could thereby cut Soviet communications with the Pacific. In any plan for a long-range war in which Japan would be responsible for sealing off this one corridor to the Pacific, Sakhalin would appear to be a valuable possession. Furthermore the island would also provide an excellent point from which a continuing surveillance of Russian naval activity might be maintained. On the other hand the possession of the island would not insure the safety of Japan. Though the movement of the Russo-Japanese border north to the fiftieth parallel or to the Asia mainland would be of great benefit to Russia's enemies in a global conflict, it would not preclude Soviet missiles whether land-, sea-, or air-based from striking a fatal blow at Japan. In all, it seems that Japan can hope to gain very little strategically from the acquisition of South Sakhalin.

With respect to the economic importance of the island the situation seems to be quite different. Japan was severely hurt by its defeat in World War II. The economy was practically destroyed during the war and has since recovered slowly. One of the major problems in this recovery has been the lack of raw materials and food in Japan. Before the war South Sakhalin, along with the other colonies, had played a large part in supplying these needs—at low cost. Today the Japanese government claims that a large portion of the country's difficulties lies in the fact that it can no longer look to these colonies for its needs.

Sakhalin has four valuable commodities, all of which Japan could use: petroleum, coal, lumber and fishery products. Japan imports over twenty per cent of its food supply, and the loss of the fishing grounds off South Sakhalin has had serious consequences. In the years before World War II almost three per cent of Japan's fishery production came from South Sakhalin (see Table 1). Since the war fishing production has dropped considerably in Japan, mainly because of the loss of former fishing grounds such as South Sakhalin and the establishment by the Soviets of a twelve-mile offshore limit around their possessions. So severe have the Russian restrictions become that in 1955 they seized 221 Japanese fishing boats and 2,230 fishermen for having trespassed on the new Soviet fishing grounds.[110]

TABLE 1[*]

JAPANESE FISHING PRODUCTION 1935-1940
(1,000 TONS LANDED WEIGHT)

YEAR	Total Fisheries Based on Japanese Property (excludes colonies)	KARAFUTO
1935............	4,574	155
1936............	4,988	135
1937............	4,936	107
1938............	4,615	97
1939............	4,660	144
1940............	4,922	137
Average	4,781	129

[*]Edward A. Ackerman, Japan's Natural Resources and Their Relation to Japan's Economic Future, (Chicago, 1953), pp. 132, 140.

The resumption of fishing operations in South Sakhalin could therefore be of considerable aid in bolstering the Japanese economy. The fish products from that area when exchanged for Japanese manufactures and services would provide a step toward solving the problem of feeding Japan's growing population. Besides, the canned fish from Sakhalin, which has generally commanded a high price (see Table 2), would provide another fairly stable export upon which Japan might draw in exchange for needed commodities.

The forest resources of Sakhalin would also be of great value to Japan. After World War I the Japanese became increasingly dependent upon the forests of Sakhalin to provide

SAKHALIN

TABLE 2*

JAPANESE MARINE PRODUCTS 1933-1938
(Value in yen)

YEAR	JAPAN TOTAL	KARAFUTO
1933.............	170,613,000	13,195,350
1934.............	173,137,000	15,673,760
1935.............	181,802,000	18,737,619
1936.............	212,648,000	19,812,145
1937.............	219,649,000	19,108,539
1938.............	248,895,000	21,651,655
Average	201,124,000	18,029,844

*Financial and Economic Annual of Japan 1933-1940, the Department of Finance, Government Printing Office, Tokyo.

lumber for their growing industries. In the years from 1928 to 1936 production in Japan averaged 6,700 million board feet while South Sakhalin supplied 1,800 million feet.[111] The paper industry in Japan made the most exacting demands on the supplies, taking nearly ten per cent of the combined lumber and pulpwood output of both Japan and South Sakhalin. Up to the end of World War II South Sakhalin produced more than half of the pulpwood produced in Japan (see Table 3).

TABLE 3*

PRODUCTION OF PULPWOOD 1930-1945
(Tons)

YEAR	JAPAN	KARAFUTO
1930.............	343,725	340,950
1931.............	301,412	316,400
1932.............	309,845	290,409
1933.............	351,805	324,629
1934.............	402,553	371,343
1935.............	426,313	403,170
1936.............	442,928	435,964
1937.............	485,625	465,449
1938.............	529,175	489,777
1939.............	632,605	476,457
1940.............	706,007	470,378
1941.............	844,684	456,561
1942.............	730,535	387,829
1943.............	635,773	288,780
1944.............	397,203	223,965
1945.............	190,800	69,531
Average	483,186	336,224

*Oji Paper Manufacturing Co., Ltd., Natural Resources Section Report 56, p. 28; and Japan's Economic Statistics, December, 1950, p. 50, in: Ackerman, Japan's Natural Resources and Their Relation to Japan's Economic Future, p. 247.

The great reduction in this outside supply has brought about a dangerous overcutting of the forests in Japan during the post-war period, and, according to E. A. Ackerman, if prompt remedial measures are not taken in the near future Japan cannot hope to maintain its supply.[112] One obvious measure, to which the Foreign Ministry itself has pointed, would be the recovery of the forests of South Sakhalin. In a recent brochure they have stated that not only did "Sakhalin account for more than seventy per cent of the pulp consumed by Japan's paper industry," but that with the growth of the artificial fiber industry "Sakhalin was in a position to supply more than sixty per cent of the wood used by it as raw material."[113]

Although Japan at one time exported a large quantity of its coal production, the gigantic growth in Japanese industrial uses for coal have made it necessary to import much of its coal supply as well as push domestic production to the maximum. Coal production in Japan dropped greatly during World War II, but since the war it has climbed steadily so that once again it has taxed the country's reserves, (see Table 4). In 1951 the annual production was 43,319,000 metric tons, still far below the peak pre-war years but already creating a drain on the not too adequate or workable reserves in Japan. Since World War II some coal has been brought to Japan from Sakhalin as a result of short-term trade agreements with the Soviet Union. However the insecurity of the agreements and the high freight charges have discouraged reliance on these imports. As yet the Japanese are unable to take advantage of the 3.5 billion ton coal reserves in Sakhalin.

TABLE 4*

COAL PRODUCTION IN JAPAN
(1000 metric tons)

Year	Production	Year	Production
1940	57,318	1946	20,368
1941	55,602	1947	27,235
1942	54,179	1948	33,860
1943	55,539	1949	37,973
1944	49,335	1950	38,459
1945	22,371	1951	43,319

*United Nations Statistical Year Book 1953, p. 106.

Japan's future requirement for oil represents the most difficult item of the four to judge, but it is probably the most important. For a highly mechanized country Japan is notoriously short of oil. In 1948 the annual production of oil in Japan was 1,291 million barrels. On January 1, 1949 the entire oil reserves in Japan were estimated at fifteen million barrels or less than a thirteen-year supply if production were maintained at the 1948 level.[114] It is obvious that Japan will be almost entirely dependent upon outside sources within a few years. Prior to World War II the Japanese were able to import a large portion of their oil from Sakhalin. The concessions companies alone were able to supply more than one million barrels of oil annually to Japan. Current estimates of proved oil reserves for North Sakhalin suggest amounts of as much as 350 million barrels and some estimates place the reserves in South Sakhalin higher. At the present, however, Soviet control over the island and the impasse in Russo-Japanese negotiations has for all practical purposes cut off Japan from this rich supply.

Strategically the island of Sakhalin is more important to the Soviet Union than it is to Japan. Stretching for six hundred miles north and south opposite the mouth of the Amur River, it provides an excellent cover for Russian naval operations out of the Soviet Far East. The Amur River has a total length of 1,485 miles from the point of confluence of the Argun and Shika Rivers. Connected with these rivers the Amur system has a total of three thousand miles of navigable waters, providing water communication with a large portion of the Soviet Far East. Ocean-going ships can sail up the river as far as the major city of Khabarovsk. With Sakhalin in enemy hands it would be virtually impossible for Russian forces to use the lower Amur River.

Besides acting as a shield for the Amur River, Sakhalin is also well suited as a base for Soviet naval operations in the Pacific. A geographer has described the topography of Sakhalin by noting that "wide lagoons, separated from the ocean by long and narrow sand spits, and kept fresh by the rivers which empty into them, are very characteristic of the eastern coast.... They afford easy and safe communication for tens of kilometers."[115] Provided with these natural bases for operation, fleets of Soviet submarines and other small craft have easy and protected access to the Pacific throughout the year.

There are some indications that the Soviets have already taken advantage of this new opportunity to gain access to the Pacific. In 1946 a number of Chinese repatriates from Sakhalin reported that the Russian occupation forces had established a large submarine base in the southern part of Sakhalin and that the base was guarded by approximately thirty thousand Soviet troops.[116] Although there is little specific information concerning the building of further naval installations on the island, work apparently has progressed far enough to make it possible for Russian naval forces to retire from Chinese ports. The evacuation of Soviet troops from Port Arthur on May 31, 1955 seems to indicate that Russia has become able to supply adequate port facilities within its own possessions in the north. The most likely of these possessions would be Sakhalin.

Although defense of the Soviet Far East is one of the prime reasons for Russian interest in the continued possession of Sakhalin, it must not be forgotten that Sakhalin also furnishes a springboard for communist expansion into the Pacific. As such it puts the Soviet Union one step closer to Japan, formerly its greatest opponent in the Far East. In 1946 it was reported that a force of 400,000 Russian troops had been massed on the island.[117]

The Soviet Union's interest in the economy of Sakhalin, though not so great as its strategic interests, has become quite important in the post-war period. Special emphasis has been placed on the expansion of the fishing and petroleum industries and the development of manufacturing and construction. Since the end of the war Russian authorities have claimed huge successes in their efforts to modernize and expand the fishing industry on the island. An article in _Pravda_ on October 4, 1955 claimed that during the current five-year plan the fishing fleet on Sakhalin had more than doubled its numbers and had increased its capacity more than five times.[118] Between 1945 and 1947 the Russian government boasted that it had increased the number of canneries on the island from eight to twenty-eight and that Sakhalin had become the foremost supplier of herring, cod, plaice and sea mammals in the Far East.[119]

A similar effort has been made to modernize the oil industry on Sakhalin. A systematic exploration of the island has raised estimates of proved oil deposits to 350 million barrels. In _World Geography of Petroleum_ it has been estimated that "the principal oilfield area in eastern Soviet Asia is the island of Sakhalin."[120] This supply has been made readily available to the major cities of Eastern Siberia by the installation of a submarine pipeline across the straits to the mainland. This pipeline has been extended to Khabarovsk whence the oil can be transported easily by rail or water to the other Soviet centers in the area. The fortunate location of these rich oil deposits on Sakhalin has made them extremely valuable to the Soviet armed forces in the Far East. Placed at the point most suitable for the development of a naval base, these deposits provide oil which would otherwise have to be transported from western and central Asia, greatly increasing the cost of supply as well as taxing the already burdened transportation systems in Siberia. The location of the deposits in this outlying region also fits in well with the Soviet plans to disperse industry and thereby eliminate its traditional transportation weakness.

The Russian efforts to foster the growth of industry on Sakhalin have also had some success since the war. As a preliminary step to building large-scale industrial operations on the island, the Soviet authorities have taken measures to improve the production of coal and lumber. As early as September, 1946 there were claims that improvements in forestry techniques and management had increased lumber cutting to 124 per cent of the annual quota.[121] With respect to the coal mines much more effort had to be devoted to renovating the facilities which had fallen into disrepair during the war. In 1946 the government spent almost fifty million rubles in repairing and expanding the existing coal mines.[122] By the third quarter of that year the eight mines which had remained in order after the war had been increased to twenty-five, and the Kolm mines had reached their 1941 output—the year of their greatest productivity.

One of the newer industries which received significant government aid after the war was shipbuilding. The need for fishing boats, refrigerator ships, and naval craft led the Soviets to establish shipyards on the island. By the end of June, 1946 two new shipyards had been completed and others were being planned. The building of shipyards and other industrial units has been accompanied by a general increase in the construction industry as a whole. The establishment of new concerns and the expanding of older businesses has brought about a substantial increase in the urban population and has necessitated a large building program. During 1950 there were twenty thousand square meters of new living space put into use in South Sakhalin and "city dwellers" were promised another thirty thousand square meters of space in 1951.[123]

On the whole it would appear that the Soviet Union has had fair success in developing industry on Sakhalin. A speech before the Nineteenth Party Congress in 1952 included the statement that the gross industrial output of the island had increased 63.2 per cent in the period from 1947 to 1950.[124] However, the progress which the Soviets have made in expanding the industries of the island has been extremely expensive. In 1951 P. F. Cheplakov reported to the Communist Party that during the first five years of Sakhalin Province (1947-1951), the capital investments in its economy had amounted to several billion rubles. Later in a report to _Pravda_ on October 14, 1955, V. Averin, a special correspondent, lamented that the U.S.S.R. had to spend an extra 100 million rubles for fish production during the first half of 1955.[125]

The Soviet Union's willingness to take on such large expenditures to build the economy of Sakhalin indicates a fixed decision to maintain control over the whole island. There are other indications which seem to substantiate the firmness of Soviet intentions. First of all they have conducted a thoroughgoing political reorganization of the island. In 1946 they absorbed South Sakhalin into the Soviet Union as electoral district number 177. Then in 1947 the whole of Sakhalin plus the Kurile Islands were constituted as Sakhalin Oblast and were given the standing of a separate province within the Russian Soviet Federated Socialist Republic.[126] As part of the program of political reorientation many of the towns in South Sakhalin were renamed.

The political reorganization was carried over into the fields of business and land ownership as well. Repatriates reported in 1946 that the Soviet authorities had taken over the management of all industry, and work quotas were maintained by a policy of distributing food only at the place of employment. During the May to September fishing season house-to-house labor requisitions were made, and all who were found at home were assigned to the fishing fleets. All farm lands were re-registered in 1945, and allotment was made according to the ability of the farmers to produce crops. All land was nationalized, and the farmers were made to turn over their crops to the Soviet administration. The farmer was not paid for the crops as such but was given regular wages.

SAKHALIN

93

To facilitate the changeover from the predominantly Japanese economy of the pre-war years, the Russian government also sponsored a program of migration from Siberia and European Russia. It was hoped that the Japanese workers and farmers in Sakhalin would eventually be replaced by Soviet nationals. Although there have been numerous difficulties in transporting the great numbers of people needed to colonize Sakhalin, a certain degree of success has been registered. On October 23, 1946 it was reported that four thousand Russian families from throughout the Soviet Union had settled in former Japanese territory in South Sakhalin.[127] Among those listed were officials, mechanics, teachers, carpenters, stovemakers, and bookkeepers. Other reports indicate that more than one hundred thousand Russian civilians have migrated to South Sakhalin. Japanese repatriates have stated that they felt the Soviet immigration from the mainland was progressing rapidly. In 1946 the Russian population had already grown to outnumber the Japanese three to one in some of the major cities.[128]

Both Russia and Japan seem to have a real need for Sakhalin. To Japan Sakhalin could be of significant aid in its attempt to solve the economic problems with which it has been plagued since World War II. The raw materials and markets which Sakhalin could supply Japan seem hardly large enough to provide any very complete solution; however, a source of additional food, coal, oil and lumber which Japan could pay for with its own goods would certainly give at least temporary relief from its economic difficulties. For Russia, Sakhalin's significance lies in the strategic position which it holds in the North Pacific. To a Russia which is resolved in its plans for world conquest, the acquisition and maintenance of a protected, year-round base on the Pacific is absolutely essential. Sakhalin is at present the best suited of any Russian possession in the Pacific area for such a base. Only a drastic alteration in Soviet plans or strength would diminish the strategic importance of Sakhalin to the Soviet Union.

Conclusion

During the negotiations between Japan and the Soviet Union concerning the final disposition of Sakhalin, neither side has shown convincingly that it will give up its designs on Sakhalin. The Japanese have intimated that they would be willing to renounce their title to the island if agreements were made that the final settlement of the issue would take place at a general conference. The implications involved are that Japan is not willing to give up title unless some substantial concessions are made in return, and it seems probable that those concessions would be granted only at a general conference with friendly backing. Soviet leaders on the other hand have said nothing to indicate that they are even remotely interested in yielding to Japanese demands for the return of Sakhalin. In fact, they have been adamant in their refusal to discuss the matter seriously.

The historical arguments for possession of the island are inconclusive and probably beside the point at present and in the near future. The maps, diaries, and histories which have been produced to prove prior and more continuous settlement by one side or the other actually prove very little. The early period of exploration and colonization in the Sakhalin area was sporadic and poorly organized. No really consistent effort to colonize the island was made by either side until comparatively modern times, and by then each side had made sufficient contact with Sakhalin to provide it with an historical case for its ownership. Continuous ownership has been equally complicated by the numerous agreements by which possession has passed back and forth between the two parties.

In the long run these arguments will probably have little to do with the final disposition of Sakhalin. Ownership will more likely be based on some form of ratio between either side's need for the island as compared to its ability to impose its wishes on the other. In the past, control of Sakhalin, or portions of it, has alternated between Japan and Russia in a manner that appears to be almost proportional to their comparative strengths at various times. In reference to an island frontier which has never had a completely acceptable definition for either side, this continuous imbalance and passing back and forth seems to be partially understandable. And since no apparently lasting agreement has yet been made, it seems reasonable that the settlement of the Sakhalin issue might still depend upon the comparative strengths or interests of Russia and Japan. The needs of the two countries are fairly clear. Japan could very definitely use South Sakhalin or the whole island to bolster its economy. On the other hand Russia has displayed an equal use for the island—both economic and strategic. At present the U.S.S.R. has control of the island and seems quite able to retain it so long as she wishes. Although there are imponderables of policy and propaganda which might make the Soviet leaders decide to accede to Japanese wishes and return South Sakhalin, it seems safe to assert that the island will not be returned to Japan in the near future.

NOTES

1. New York Times, March 17, 1947, p. 77:7.

2. Ibid., February 17, 1952, p. 6:6.

3. A recent illustration of the Japanese approach to this controversy can be seen in Ministry of Foreign Affairs, The Northern Islands (Tokyo, 1955), pp. 1-28.

4. A good, brief discussion of the geography of Sakhalin may be found in Theodore Shabad, Geography of the U.S.S.R. (New York, 1951), pp. 329-33.

5. James Murdoch, A History of Japan (London, 1926), III, p. 511.

6. The name is rendered in other accounts as Dembei or Denbei.

7. Harry Emerson Wildes, Aliens in the East (Philadelphia, 1937), p. 75.

8. Ibid., p. 77.

9. Yosaburo Takekoshi, The Economic Aspects of the History of the Civilization of Japan (London, 1930), III, 181.

10. John A. Harrison, Japan's Northern Frontier (Gainesville, 1953), pp. 7-9.

11. Ibid., p. 13.

12. W. G. Aston, "Russian Descents in Saghalien and Itorup in the Years 1806 and 1807," Asiatic Society of Japan. Transactions. (Yokohama, 1874), p. 94.

13. Takekoshi, loc. cit.

14. George Alexander Lensen, "Early Russo-Japanese Relations," Far Eastern Quarterly (November, 1950), X, pp. 3-37.

15. John A. Harrison discusses at length the controversy of whether Spanberg had actually touched on the Japanese coast or on the coast of Korea as the admiralty later contended. The weight of evidence seems to indicate that Spanberg did sail to Japan. Harrison, op. cit., pp. 150-1.

16. Wildes, op. cit., p. 81.

17. Yoshisaburo Kuno, Japanese Expansion on the Asiatic Continent (Berkeley, 1937), I, pp. 226-7.

18. Lensen, op. cit., pp. 21-22.

19. Takekoshi, loc. cit.

20. Harrison, op. cit., p. 20.

21. Joseph L. Sutton, "Territorial Claims of Russia and Japan in the Kurile Islands," Occasional Papers (Ann Arbor, 1951), I, p. 44.

22. Takekoshi, op. cit., pp. 184-5.

23. Harrison, op. cit., pp. 20-21.

24. Lensen, op. cit., p. 29.

25. Harrison, loc. cit. The quotation was taken from Michael Dobrynin, translator: "Historical Review of the Activities of the Russian-American Company and Its Activities Up to the Present Time" (Bancroft Library: University of California at Berkeley), pp. 207-8.

26. Harrison, op. cit., p. 20.

27. Lensen, op. cit., p. 30.

28. H. B. Morse and H. F. MacNair, Far Eastern International Relations (New York, 1931), pp. 65-6.

29. Takekoshi, op. cit., pp. 183-4.

30. Harrison, op. cit., p. 24.

31. Kuno, op. cit., p. 236.

32. Takekoshi, op. cit., p. 186.

33. Harrison, op. cit., p. 23.

34. David J. Dallin, The Rise of Russia in Asia (New Haven, 1949), p. 26.

35. Harrison, op. cit., p. 23.

36. Wildes, op. cit., pp. 163-4.

37. George Alexander Lensen, Russia's Japan Expedition of 1852 to 1855 (Gainesville, 1955). XXII-XXIII.

38. Paul E. Eckel, "The Crimean War and Japan," Far Eastern Quarterly (February, 1944), III, p. 109.

39. Dallin, op. cit., pp. 17-18.

40. Ibid., p. 18.

41. Takekoshi, op. cit., p. 323.

42. George Alexander Lensen, Russia's Japan Expedition of 1852 to 1855 (Gainesville, 1955), VII.

43. Eckel, op. cit., pp. 109-10.

44. Lensen, op. cit., p. 7.

45. Kuno, op. cit., p. 244.

46. Harrison, op. cit., pp. 41-2.

47. Ibid., loc. cit., p. 42.

48. Lensen, op. cit., pp. 79-80.

49. Ibid., pp. 122-5.

50. Roy Hidemichi Akagi, Japan's Foreign Relations, 1542-1936; A Short History (Tokyo, 1936), p. 37.

51. Harrison, op. cit., pp. 49-50.

52. Another version of the negotiations holds that while in St. Petersburg, Count Matsudaira found a globe at the Governmental Astronomical Observatory which had Sakhalin divided in two colors at the fiftieth parallel. Upon pressing the issue, he found Ignatiev willing to accede to that line in principle on the condition that a commission be sent to determine the natural boundary with reference to topography. Matsudaira's aides urged caution, so he allowed the matter to drop. Akagi, op. cit., p. 62.

53. Harrison, op. cit., pp. 168-9, Appendix II.

54. Akagi, op. cit., p. 63.

55. Ibid.

56. Harrison, op. cit., pp. 55-6.

57. Akagi, op. cit., p. 65 and MacNair, op. cit., pp. 72-3.

58. MacNair, op. cit., p. 82.

59. John Albert White, The Siberian Intervention (New Jersey, 1950), pp. 61-2.

60. Dallin, op. cit., pp. 85-6.

61. Andrei Lobanov-Rostovsky, "Foreign Policies of Japan," Foreign Policies of the Great Powers (Berkeley, 1939), p. 126.

62. White, op. cit., p. 68.

63. Dallin, op. cit., pp. 121-2, and New York Times, December 29, 1915, p. 1:6.

64. White, op. cit., pp. 182-3, pp. 362-5.

65. Ibid., p. 176.

66. Dallin, loc. cit.

67. Louis Fischer, The Soviets in World Affairs (New York, 1930), I, p. 304. Quoted from: Conference on the Limitations of Armaments. Official Protocol of the Sessions. (Washington, 1921), pp. 340-54.

68. White, op. cit., pp. 306-7.

69. Ibid., pp. 411-2. A complete list of the demands can be found in Appendix III.

70. Ibid.

71. Dallin, op. cit., p. 176. The methods which the Far Eastern Republic used to win United States backing are discussed in Fischer, op. cit., I, pp. 302-3.

72. Dallin, op. cit., pp. 177-8 and Harriet Moore, Soviet Far Eastern Policy 1931-1945 (New Jersey, 1945), pp. 175-80.

73. David J. Dallin, Soviet Russia and the Far East (New Haven, 1948), p. 3.

74. Max Beloff, The Foreign Policy of Soviet Russia, 1929-1941 (New York, 1947), I, p. 28. From: O. Hoetzch, Le Caractere et la Situation Internationale de l' Union des Soviets, p. 84.

75. Dallin, op. cit., p. 23.

76. Ibid.

77. Bernard Pares, Russia Past and Present (New York), p. 125-26.

78. Ibid.

79. Dallin, op. cit., p. 15.

80. Moore, op. cit., Appendix I, pp. 187-8.

81. Dallin, op. cit., p. 38.

82. Ibid., pp. 42-3; 148-9.

83. Ibid., p. 164.

84. Moore, op. cit., p. 141.

85. Dallin, op. cit., p. 164. The quote is credited to United States, Department of State. Nazi-Soviet Relations (Washington, 1948), pp. 323-4 and K. Eidus, Yaponiya ot pervoi do vtoroi mirovoi voiny (Moscow, 1946), p. 236.

86. Ibid., p. 175.

87. Ibid., p. 176. Quoted from Pravda, April 13, 1942.

88. Moore, op. cit., p. 200-10.

89. New York Times, March 17, 1947, p. 77:7.

90. Ibid.

91. New York Times, February 20, 1955, IV, p. 5:4.

92. Ibid., January 23, 1952, p. 4:1.

93. Ibid., February 17, 1952, p. 6:6.

94. Ibid., August 6, 1945, p. 3:1.

95. Dallin, op. cit., p. 214.

96. New York Times, February 4, 1946, p. 4:6.

97. Ministry of Foreign Affairs, The Northern Islands (Japan, 1955), pp. 9, 20.

98. Robert A. Fearey, The Occupation of Japan Second Phase: 1948-50 (New York, 1950), pp. 14-17.

99. New York Times, September 23, 1955, p. 7:1.

100. Ibid., January 28, 1955, p. 1:7.

101. Ibid., May 27, 1955, p. 6:4.

102. Ibid., June 17, 1955, p. 1:8.

103. Japan Information. Information Section of the Embassy of Japan (Washington, 1955), II, No. 12, p. 2.

104. New York Times, August 20, 1955, p. 2:6.

105. Ibid., September 22, 1955, p. 5:2.

106. Ibid., January 24, 1956, p. 13:1.

107. Ibid., February 11, 1956, p. 3:8.

108. Japan Information, loc. cit.

109. W. W. Lockwood, The Economic Development of Japan: Growth and Structural Change 1868-1938 (Princeton, 1954), p. 51.

110. New York Times, February 12, 1956, p. 16:2.

111. Lockwood, op. cit., p. 362.

112. E. A. Ackerman, Japan's Natural Resources and Their Relation to Japan's Economic Future (Chicago, 1953), p. 245.

113. Ministry of Foreign Affairs, op. cit., p. 23.

114. W. E. Pratt and D. Good, World Geography of Petroleum (New York, 1950), pp. 235-7.

115. L. S. Berg, Natural Regions of the U.S.S.R. (New York, 1950), p. 239.

116. New York Times, January 18, 1946, p. 10:1.

117. New York Times, January 18, 1946, p. 10:1.

118. V. Averin, Pravda, October 14, 1955, p. 2; tr., The Current Digest of the Soviet Press: Vol. VII, no. 41 (November 23, 1955), p. 29.

119. V. Ogarkov, "South Sakhalin Today," Trud, September 2, 1947; tr., Soviet Press Translations: Vol. II, no. 19 (November 15, 1947), p. 233.

120. Pratt and Good, op. cit., p. 235.

121. Izvestia, September 3, 1946; tr., Soviet Press Translations: Vol. I, no. 1, pp. 15-6.

122. V. Medvedovsky, "Life Returns to the Mines," Izvestia, August 15, 1946; tr., Soviet Press Translations: Vol. I, no. 2, p. 23.

123. M. Samunin, Izvestia, September 26, 1951; tr., Soviet Press Translations: Vol. 6, no. 26 (November 15, 1951), p. 632.

124. Leo Grulio, Current Soviet Policies (New York, 1953), p. 225.

125. Averin, loc. cit.

126. Shabad, op. cit., p. 314.

127. New York Times, October 24, 1946, p. 12:2.

128. Ibid., December 10, 1946, p. 1:6.

JAPANESE LEGAL HISTORY OF THE TOKUGAWA PERIOD:
SCHOLARS AND SOURCES

Dan F. Henderson

During the Tokugawa Period (1603-1868) the output in Japan of official documents and commentaries in the field of law was prodigious. The study of these materials provides an important means of gaining an understanding of Tokugawa political and social institutions; yet for at least three reasons most of the materials have been little cited and presumably little used by Westerners. First, their use requires not only special skills in the grammar, diction and cursive style of the Tokugawa official language, but also a considerable background in the history of the period. Because the records are often little more than official notes, they are elliptical and ambiguous unless the reader has knowledge almost as detailed as that of the official writer himself. Second, many of them exist in a single brush-written copy stored in one of the libraries of Japan. Third, the few Western scholars qualified to make use of these materials have quite properly conceived their role to be that of the middle man between Japanese historians and the Western world. They have avoided the primary sources and left much spade work to their Japanese co-workers. It may well be that such an allocation of functions should continue for some time in the future.

At any rate it goes without saying that primary legal materials are not essential to the beginning student of Tokugawa institutions. There is a wealth of secondary material in the form of texts, monographs, essays and periodical literature by Japanese concerning most of the major institutions of the Tokugawa period. But whether or not the primary legal documents of the period become part of the working materials of the Western student of pre-modern Japanese institutions, it is still of importance that he have an understanding of Tokugawa legal patterns and the type of primary sources available to him. It is with this need in mind that the following guide has been prepared.

In this survey of Tokugawa legal documents, emphasis has been placed on primary sources. Secondary material has not been treated except for the listing of leading Japanese bibliographies, where reference to specific topics can be found, and for comments on the work of individual modern scholars in the field. A list of the main collections of essays by leading modern scholars has also been provided. For a selective list of monographs and articles, with translated titles, the reader is referred to the writer's unpublished Ph.D. dissertation, "The Pattern and Persistence of Traditional Procedures in Japanese Law" (University of California, Berkeley, 1955, pp. 325-435). Since any study of Tokugawa law and institutions also requires constant reference to the numerous collections of general historical materials that have been compiled and printed in Japan since the Restoration, the reader is also referred to a convenient guide to these materials contained in John W. Hall's <u>Japanese History: A Guide to Japanese Reference and Research Materials</u> (University of Michigan Press, Ann Arbor, 1954, 165 pp.).

1. <u>Western Studies</u>

Little has been done by Westerners in the field of Tokugawa laws as such. Otto Rudorff of Germany was a pioneer, and his translations and work on the Tokugawa judicial system are still of considerable value. His German translation of the <u>Osadamegaki, jōkan</u> is the only translation in print of an important collection of decrees, although the present writer has made an English translation which exists in typescript. Rudorff also participated in the drafting of the court organization laws of the Meiji period.

Soon after Rudorff's work, John Henry Wigmore, known to the legal profession for his work on evidence, spent three years (1889-1892) in Japan at Keiō University. There he gained a remarkable understanding of the Tokugawa legal system and recognized the universal value of that unique system of judge-made law for a study of legal development. His work was primarily in the field of customary private law and thus supplemented Rudorff's work on the public law, the Osadamegaki, and other written law. Wigmore's translation project requires further notice in connection with the primary sources on Tokugawa law described below.

The study of feudal documents by Kanichi Asakawa in his Documents of the Iriki (New Haven, 1929) is of high quality. John Carey Hall's translations of some of the major Tokugawa "legislation" are also notable, though they must always be checked for errors against the Japanese text.

2. Japanese Legal Historians

In the Meiji period the Japanese legal scholars were preoccupied with the adoption of Western-style legal codes acceptable to the Western nations in order to induce these nations to give up extraterritorial rights. As a result the history of their indigenous institutions was almost completely neglected. Miyazaki Michisaburō, who held the first chair in comparative law at Tōkyō University (1883), is said to be the first Japanese academician to make legal history his specialty. Miyazaki concentrated on the period from 986-1467. His studies are collected in Miyazaki sensei hōseishi ronshū, 1929 [No. 109]. Also notable in the Meiji period is the work of Konakamura Kiyonori, Nihon kodai hōten, 1892 [No. 28], and the two collections of essays compiled by the Kokugakuin, Hōsei ronsan, 1903 [No. 102], and Hōsei ronsan zokuhen, 1904 [No. 103]. The articles in the above volumes by Komiyama Yasusuke and Naitō Chisō are especially interesting. Naitō Chisō was a Tokugawa vassal, whose experiences during the shogunate and through the transitional period make his view valuable. Miura Kikutarō, Nihon hōseishi, 1900, and Ikebe Yoshikata, Nihon hōseishi, 1912, are early surveys.

But it is with the work of Miura Kaneyuki of Kyōto University and Nakada Kaoru of Tōkyō University and their later students that legal history came into its own in Japan. Miura's Hōseishi no kenkyū, 1919 [No. 101], and Zoku hōseishi no kenkyū, 1925 [No. 116] contain many fine articles on various phases and periods of Japanese legal history. Some of them are still very valuable. "Rekidai hōsei no kōfu to sono kōshiki" and "Edo jidai no saiban seido," among many others, are still the best introductory studies on those topics. Unfortunately Miura's work is not well documented, and the method of citation is too general for ready use in checking sources.

Miura was a doctor of literature, and his school of legal historians has been contrasted with that of Tōkyō University, which is more legalistic. The Tōkyō University scholars trace, in Confucian fashion, from Miyazaki Michisaburō through Nakada Kaoru to his disciples, Ishii Ryōsuke, Takayanagi Shinzō, Kaneda Heiichirō and others. Nakada's Hōseishi ronshū, 1926-1943 [No. 104], contains a wealth of scholarly research on all of the conventional periods of Japanese history. His "Tokugawa jidai no minji saiban jitsuroku" (Vol. 3) is especially valuable as a study of actual practices in the shogunal courts. Ikebe Yoshikata published the Nihon hōseishi shomoku kaidai [No. 5] in 1918. It is largely outdated now, but was an important guide to the primary sources at the time.

Building on the work and training of Miura and Nakada, the contemporary Japanese legal historians have logically devoted most of their time to the task of bringing Japanese legal history up to date. This has meant that most of the prominent scholars, such as Ishii Ryōsuke (Tōkyō University), Takigawa Masajirō (Kokugakuin) and Maki Kenji (formerly of Kyōto University), have not made their major specialized studies on Tokugawa law, but rather on the law of prior periods. Notable exceptions are certain studies of three scholars, Takayanagi Shinzō (Tōhoku University, Sendai), the late Kobayakawa Kingo (Kyōto University) and Kaneda Heiichiro (Kyūshū University). Takayanagi has published a series of articles on Tokugawa criminal law and another on family law in the journal Hōgaku. Kobayakawa Kingo did a voluminous pioneer job in the 1930's and early 1940's in the field of Tokugawa civil litigation. His articles in the journal Hōgaku ronsō are profusely and accurately documented. These articles serve as an introduction in the early stages of Tokugawa civil litigation. Kaneda's major studies were on the law of obligations in the Tokugawa period and may be found in the journal Hōsei kenkyū.

Many younger scholars have begun to work intensively on Tokugawa law. For example, Hiramatsu Yoshirō (Nagoya University) is working on Tokugawa jurisdiction and also criminal law. Ōtake Hideo (Kōbe) has worked on the law of Tokugawa water rights, and Maeda Masaharu (Kansai Gakuin University) has done valuable work on village law of the Tokugawa period. Inokuma Kaneshige (Kyōto University) specializes in Imperial court history and Kyōto lore.

3. Primary Sources for Tokugawa Laws and Precedents

Since the Meiji Restoration many of the collections of shogunal decrees and precedents have been copied from the brush-written manuscripts and printed either by Japanese government ministries or legal historians. By multiplying the copies as well as rendering them much easier to read, even for experts, this painstaking work has been of great service to later students. Ishii Ryōsuke's chapter, "Legal Sources" in his Nihon hōseishi gaisetsu [No. 3, pp. 369-378] furnishes a good brief introduction to many of these original sources, both printed and manuscript.

The functions and sources of the various types of decrees and cases and their relationships to each other require a brief explanation to supplement the listing in the appended bibliography. It is first necessary to understand the relationship between the Kujikata osadamegaki 公事方御定書, the Kajō ruiten 科條類典 and the Tokugawa kinreikō 德川禁令考.

The Kujikata osadamegaki, usually abbreviated Osadamegaki, was drafted in 1742 in two parts, First Book (jōkan) and Second Book (gekan). The Second Book was popularly known as the Osadamegaki hyakkajō and must not be confused with what has been called the Kunōzan hyakkajō (the so-called Legacy of Ieyasu), an unofficial document sometimes attributed to Ieyasu but actually of uncertain origin. Certain inconsistencies indicate that at least part of it was written after Ieyasu's death (See Naitō Chisō, "Kunōzan Hyakkajō wa itsuwari naru koto," in Hōsei ronsan zokuhen [No. 103, pp. 529-534]).

The two parts of the Osadamegaki correspond roughly to the distinction in the Ritsuryō of the Taihō Code (702) between administrative decrees (ryō) and criminal prohibitions (ritsu). The Osadamegaki, First Book corresponds to the administrative ryō and the Second Book to the criminal ritsu. However, the ritsu and ryō classification is very crudely observed. In the Second Book, for instance, there are many provisions on procedure and even some civil law. The First Book is important because it contains a number of basic decrees on court organization and practice. It also covers most of the administrative problems, as seen by the drafters in 1742.

Historically, the Osadamegaki was an attempt by Yoshimune, the eighth shōgun, to select the important decrees and precedents in the legal records which had accumulated for over a century and to arrange them in a codified form as a guidebook for his judges. To the extent that the process of compilation involved a certain amount of selection between two or more inconsistent precedents, the Second Book may be regarded as a "code," but the First Book was little more than a collection of decrees. In neither book was there any idea of legislating a change. (See Koide Yoshio, "Osadamegaki hyakkajō hensan no jijō ni tsuite," 4 Shichō 4, 3 [Nov., 1934], pp. 112-137.)

Before the time of the Osadamegaki, there were several private collections of decrees and precedents serving as judicial guides. Judges were encouraged in the early

Tokugawa period to decide cases on their "merits" (dōri), but such a subjective process caused confusion and inconsistencies in the results. In order to standardize their own practice at least, many judges kept private records of their cases to guide them in subsequent decisions. Those individual collections are extremely important to a study of the judicial practice of the first century of the Tokugawa period. Several of the most important of them have been printed (See Ishii Ryōsuke, Kinsei hōsei shiryō sōsho, Tōkyō, 1938-1941). For example, the Genroku gohōshiki is such a private collection of case notes. This work has been translated into English by Hiramatsu Yoshirō (Nagoya University) and Dr. Mario Schubert (Italy), but has not yet been published.

After 1842 judicial practice in Edo was guided by the standards of the Osadamegaki plus subsequent precedents or court opinions (sashizu) in novel cases and later proclamations (ofuregaki), memoranda (kakitsuke) and orders (tasshi).

With this much background it is possible to understand the relationship between the Osadamegaki and the Kajō ruiten. Yoshimune in preparing for the compilation of the Osadamegaki had ordered that all pertinent decrees and precedents be assembled for reference. In 1767 these materials previously used by Yoshimune's compilers were arranged under each controlling article of the Osadamegaki, and the whole became known as the Kajō ruiten and was used for reference in the courts. Some confusion has resulted from the fact that the Meiji editors of the Tokugawa Kinreikō [No. 35] and the Tokugawa kinreikō kōshū [No. 36] first regarded the Kajō ruiten as a code used by the judges of the Tokugawa period and also as a revision of the shogunal law, erroneously assumed to have been made when the Kajō ruiten was compiled in 1767. This mistake is corrected in the preface of the modern printed edition of the Tokugawa kinreikō kōshū.

The relationship between the Kajō ruiten and the Tokugawa kinreikō kōshū lies in the fact that the latter is the only printed version of the Kajō ruiten, although it also contains Tokugawa precedents made subsequent to 1767 which the Meiji editors of the Ministry of Justice considered relevant. There is a manuscript copy of the Kajō ruiten at the Naikaku Bunko, and the statement by Takigawa Masajirō, Nihon hōseishi kenkyū [No. 111], that all copies have been lost is thus an error.

The Tokugawa kinreikō contains seventy-two titles, under which have been collected decrees and precedents covering the whole Tokugawa period on all sorts of subjects from regulation of the Imperial Court to shogunal hawking expeditions, foreign trade, and outcasts (eta). The whole project of compiling the twelve volumes of the Tokugawa kinreikō and kōshū was carried out by the Ministry of Justice (Shihōshō) between 1878 and 1894, and the work was first printed in 1894-1895. There is a neatly bound reprint dated 1931. The subject matter headings by which this work is organized make it very convenient to use as a source for both decrees and court precedents.

The Ofuregaki shūsei, now conveniently printed in five large volumes under the editorship of Takayanagi Shinzō and Ishii Ryōsuke [No. 29], is another important source of Tokugawa law applicable to the commoners. In order to understand the character of these collections, it must first be remembered that ofuregaki were proclamations of the Senior Council (Rōjū), promulgated through fixed channels of authority to the people in general. The Ofuregaki shūsei then are decrees rather than court precedents. Furthermore, the ofuregaki were a special type of decree, in general promulgated at large as distinguished from kakitsuke, which were usually administrative memoranda to the officials and tasshi which were orders addressed to specific persons. The first compilation of ofuregaki (Kampo 1741-1744) was ordered by Yoshimune, and the other three compilations were continuations of the practice in Hōreki (1751-1764), Temmei (1781-1789) and Tempō (1830-1844).

The later Tokugawa "courts" relied heavily on precedents, and the practices which grew up in the "court" system were based largely on judge-made law. Hence authoritative precedents were recorded and compiled into categories roughly corresponding to the criminal-civil distinction. The civil cases of the Tokugawa Conference Chamber (hyōjōsho) were recorded in the Saikyodome. Forty-five volumes of these records existed for the years between 1702-1867. Unfortunately all of the original forty-five volumes were lost in the Tōkyō earthquake of 1923. At the time of the earthquake there were extra copies of only two parts. One copy, covering the period from 1720-1729, is now at the Kyōto University Library. It has, however, a large gap from 1721-1727. The other copy is at Tōkyō University and covers the period 1781-1782. These remnants were printed by the Ministry of Justice as Shihō shiryō, Bessatsu No. 19 [No. 31] along with those parts of the Saikyodome which fortunately had been quoted at length in the Tokugawa kinreikō kōshū. These cover four parts of the Saikyodome for the period from 1796-1865. Although the loss of this major source of civil decisions is irreparable, these remnants in the printed volume give a sampling for the period from 1720-1865.

As expected criminal precedents of the Tokugawa period are more voluminous because of the usual preponderance of criminal elements of the written law in early stages of legal growth. The Oshioki reiruishū contains collections of Conference Chamber opinions rendered in response to questions put to the Chamber by the Senior Council concerning requests (ukagai) originally referred to the Council by other lesser shogunal officials and Commissioners. These criminal opinions were compiled by the Chamber itself on five different occasions in order to have the precedents in ready form for reference. The five compilations are as follows:

1. Koruishū 古類集, sometimes referred to as Chahyōshi zenshū 茶表紙前集, covering the period from 1771-1802; compilation began in 1804.

2. Shinruishū 新類集, or Aobyōshi 青表紙, covering 1803-1814.

3. Zokuruishū 續類集, sometimes referred to as Kibyōshi 黄表紙, covering 1815-1826.

4. Tempo ruishū 天保類集, sometimes called Chahyōshi kōshū 茶表紙後集, covering 1826-1839.

5. The fifth compilation was destroyed in the Tōkyō earthquake of 1923. No copies remain.

Copies of the first four of these compilations may be found at Kyōto University and at the Naikaku Bunko. Only the Koruishū (1771-1802, 4 vols.), and the Shinruishū (1803-1814, 2 vols.) have been printed as Shihō shiryō, Bessatsu Nos. 8, 10, 11, 12, 18, 20 [No. 30].

Besides the Oshioki reiruishū, there are two volumes of criminal precedents printed as Tokugawa jidai saiban jirei (Shihō shiryō, Nos. 221, 273) [No. 34]. There is also a compilation of both decrees and precedents by the North Town Commissioner of Edo. This is known as the Senyō ruishū and covers the period from 1716-1753. The first three of its thirty-two books have been printed (Ishii Ryōsuke, Kyōho senyō ruishū, Tōkyō 1944) [No. 24].

Besides the official shogunal compilations mentioned above, the Meiji compilation, Tokugawa jidai minji kanreishū is a valuable source of both civil precedents and civil decrees, classified by subject matter. Originally these materials were compiled from a variety of shogunal legal materials by the Ministry of Justice in 1878 for reference during the Meiji codifications. Each item included in the compilation cited its source in a shogunal law book or private guidebook. Since many of the sources cited were lost in the 1923 earthquake, this compilation, drawing from such a wide variety of materials, is one of the most valuable sources for the modern study of Tokugawa law. The compilation was finally printed in 1934-1936 as Shihō shiryō, Nos. 187, 192, 205, 213, 216 [No. 33]. The arrangement is by subjects as follows:

1. No. 187, Jinji 人事 (Personal affairs)

2. No. 192, Dōsan 動産 (Movable property)

3. No. 205, Fudōsan 不動産 (Immovable property)

4. No. 213, Fudōsan (part two)

5. No. 216, Soshō 訴訟 (Procedure)

These works contain dated decrees on given topics, followed by supporting documents, if any; these are followed by dated precedents and finally undated decrees and precedents.

In the field of Tokugawa customary law it is fortunate that the Ministry of Justice, in preparation for the Meiji codification, compiled three sets of local customary law which have since been printed. These are entitled: Minji kanrei ruishū, 1877 [No. 25]; Zenkoku minji kanrei ruishū, 1880 [No. 38]; and Shōji kanrei ruishū, 1883-1884 [No. 32]. More recently the Minji kanrei ruishū and Zenkoku minji kanrei ruishū have been consolidated into a single volume based primarily on the Zenkoku minji kanrei ruishū, but using whatever superior features the compiler felt were contained in the classification system of the Minji kanrei ruishū. The consolidated version seeks to avoid overlapping and at the same time to provide a better geographical coverage and index than either of the originals (See Kazahaya Yasoji, Zenkoku minji kanrei ruishū, 1944 [No. 39]). These collections were made by traveling commissions from the Ministry of Justice, which recorded practices in the various provinces of Japan as related to them by the local officials. Although the gathering of these records was begun in 1875, well into the Meiji period, they may be considered fairly representative of the prior Tokugawa local practices and are indeed an unusual set of materials. Too often customary law is neglected in times of transition until it finally becomes lost entirely.

One of the most remarkable products of Western legal scholarship in Japan was the English translation of the Minji kanrei ruishū and the Tokugawa jidai minji kanreishū supervised by John Henry Wigmore. Wigmore's work was carried out in two stages, the first during his stay (1889-1892) at Keiō University and the second under the sponsorship of the Society of International Cultural Relations (Kokusai Bunka Shinkōkai) between 1935 and 1941. During the first period he translated parts of both the Minji kanrei ruishū and Tokugawa jidai kanreishū and had them printed with an introduction on Tokugawa institutions as "Materials for the Study of Private Law in Old Japan," TASJ, 20, Supplement (1892). It should be noted that this translation of the Minji kanrei ruishū was from the original Japanese report, while the Japanese printed copy of 1877 is abridged.

In 1935 Wigmore came to Japan for two months at the invitation of the Kokusai Bunka Shinkōkai and organized a team of translators who in the following six years sent him their translations to be edited in Chicago. By 1941 the translation project was completed. The material translated in this fashion was organized by Wigmore as follows: Part 1. Introduction; Part 2. Contract: Civil Customary Law; Part 3. Contract: Legal Precedents; Part 4. Contract: Commercial Customary Law; Part 5. Property: Civil Customary Law; Part 6. Property: Legal Precedents; Part 7. Persons: Civil Customary Law; Part 8. Persons: Legal Precedents; Part 9. Procedure: Legal Precedents; Part 10. Vocabularies and Indexes.

It can be seen that Wigmore's project consolidated two types of sources. What is called "precedent" by Wigmore comes from the Tokugawa jidai minji kanreishū, which had been printed in Japanese in 1934-1936 [No. 33]. What Wigmore called "civil customary law" derives from the Minji kanrei ruishū, except for a selection from the Shōji kenrei ruishū. Also it should be noted that what was termed "movable property (dōsan)" in the Tokugawa jidai kanreishū is called by Wigmore "Contract: Legal Precedents." Hence the Minji kanrei ruishū became parts 2, 5 and 7, and the Tokugawa jidai kanreishū became parts 3, 6, 8 and 9 of Wigmore's organization.

In the above outline of Wigmore's work parts 1, 2, sections of part 3, and part 5 had been printed in 1892 in TASJ. Part 7 was printed in 1941 by the Kokusai Bunka Shinkōkai. The whole of the manuscript is presently located at the Kokusai Bunka Shinkōkai office in Tōkyō (Ōsaka Shōsen Building). Linguists will doubtless find grounds for questioning many passages of the translations, and historians may reasonably expect persons who work with these primary sources to read them in the original or printed Japanese.

Besides the civil customary law, considerable "statutory" material on local law and administration has been printed by the Japanese in recent years. Certain shogunal regulations for rural villagers were regularly promulgated by oral readings from the preface of the five-man-group registry. A large number of these have been collected and printed: Hozumi Nobushige, Goningumi hōkishū, 1921 [No. 18]; Hozumi Shigetō, Goningumi hōkishū zokuhen, 1944 [No. 19]; and Nomura Kentarō, Goningumichō no kenkyū, 1944 [No. 17]. Maeda Masaji"s Nihon kinsei sompō no kenkyū, 1952 [No. 27] is an important addition to the printed primary sources available on local law, since it deals with the autonomous law of the village as opposed to that in the five-man-group registries which originated in the shogunate.

Finally it should be noted that there exist a number of important collections of regulations on local government which were compiled by writers in the Tokugawa period. Some of these have been printed in recent times: Bokumin kinkan [No. 16], Kōsei jikata ochiboshū [No. 52], and Jikata hanrei roku [No. 48]. Also certain unprinted manuscripts, such as Mokuhi [No. 87], Soshō hikan tsuika [No. 97], and Bunshō hikan [No. 64], are very important to a study of shogunal litigation, but they will be described in the appropriate section of the appended listings and require no comment here.

For more detailed information on the growth of the study of legal history in modern Japan and on some of its chief figures the reader is referred to the following sources:

Fuse Yaheiji 布施彌平治. "Nihon hōseishiryō ichiran shiryō 日本法制史料一覽 [資料] (A glance at the historical materials of Japanese legal history: source material). Nihon hōgaku 18, 217-244; 357-368 (1952).

Hiramatsu Yoshirō 平松義郎. "Nihon hōseishi ni tsuite-nani wo yomu beki ka"日本法制史について —何を讀むべきか (Concerning Japanese legal history--what should one read?). Jurisuto 18, 31-34 (Sept. 16, 1952).

Ishii Ryōsuke 石井良助. "Nihon hōseishi kenkyū no hattatsu" 日本法制史研究の發達 (Development of Japanese legal history). In Tōkyō Teikoku Daigaku gakujutsu taikan, 277-293 (1942).

Kumagai Kaisaku 熊谷開作. "Iwayuru Nihon hōseishi no seiritsu to sono genkai"いわゆる日本法制史の成立とその限界 (The establishment of the so-called Japanese legal history and its proper sphere). Hōritsu bunka 4, 1, 62-66 (1949).

Kumasaki Wataru 隈崎渡. "Nihon hōseishi gakkai no atarashii shūkaku—Ishii, Takayanagi ryō kyōju no shinchō ni tsuite—" 日本法制史學界の新しい收穫— 石井,高柳兩教授の新著について(A new harvest for the field of Japanese legal history—the new writings of Professors Ishii and Takayanagi). Hōgaku shimpō 56, 741-746 (1949).

Takayanagi Shinzō 高柳眞三. "Hikakuhō no taishō to shite no Nihon hōseishi" 比較法の對象としての日本法制史 (Japanese legal history as an object for comparative law). Hōritsu taimuzu 4, 3.

Takigawa Masajirō 瀧川政次郎. "Meiji igo ni okeru hōseishigaku no hattatsu" 明治以後における法制史學の發達 (Development of legal history since Meiji). In Nihon hōseishi kenkyū, 607-667 (1941).

4. Japanese Law Libraries and Collections

A word should be said about Japanese libraries. By far the most convenient for modern legal sources is the Saikō Saibansho Toshokan 最高裁判所圖書館 (Supreme Court Library). In general Japanese library catalogues do not contain all of the data required by American standards of citation and bibliography. Hence the student usually must collect the data from each book itself. However, the Supreme Court Library is a pleasant exception. Catalogues such as the Hōritsu tosho mokuroku, 1950 [No. 7], and Ippan tosho mokuroku, 1953 [No. 8], published by the Supreme Court, not only have all of the usual data needed on the listed items, but also have author indices in alphabetical order and rōmaji headings for the convenience of foreigners.

The Hōmu Toshokan 法務圖書館 (Ministry of Justice Library) has the most complete collection of legal sources in Japan. It is also quite convenient to use. Its catalogues, however, are not as adequate as those of the Supreme Court. For the usual tools of the practicing lawyer, the Tōkyō Bar Association and First Tōkyō Bar Association libraries are convenient. The Kokuritsu Kokkai Toshokan, Miyakezaka Bunshitsu, Hōritsu Seiji-bu 國立國會圖書館三宅坂分室 法律政治部 (National Diet Library, Miyakezaka Branch, Law and Politics Section) is useful for post-war government records.

For Tokugawa sources the collections at the Ministry of Justice Library, the Naikaku Bunko (inside the Imperial Palace), Ueno Library and Tōkyō and Kyōto University libraries are the best. All of the libraries mentioned above have extremely helpful staffs, and what is lacking in organization is often more than compensated for by staff assistance in locating material.

The foreign lawyer in Japan will have trouble in finding the legal works he needs on his own law. The Ministry of Justice Library has quite a large collection and is probably the best place to start looking for foreign language books. The catalogue entitled Ōbun tosho mokuroku [No. 11] is helpful for that purpose.

ANNOTATED BIBLIOGRAPHY

a. Bibliographies of Legal History:

1. Daigokai bunken mokuroku 第五回文獻目錄 (Fifth list of literature). Edited by Hōseishi Gakkai 法制史學會 (Legal History Association), n.p.: mimeographed, 1953, 68 pp.

   There are four prior annual lists starting with 1949. These annual bibliographies are the most convenient available to keep abreast with the current scholarly output by contemporary Japanese legal historians.

2. Nihon hōseishi 日本法制史(Japanese legal history). Takayanagi Shinzō 高柳眞三. Tōkyō: Yūhikaku 有斐閣, 1948. 383 pp.

   A list of literature on Japanese legal history is included, pp. 367-383. Since Takayanagi lists all of the Tokugawa sources together, instead of mixing them with those on the same subject from other periods, this work is more convenient to use but not quite as comprehensive as Ishii's. [See No. 4.]

3. Nihon hōseishi gaisetsu 日本法制史概説(General survey of Japanese legal history). Ishii Ryōsuke 石井良助. Tōkyō: Kōbundō 弘文堂, 1948. 607 pp.

   The chapter on sources of law, pp. 369-378, lists many of the primary sources of Tokugawa law, both printed and unprinted.

4. Nihon hoseishi gaiyō 日本法制史概要 (General essentials of Japanese legal history). Ishii Ryōsuke 石井良助. Tōkyō: Sōbunsha 創文社, 1952. 247 pp.

   In arabic paging the author includes 20 pages of bibliography. This list is the most comprehensive coverage of literature on the whole of Japanese legal history to be found in one place. The materials are classified in subject matter divisions with chronological listing in each division.

5. Nihon hōseishi shomoku kaidai 日本法制史書目解題 (Annotated bibliography on Japanese legal history). Edited by Ikebe Yoshikata 池邊義象. Tōkyō: Daitōkaku 大鐙閣, 1918. Paper bound, 2 vols.

   Consists of three parts: 1) primary sources; 2) general historical sources; 3) special subjects.

6. Zōtei kokusho kaidai 増訂國書解題 (Revised and supplemented, annotated bibliography of national literature). Edited by Samura Hachirō 佐村八郎. Revised by Samura Toshirō 佐村敏郎. Tōkyō: Rokugōkan 六合館, 1926. 2 vols.

   The second volume has a subject matter index of 154 pages (separate pagination). See 27-33 for descriptions of pre-Meiji works on legal subjects. Nowhere near all of the important sources of legal history are listed, but occasionally a helpful description of a manuscript may be found.

b. General Bibliographies, Catalogues, and Indices to Sources:

7. Hōritsu tosho mokuroku, washo no bu 法律圖書目録和書の部(Catalogue of legal books held, part on Japanese books). Tōkyō: Saikō Saibansho Jimusōkyoku 最高裁判所事務總局, 1950. 278+100 pp.

   This catalogue has an alphabetical author index.

8. Ippan tosho mokuroku, washo no bu 一般圖書目録和書の部(Catalogue of general books held, part on Japanese books). Tōkyō: Saikō Saibansho Jimusōkyoku, 1953. 1207 pp.

9. Kinsei kangakusha chojutsu mokuroku taisei 近世漢學者著述目錄大成 (A complete catalogue of the works of Chinese scholars of the recent era). Compiled by Seki Giichirō 關儀一郎 and Seki Yoshinao 關義直. Tōkyō: Tōyō Tosho Kankōkai 東洋圖書刊行會, 1946. 573 pp. plus an appendix with 100 pp. of genealogies of Confucianists.

10. Nihon sōsho sakuin 日本叢書索引 (Index to collections of Japanese books). Compiled by Hirose Bin 廣瀬敏 Tōkyō: Musashino Shoin 武蔵野書院, 1939. 573+93 pp.

　　An old but reliable index.

11. Ōbun tosho mokuroku 歐文圖書目錄 (Catalogue of western books held). Tōkyō: Shihōshō 司法省, 1936. 958 pp.

12. Sōgō shiryō mokuroku 綜合史料目錄 (Consolidated list of historical materials). Compiled by Watanabe Shigeru 渡邊茂. Hakodate: Hokkaidō Gakugei Daigaku Hakodate Bunkō Shigaku Kenkyūkai 北海道學藝大學函館分校史學研究會 1954. 85 pp.

　　A convenient small catalogue of the contents of important Japanese collections of historical sources listed by kana. It is, therefore, useful when the name of a manuscript is known, and the collection in which it is printed needs to be found.

13. Sōsho zenshū shomoku 叢書全集書目 (List of books collected in sōsho). Edited by Kawashima Gosaburō 川島五三郎. Tōkyō: Tōkyō Kosekishō Kumiai 東京古籍商組合. 1934-1935. 5 vols.

　　Volumes 4 on history and 5 on law and politics are valuable for the standard collections and the list of books printed in them.

14. Wakan tosho mokuroku 和漢圖書目錄 (Catalogue of Japanese and Chinese books held). Tōkyō: Shihōshō, 1935. 2748 pp.

　　Usually the publisher and main pagination are not given in this catalogue but it lists more books on law than that of the Supreme Court. There are important supplements to bring it up to date.

15. Zōtei zenshū sōsho kakaku sōran 増訂全集叢書價格總覽 (Revised and supplemented list of collections and compilations). Compiled by Kawashima Gosaburō 川島五三郎 and Yagi Toshio 八木敏夫. Tōkyō: Nihon Kosho Tsūshinsha 日本古書通信社, 1949. 236 pp.

　　Convenient and up-to-date, but not so accurate as the Sōsho zenshū shomoku and Nihon sōsho sakuin [Nos. 13 and 10].

c. Printed Primary Sources: Collections of Tokugawa Laws and Precedents

16. Bokumin kinkan 牧民金鑑 (Golden guide of rustic folk). Originally compiled by Arai Akimichi 荒井顯道 (1853). Edited by Yokogawa Shirō 横川四郎 and supervised by Takigawa Masajirō 瀧川政次郎. Tōkyō: Seibundō Shinkōsha 誠文堂新光社, 1935. 2 vols.

　　This is a valuable work on rural administration by Arai Akimichi, a Deputy. The manuscript copy is available at the Naikaku Bunko.

17. Goningumichō no kenkyū 五人組帳の研究 (Study of the five-man-groups registry). Nomura Kentarō 野村兼太郎, author and editor. Tōkyō: Yūhikaku 有斐閣, 1944. 682 pp.

18. Goningumi hōkishū 五人組法規集 (Collection of regulations for the five-man-groups). Compiled by Hozumi Nobushige 穂積陳重. Tōkyō: Yūhikaku 有斐閣, 1921. 705 pp.

19. Goningumi hōkishū zokuhen 五人組法規集續編 (Later collection of laws for the five-man-groups). Compiled by Hozumi Shigetō 穂積重遠. Tōkyō: Yūhikaku 有斐閣, 1944. 2 vols.

20. Ijō nami buke gofuchinin reisho 以上並武家御扶持人例書 (Book of precedents for warriors over [the rank of audience, omemie 御目見]). This is summarized by Miura Kaneyuki 三浦周行 in Ushinawaretaru kinsei hōsei shiryō 失はれたる近世法制史料 (Lost materials of legal history of the modern age), in Hōseishi no kenkyū 1389-1458. 1418 pp.

21. Kempō shiryō 憲法志料 (Materials of [ancient] law). Originally compiled by Kimura Seiji 木村政辭. Translated from kambun to Japanese by Hashimoto Hiroshi 橋本博. Tōkyō: Shihōshō 司法省, 1935. 2 vols.

This is a collection of legal materials from the time of the Empress Suiko 推古 (7th century) to the Keichō period (1596-1614), not to be confused with Kempō shiryō 憲法資料 (Source of material on the [Meiji] constitution).

22. Kinsei hampō shiryō shūsei 近世藩法資料集成 (Compilation of materials on the law of the feudal domains of the recent era). Edited by Kyōto Daigaku, Hōgakubu 京都大學法學部. Kyōto: Kōbundō 弘文堂, 1942-1944. 3 vols.

Volume 1 includes the code of the Kameyama domains and Morioka 盛岡 domain; Volume 2, the Kumamoto 熊本 domain; and Volume 3, the Matsue 松江 domain.

23. Kinsei hōsei shiryō sōsho 近世法制史叢書 (Compilation of writings on legal history of the recent era. Compiled by Ishii Ryōsuke 石井良助. Tōkyō: Kōbundō Shobō 弘文堂書房, 1938-1941. 3 vols.

These volumes include important early collections of laws and precedents. They are mostly private compilations by officials before the Osadamegaki (1742).

24. Kyōho senyō ruishū 享保撰要類集 (Classified collection of essential regulations of the Kyōho era, 1716-1735). Edited by Ishii Ryōsuke, Tōkyō: Kōbundō 弘文堂, 1944. 236 pp.

This is a printed copy of part of a collection of important regulations issued by the North Edo Town commissioner from 1716-1753. Only 3 books (kan) of 32 are printed in this volume.

25. Minji kanrei ruishū 民事慣例類集 (Classified collection of civil customary practices). Edited by Takimoto Seiichi 瀧本誠一. Tōkyō: Hakutōsha 白東社, 1932. 390 pp.

Originally compiled by a commission from the Ministry of Justice in 1877.

26. Nihon kindai keiji hōreishū 日本近代刑事法令集 (Collection of criminal law of modern Japan). Compiled by Shihōshō Hishoka 司法省秘書課. Tōkyō: Shihōshō, 1945. 641 pp.

This volume contains one of the best versions of the Osadamegaki, gekan 御定書下巻 (Written decisions, second book). It also contains the body of precedents (Osadamegaki reisho 御定書例書) which grew up in applying the Osadamegaki after 1742 (see pp. 145-205) and Sharitsu 赦律 (Law of amnesty) promulgated near the end of the Tokugawa period and important to studies of criminal law.

27. Nihon kinsei sompō no kenkyū 日本近世村法の研究 (A study of village law of the Japanese recent era). Maeda Masaji 前田正治, author and compiler. Tōkyō: Yūhikaku 有斐閣, 1952. 319 pp.

This is an important assemblage of laws established by the villages and hence supplements the collections of shogunal regulations for the five-man-groups.

28. Nihon kodai hōten 日本古代法典 (Compilation of ancient Japanese laws). Compiled by Konakamura Kiyonori 小中村清矩 and others. Tōkyō: Hakubunkan 博文館, 1892. 986 pp.

This volume contains some of the more important "legislation" of the various periods in Japanese history. It contains the Buke Shohatto, Osadamegaki Hyakkajō, etc.

29. Ofuregaki Kampo shūsei 御觸書寛保集成 (Compilation of proclamations of the Kampo era, 1741-1743). Edited by Ishii Ryōsuke 石井良助 and Takayanagi Shinzō 高柳眞三. Tōkyō: Iwanami Shoten 岩波書店, 1934. 1356 pp.

This volume, covering decrees from 1615-1743, is one of five volumes. The other four were compiled by the Tokugawa Conference Chamber (Hyōjōsho) in the periods of Hōreki (1751-1763) 1 vol., Temmei (1781-1788) 1 vol., and Tempō (1830-1843) 2 vols.

30. Oshioki reiruishū 御仕置例類集 (Classified collection of precedents on executions), in Shihō shiryō bessatsu, vols. 8, 10, 11, 12, 18, 20. Tōkyō: Shihōshō Chōsabu 司法省調査部 1941-1946. 6 vols.

These precedents are the instructions of the Conference Chambers in response to requests put to the Senior Council by the various Commissioners and in turn referred to the Chamber for opinions.

31. Saikyodome 裁許留 (Records of Judgments), in Shihō shiryō bessatsu, vol. 19. Tōkyō: Shihōshō Hishoka 司法省秘書課, 1943. 607 pp.

This is a printed copy, all that remains of the 45 volumes of records kept between 1702 and 1867 of civil cases in the Conference Chamber. The greater part were lost in the Tōkyō earthquake of 1923.

32. Shōji kanrei ruishū 商事慣例類集 (Classified collection of commercial customary practices). Edited by Takimoto Seiichi 瀧本誠一. Tōkyō: Hakutōsha 白東社, 1932. 1130 pp.

    This collection also may be found in 49 Nihon keizai taiten 3-732 and 50 id. 735-1130. The original collection was made by teams of investigators from the Ministry of Justice 1883-1884.

33. Tokugawa jidai minji kanreishū 德川時代民事慣例集 (Collection of civil customary precedents of the Tokugawa period), in Shihō shiryō, vols. 187, 192, 205, 213 and 216. Tōkyō: Shihōshō Chōsaka 司法省調査課 1936. 5 vols.

    This collection is mostly court decisions. Volume 216 on procedure is of great value to the study of Tokugawa procedure.

34. Tokugawa jidai saiban jirei 德川時代裁判事例 (Precedents of trials in the Tokugawa period), in Shihō shiryō, vols. 221, 273. Tōkyō: Shihōshō Chōsaka 司法省調査課, 1936 and 1942. 2 vols.

    These are criminal precedents.

35. Tokugawa kinreikō 德川禁令考 (A consideration of Tokugawa regulations). Kikuchi Shunsuke 菊池駿助, editor-in-chief. Compiled between 1878-1895. Tōkyō: Yoshikawa Kōbunkan 吉川弘文館, 1931-1932. 6 vols.

36. Tokugawa kinreikō kōshū 德川禁令考後聚 (Consideration of Tokugawa regulations, supplement). Edited by Shihōshō. Tōkyō: Yoshikawa Kōbunkan, 1931-1932. 6 vols.

37. Toyotomi shi hattokō 豐臣氏法度考 (Consideration of the decrees of the House of Toyotomi). Edited by Miyake Chōsaku 三宅長策. Tōkyō: Tetsugaku Shoin 哲學書院, 1893. 122 pp.

38. Zenkoku minji kanrei ruishū 全國民事慣例類集 (Country-wide classified collection of civil customary practices). Compiled by Shihōshō 司法省 in 1880. Found in 50 Nihon keizai taiten 3-390.

39. Zenkoku minji kanrei ruishū 全國民事慣例類集 (Country-wide classified collection of civil customary practices). Compiled by Kazahaya Yasoji 風早八十二. Tōkyō: Nihon Hyōronsha 日本評論社, 1944. 353 pp.

    This compilation is based primarily on the Shihōshō version by the same name, but it assimilates the best features of the Minji kanrei ruishū (1877) also. Hence it is the most convenient source for the Tokugawa customary law.

d. Printed Primary Sources: Specific Legal Writings Included in Collections

    Many of the writings by Tokugawa authors listed below are printed in the Nihon keisai taiten. Also several of the important legal guidebooks of the middle of the Tokugawa period are printed in Ishii, Kinsei hōsei shiryō sōsho. Both of these collections provide introductions to each printed document, revealing facts about the authors and circumstances which produced the document. Further data on the works listed below may be found, as indicated, in the prefaces of the printed copies.

The Tokugawa guides to practice for officials were usually books of decrees and precedents, privately selected and systematically arranged by some studious clerk in one of the offices. Copies were circulated to other officials. Hence, such books become an important source of insight into the practices of Tokugawa courts.

40. Buke myōmokushō 武家名目抄 (Titles of warrior houses). In Zōtei kojitsu sōsho, 8 vols.

41. Bunden sōsho 聞傳叢書 (Collected written traditions heard). In 25 Nihon keizai taiten.

    The Bunden sōsho was edited by Bunyō Inshi (pen name) together with Jikata ochiboshū and Zoku jikata ochiboshū. All together the three writings constitute about 1600 pp. in volumes 24-25 of the Nihon keizai taiten. A manuscript copy may be found at Naikaku Bunko.

42. Chōseidan 廳政談 (Discussion on administration). In vol. 3 of Ishii, Kinsei hōsei shiryō sōsho 257-276 (1941).

    From a note in the back of the manuscript this was approved by Yoshimune as a legal guide in 1737, but it may have been a private collection adopted by the Conference Chamber then. It has 370 articles. A manuscript copy is available in the Naikaku Bunko.

43. Genroku gohōshiki 元禄御法式 (Rules of the Genroku period, 1688-1703). In vol. 1 of Ishii, Kinsei hōsei shiryō sōsho 451-464 (1938).

    Abstracts from the prison records of convictions by the Town Commissioners in Edo.

44. Gotōke reijō 御當家令條 (Articles of the Incumbent House [Shogunate]). In vol. 2 of Ishii, Kinsei hōsei shiryō sōsho 1-295 (1939).

    This collection of decrees and precedents was written by Fujiwara Chikanaga 藤原親長. If we can assume that it was written when the introduction was signed, its date is about 1711. It consists of 600 articles with dates ranging from 1597-1696.

45. Heirisaku 平理策 (Policy for peace through reason), by Niwa Tsutomu 丹羽勗. In vol. 33 of Nihon keizai taiten.

    Niwa Tsutomu wrote this short passage in 1819 as an instruction for Deputies and headmen. He was a clerk (yūhitsu 右筆) of the Owari domain and was quite accomplished in literature, but very conservative in politics.

46. Honchō tōin hiji, in Kinsei bungei sōsho 本朝藤陰比事近世文藝叢書 (Compilation of literature of the recent era). 1911.

    An anonymous writing on trials. The title is styled after a Chinese title.

47. Imagawa kanamokuroku, tsuika 今川かな目録追加 (Supplement to the code of the Imagawa domain). In Zoku gunsho ruijū.

48. Jikata hanrei roku 地方凡例録 (Records of common precedents of rural administration). In vol. 13 of Nihon keizai taiten.

   A very valuable source book of regulations and practices in the local areas by Ōishi Hisataka 大石久敬, a vassal of the Tokugawa clan. Ōishi died in 1794, before it was finished.

49. Kannō wakumon 勧農惑問 (Problems in the advancement of farming), by Fujita Yūkoku 藤田幽谷. In vol. 32 of Nihon keizai taiten.

   Fujita was born in 1773, died 1826, and served as a local administrator in the Mito domain and later as director of the Mito school.

50. Kōdōkanki 弘道館記 (Records of the Kōdōkan School of the Mito domain). In vol. 3 of Kinnō bunko.

   This is an introduction by Tokugawa Nariaki 徳川斉昭 to Kōdō kanki jutsugi by Fujita Hyō 藤田彪, pp. 121-190.

51. Kentei hikki 謙亭筆記 (Notes of Kentei), by Komiyama Kentei 小官山謙亭. In vol. 13 of Nihon keizai taiten.

   Komiyama Kentei became a Deputy for the shogunate in the Kyōho period (1716-1736). This and the book of Zōho denen ruisetsu are on local administration.

52. Kōsei jikata ochiboshū 校正地方落穂集 (Miscellaneous gleanings on rural administration). In vols. 24-25 of Nihon keizai taiten.

   Edited under pen name of Bunyo Inshi (1751-1764). There is a supplement, Zoku jikata ochiboshū, also in vols. 24-25 of Nihon keizai taiten.

53. Kyōho nenkan zakki 享保年間雑記 (Miscellaneous notes on the Kyōho period, 1716-1736). In vol. 17 of Mikan zuihitsu hyakushū.

54. Minkan seiyō 民間省要 (Essence of administering amongst the populace), by Tanaka Kyūemon 田中丘右衛門. In vol. 5 of Nihon keizai taiten.

   Tanaka Kyūemon worked as an engineer for the shogunate. He recorded his experience in the Minkan seiyō, which pleased the shogunate, and Tanaka received a rice stipend. He was later given charge of certain lands for the shogunate near Edo.

55. Ritsuryō yōryaku 律令要略 (Essentials of the prohibitions and regulations). In vol. 2 of Ishii, Kinsei hōsei shiryō sōsho.

   Dated 1741, this collection has several passages of interest on court practice and the basic ideas of law of the time.

56. Seken tedai katagi 世間手代氣質 (Disposition of the world's clerks). Written in 1730 by Ejima Kiseki 江島其磧 (1679-1736). In vol. 1 of Teikoku bunko kōtei Kiseki Jisho kessakushū.

57. Suijinroku 吹塵録 (Records of blowing dust). In vols. 3 and 4 of Katsu zenshū (1928).

   A miscellaneous collection of source material assembled by Katsu Kaishū for the Finance Minister during the Meiji period. There are statistics on population and rice production divided by province in the Tokugawa period. Despite inaccuracies, it is an important source of material on various subjects.

58. Tamakushige 玉くしげ (Jewel box [means innermost thought]), by Motoori Norinaga 本居宣長. In vol. 23 of Nihon keizai taiten.

   Motoori Norinaga (1730-1801) wrote this book in 1787 in response to questions on administration put to him by the Daimyō of Kii, who gave him a 300-koku stipend. His criticism is quite frank and concrete.

59. Tokugawa jikki 德川實紀 (Actual records of the Tokugawa). In vols. 38-44 of Shintei zōho kokushi taikei.

   A daily chronicle of affairs of the shogunate in the first part of the Edo period.

60. Tsurumi kyūko isaku 鶴見九皐遺策 (Remaining works of Tsurumi Kyūko), by Tsurumi Heizaemon 鶴見平左衛門. In vol. 5 of Nihon keizai taiten.

   Tsurumi was a Mito retainer. Although the date of this book is not given, we know that it was presented after Tsurumi's death to the Mito elders in 1799 by a Tachibana Suiken.

61. Yabureya no tsuzukuri banashi 破れ家のつゞくり話 (A tale of patching a tumble-down house), by Shingū Ryōtei 新宮涼庭. In vol. 33 of Nihon keizai taiten.

   Shingū Ryōtei wrote this book in 1845. He was a famous Kyōto physician and quite critical of the shogunate.

62. Zōho denen ruisetsu 增補田園類説 (Supplemented classified explanations of rice lands), by Komiyama Kentei 小宮山謙亭. In vol. 13 of Nihon keizai taiten.

   This book has been erroneously attributed to the author who revised it, Tanimoto Oshie 谷本教.

e. Unprinted Primary Sources: Tokugawa Legal Manuscripts

   The most important depositories for Tokugawa shogunal manuscripts and documents are the Naikaku Bunko, the Ueno Branch of the National Diet Library, the Ministry of Justice Library, Tōkyō University Library and Kyōto University Library. At Tōkyō University there is a room set aside for legal materials called Hōseishi Shiryō Shitsu 法制史資料室 (Room for Materials on Legal History). A similar room at Kyōto is the Kyōto

Daigaku Hōri Hōsei Kenkyūshitsu 京都大學法理法制研究室 (Kyōto University Jurisprudence and Legal Institutions Research Room). Most of the manuscripts listed below are at Kyōto University, but other important ones are at other libraries as indicated.

The Kiuchi 木内 second-hand book shop in front of Tōkyō University usually has quite a stock of Tokugawa manuscripts, and the Shibunkaku 思文閣 in Kyōto also deals in such materials.

63. Aoyama hiroku 青山秘録 (Private records of Aoyama). 5 vols.

  The present writer has a manuscript copy of this private guide of a member of the Senior Council.

64. Bunshō hikan 聞詔秘鑑 (Private guide of petitions heard). 2 vols.

  This appears to be a summary of the Jichōkan hibunshū 寺町勘秘聞集. The general coverage of the Jichōkan hibunshū and Sampishū 三秘集 is practically the same. Like many of the other manuscripts in this list, the Bunshō hikan was a private manual made by an official as a guide in his judicial work, but it is one of the most abstract, brief, and general manuscripts of its type and consequently is quite convenient on questions of jurisdiction and procedure. The present writer has a handwritten copy (1954) of the Tōkyō University original.

65. Bunshō hikanroku 聞詔秘鑑録 (Record for private guidance of petitions heard).

  The Kyōto manuscript is in two small volumes of 104 sections (ten 天) and 86 (chi 地) sections. It appears to be a copy of, or at least of the same origin as, the Bunshō hikan.

66. Chōso hiroku 聽訴秘録 (Private records of petitions heard).

  A Kyōto manuscript in 5 vols. (ten books). Since the material follows the order of the Osadamegaki, it was probably written after 1742.

67. Edo jidai soshō sumikuchi shōmon 江戸時代訴訟濟口證文 (Documents of settlements for lawsuits in the Edo period).

  A manuscript dated 1842 at Kyōto University.

68. Gokenin oshioki ukagai 御家人御仕置伺 (Request for execution of housemen [of the shogunate]).

  This manuscript is in several large volumes and includes cases from 1784-1788. The Kyōto version was copied under the supervision of Miura Kaneyuki 三浦周行. It served as precedents for judges to follow in their application of the Osadamegaki to the shogun's housemen.

69. Goyō dome 御用留 (Notes for official use). 1 vol.

  At Kyōto this manuscript is entitled both Goyōdome and Hōsō kōkan 法曹後鑑. This is probably an extract for the use of a certain official, hence Goyōdome.

70. Hikan 秘鑑 (Private guide).

   This is a private legal guidebook in 5 manuscript volumes (13 books). It is a collection of ordinances from about the time of Yoshimune 吉宗 (1716-1745). There are copies at Kyōto University and the Naikaku Bunko.

71. Harigami dome 張紙留 (Notes on pasted papers).   6 vols. at Naikaku Bunko.

   The Conference Chamber customarily pasted its decision to letters of inquiry. These pasted decisions were called harigami.

72. Hōsō kōkan 法曹後鑑 (Later guide for legal officers).

   A manuscript at Kyōto University including Conference Chamber decisions and opinions in answer to inquiries from daimyō and shogunate officials. It covers the period from roughly 1765 to 1800. There is a much larger manuscript by the same name at Tōkyō University containing criminal cases.

73. Hyōgiritsu 評議律 (Conferences on criminal law).

   This appears to be a private collection of criminal precedents extracted from the Oshioki reiruishū. There are copies at Tōkyō University and Kyōto University.

74. Hyōjōsho kakurei 評定所格例 (Rules and precedents of the Conference Chamber).

   This is a description of the Conference Chamber as it was after 1772. There is also a detailed description of the practice in the Chamber (dated 1788). The only copy seems to be at Kyōto University where it exists as a copy made by Miura Kaneyuki.

75. Hyōjōsho okite 評定所掟 (Conference Chamber regulations).

   Kyōto University manuscript.

76. Itakura seiyō 板倉政要 (Essentials of the administration of Itakura).

   This is a manuscript in 3 volumes (8 books) at Kyōto. Presumably this is a guidebook based on the practices established and regulations issued by the Itakuras while they were the first two Deputy Governors (Shoshidai) of Kyōto.

77. Jichōkan hibunshū 寺町勘秘聞集 (Collection of private questions asked of the Temple, Town and Finance [Commissions]).   2 vols.

   This is a private manuscript, copied by an unidentified person in 1791, and presently at Kyōto University. The contents are legal questions from the various daimyō and officials to the Temple and Shrine, Edo Town and Finance Commissioners. The Commissioners then attached their answers (tsukefuda 附札). Since it shows the legal relationship in concrete situations between private domains of daimyō and the shogunate, it is very valuable for a study of the conformity of the daimyō to Edo practice.

78. Jishakata oshioki reisho 寺社方御仕置例書 (Written precedents for execution by temple and shrine personnel).

    This is a very small manuscript, but well known as a supplemental law to implement the Osadamegaki vis-a-vis bonzes. There are copies at Kyōto and Tōkyō Universities.

79. Keizai daihiroku 刑罪大秘録 (Great private records of crimes and penalties).

    A copy of this manuscript may be found at the Naikaku Bunko.

80. Kenkyō ruiten 憲教類典 (Classified compilation of wise instructions). A private collection of shogunate laws compiled by Kondō Morishige 近藤守重.

    This is a detailed work of 122 manuscript volumes classified by subject matter and offices. It covers materials from Keichō (1596-1614) to Kansei (1789-1800). Manuscript at Naikaku Bunko.

81. Kōsai hiroku 公裁秘録 (Private records of public trials).

    A manuscript in 6 volumes at Kyōto including cases through the Bunka period (1804-1818) and valuable for details of adjudication. There is a 3-volume manuscript by the same name at Naikaku Bunko.

82. Kōsai kikan roku 公裁亀鑑録 (Records of model cases of public trials).

    This is a manuscript in 3 volumes (Ten, Chi, Jin 天地人) and appears to be another collection of precedents and rules as a guidebook for an official (Copied 1854).

83. Kōsai zuihitsu 公裁随筆 (Miscellaneous notes on public records). 2 vols. at Kyōto.

84. Kyōchōfuin kiji 京兆府尹記事 (Notes on officials of Kyōto). 3 vols. (6 books 巻).

    This manuscript by Okafuji Toshitada 岡藤利忠 has an interesting description of the duties of the Commissioners of distant provinces in 1799 and also a detailed chart of the ranks of bannermen (Vol. 2).

85. Kyōto kiroku 京都記録 (Written records of Kyōto).

    This is a small Kyōto manuscript valuable for details on Kyōto jurisdiction and the domains of the Imperial Court—a handbook of Kyōto administration. Since the eight Kansai provinces had been split for jurisdictional purposes, we can assume it was written after 1722.

86. Machi bugyōsho toiawase aisatsu dome 町奉行所問合挨拶留 (Notes of questions and answers of the Town Commission).

    The manuscript is at Tōkyō University.

87. Mokuhi 目秘 (Private articles).

   This is an unprinted manuscript, a copy of which may be found in the Kyōto University Library. It is probably the most valuable single volume of Tokugawa civil procedures. The present writer has a copy made by hand from the original in 1954.

88. Nagasaki bugyōsho shohōrei hikae 長崎奉行所諸法令控 (Copy of various decrees of the Nagasaki Commissioner Office).

   A manuscript in 2 volumes at Kyōto University.

89. Ōsaka sode kagami 大阪袖鑑 (Pocket guide to Osaka).

   The manuscript at Kyōto has a detailed list of the Ōsaka officials and their duties. There is also a copy at the Naikaku Bunko.

90. Otomegaki 御留書 (Written notes). 4 vols.

   This manuscript at Kyōto is in very poor condition and unclearly marked. However someone has numbered them 1, 2, 3, 4 in the lower left corner in red and these numbers may be used for identification.

91. Ryūei hikan 柳營秘鑑 (Private guides of the Willow Camp [shogunate]).

   There is a copy at Kyōto University. The contents concern the rank, ceremony and manners of the shogun's castle.

92. Sanbugyō mondō 三奉行問答 (Inquiries and replies of the three Commissions). 16 vols.

   This is the most comprehensive compilation of daimyō interrogations and the Commissioners' answers (Tōkyō University).

93. Shintōrei 新東令 (New eastern [shogunate] decrees). 1 vol.

   This manuscript, dated 1789, in 74 pages, can be found at Kyōto University.

94. Shōmon hinagatachō 證文雛形帳 (Form book for documents).

   Tōkyō University manuscript.

95. Shoyō ukagai tomegaki 諸用伺留書 (Written notes on requests for various purposes).

   A one-volume manuscript including legal questions referred to the shogunate up to 1852. There are 127 entries in all.

96. Sojō hentōsho uragakian 訴狀返答書裏書案 (Form book for petitions, answers, and endorsements).

   Signed by Kotani Jirozaemon 小谷次郎左衛門. Kyōto University.

97. Sosho hikan tsuika 訴所秘鑑追加 (Supplement to the private guide to the petition place).

   This is a document at Tōkyō University, which is very valuable for its detailed explanations of the trial practices in the Temple and Shrine Commission. The title indicates that it is a supplement to a prior volume, but the whereabouts of this first work is unknown. The present writer has a copy made by hand in the fall of 1954.

98. Tekirei mondō 的例問答 (Model inquiries and replies). 7 vols. at the Naikaku Bunko.

99. Tōto kanron hikan 東都官論秘鑑 (Private guide of explanation on offices of the Eastern Capital [Edo]). 5 vols. No. 1 is missing at Kyōto.

   This manuscript is a description of various offices in the Edo Shogunate and also includes a report by Etagashira Danzaemon on his genealogy and feudal duty to the shogunate in 1719.

f. Collections of Articles and Essays

   Many of the most valuable secondary studies on Tokugawa legal institutions are found in collections of essays. These are of several types: collections of articles of a single author previously printed in scholarly journals; collections of essays by different authors as contributions to a volume in commemoration of a retiring professor; essays by several authors in a cooperative research project; or essays by a single author not previously published.

100. Edo jidai shiron 江戸時代史論 (Historical essays on the Edo period). Compiled by Nihon Rekishi Chiri Gakkai 日本歴史地理學會 (Japanese History and Geography Association). Tōkyō: Jinyūsha 仁友社, 1915. 644 pp.

101. Hōseishi no kenkyū 法制史の研究 (A study of legal history). A compilation of the articles of Miura Kaneyuki. Tōkyō: Iwanami Shoten 岩波書店, 1919. 1174 pp.

102. Hōsei ronsan 法制論纂 (Compilation of essays on legal institutions). Compiled by Kokugakuin 國學院. Tōkyō: Dai Nihon Tosho Kabushiki Kaisha 大日本圖書株式會社, 1903-1904. 1446 pp.

103. Hōsei ronsan zokuhen 法制論纂續編 (Supplement to the Compilation of essays on legal institutions). Compiled by Kokugakuin. Dai Nihon Tosho Kabushiki Kaisha, 1904. 914 pp.

104. Hōseishi ronshū 法制史論集 (Collection of essays on legal history). A compilation of the essays of Nakada Kaoru 中田薫. Tōkyō: Iwanami Shoten 岩波書店, 1926-1943. 3 vols.

   Vol. 1. Family and succession law, 1926
   Vol. 2. Property law, 1938
   Vol. 3. Law obligations and miscellaneous, 1943

105. Jushūnen kinen hōgaku ronshū 十周年記念法學論集 (Collection of essays on jurisprudence as a tenth anniversary memorial). Compiled by Tōhoku Teikoku Daigaku Hōbungakubu 東北帝國大學法文學部. Tōkyō: Iwanami Shoten 岩波書店, 1934. 690 pp.

106. Kinsei Nihon no jugaku 近世日本の儒學 (Confucianism of Japan of the recent era). Compiled by Tokugawa-kō Tsugumune Shichijūnen Shukuga Kinenkai 德川公爵宗七十年祝賀記念會 (Seventieth Anniversary of Prince Tokugawa Tsugumune). Tōkyō: Iwanami Shoten, 1939. 1149 pp.

107. Kokka Gakkai Gojūshūnen kinen kokkagaku ronshū 國家學會五十周年記念國家學論集 (Collections of the essays on the national polity as a memorial on the fifth anniversary of the Political Science Association). Compiled by Kokkagakkai 國家學會. Rōyama Masamichi 蠟山政道, editor. Tōkyō: Yūhikaku 有斐閣, 1937. 815 pp.

108. Miyake hakushi koki shukuga kinen rombunshū 三宅博士古稀祝賀記念論文集 (A collection of essays in commemoration of Doctor Miyake's Seventieth anniversary). Compiled by Ōtsuka Shigakkai 大塚史學會. Tōkyō: Oka Shoin 岡書院, 1929. 830 pp.

109. Miyazaki sensei hōseishi ronshū 宮崎先生法制史論集 (Collection of essays of Professor Miyazaki on legal history). Compiled by Nakada Kaoru 中田薫. Tōkyō: Iwanami Shoten 岩波書店, 1929. 766 pp.

110. Nakada sensei kanreki shukuga hōseishi ronshū 中田先生還曆祝賀法制史論集 (Collection of essays on legal history in honor of Professor Nakada's sixtieth anniversary). Edited by Ishii Ryōsuke 石井良助. Tōkyō: Iwanami Shoten 岩波書店, 1937. 717 pp.

111. Nihon hōseishi kenkyū 日本法制史研究 (A study of Japanese legal history). Takigawa Masajirō 瀧川政次郎, author. Tōkyō: Yūhikaku 有斐閣, 1941. 790 pp.

112. Nihon keizaishi kenkyū 日本經濟史研究 (A study of Japanese economic history). Kōda Shigetomo 幸田成友, author and compiler. Tōkyō: Ōokayama Shoten 大岡山書店, 1928. 854-61 pp.

113. Saitō hakushi kanreki kinen, hō to saiban 齊藤博士還曆記念法と裁判 (Memorial to Doctor Saitō on his sixtieth anniversary, law and litigation). Compiled by Kitamura Gorō 北村五郎. Tōkyō: Yūhikaku 有斐閣, 1942. 720 pp.

114. Tokugawa seido shiryō 德川制度史料 (Historical materials on the Tokugawa system). Compiled by Ono Kiyoshi 小野清. Tōkyō: Rokugōkan 六合館, 1927. 2 parts. Part 1, 209 pp., Part 2, 273 pp.

115. Tōkyō teikoku daigaku gakujutsu taikan 東京帝國大學學術大觀 (Survey of studies at Tōkyō Imperial University). Compiled by Tōkyō teikoku daigaku, Hōgakubu, Keizaigakubu, 東京帝國大學法學部經濟學部. Tōkyō: Kokusai Shuppan Insatsusha 國際出版印刷社, 1942. 786 pp.

116. Zoku hōseishi no kenkyū 續法制史の研究 (Supplement to a study of legal history). A compilation of later articles of Miura Kaneyuki. Tōkyō: Iwanami Shoten 岩波書店, 1925. 1563 pp.